Building
Better Policies

Building Better Policies

The Nuts and Bolts of Monitoring and Evaluation Systems

Gladys Lopez-Acevedo, Philipp Krause, and Keith Mackay, *Editors*

THE WORLD BANK
Washington, D.C.

1 2 3 4 15 14 13 12

ISBN (paper): 978-0-8213-8777-1
ISBN (electronic): 978-0-8213-9505-9
DOI: 10.1596/978-0-8213-8777-1

Library of Congress Cataloging-in-Publication Data
Lopez Acevedo, Gladys.
   Building better policies : the nuts and bolts of monitoring and evaluation systems /
Gladys Lopez-Acevedo, Philipp Krause, Keith Mackay.
      p. cm.
   Includes bibliographical references.
   ISBN 978-0-8213-8777-1 (alk. paper) — ISBN 978-0-8213-9505-9
   1. Public administration—Evaluation.   2. Administrative agencies—Evaluation.
3. Human services—Evaluation. I. Krause, Philipp, 1978– II. Mackay, Keith.
III. World Bank. IV. Title.
   JF1351.L66 2012
   352.8'8—dc23   2012011907

Cover design: Debra Naylor/Naylor Design.

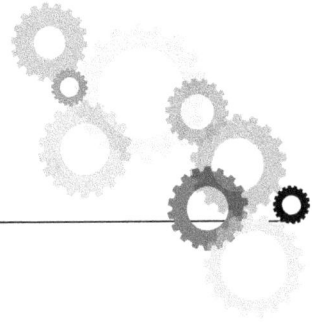

CONTENTS

Boxes

Figures

Tables

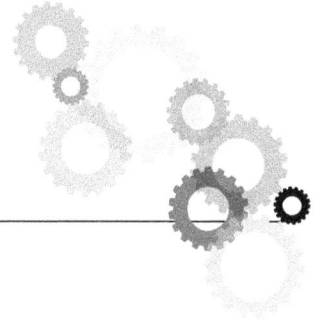

FOREWORD

Government teams from around the world—from Colombia to South Africa, from Mexico to Indonesia, from Minas Gerais to Yucatan, from Karnataka to Antioquia—are confronting many of the challenges and making progress in various dimensions of setting up and improving systems to monitor and evaluate performance. Take the example of Minas Gerais. The State for Results team has been working in recent years on the design and implementation of a system for monitoring social indicators that will make it possible to better track changes in socioeconomic conditions at a disaggregated level. It is working on instruments to facilitate the quality assurance of government interventions, such as spot surveys that indicate how and how well money was spent. And it has an ambitious agenda to evaluate the impact of key programs.

This book is useful to anyone who cares about the quality of public policies and who wants to learn and understand how public policies and programs can be shaped with the objective of improving people's welfare. You might be interested in setting development goals and specific targets for development outcomes for a country, province, city, or sectoral entity, and in the techniques that are available for doing that (as well as how these techniques might interact with the usual political pressures). Or you might want to understand the institutional and technical constraints to setting up an evaluation system that assesses the impact of different interventions and provides a sense of whether the interventions are indeed effective in achieving development targets (that is, a system that allows you to know if you are doing the right things). Or you might want to know the characteristics of a monitoring system that provides real-time information on whether goods and services are being delivered as planned and whether output targets are being reached (that is, a system that indicates whether you are doing things right).

This book discusses many of the institutional and technical challenges governments confront in building monitoring and evaluation (M&E) systems, and how to embed such systems in the decision-making process in all sectors, at all times, thereby ensuring that high-quality information effectively feeds policy design and policy decision-making.

Basing policy on evidence at all stages of the policy cycle is hard. Policy decisions should always result from a combination of political considerations along with information and evidence about the impacts and effectiveness of the policy. But (too) many times, information and evidence are not part of the equation. For instance, countries and governments have to define what is important for people's welfare. Is it reducing infant mortality? Improving citizen security? Reducing children's malnourishment? Increasing youth employment opportunities? Once a country knows the key areas of intervention, the looming question is, how much is the country capable of improving? What is realistic? What is attainable? The definition of numeric targets is a complicated endeavor, and frequently targets are set based only on political considerations. Saying, "our objective is to reduce poverty" is not the same as saying "we will reduce poverty by 10 points in the next 5 years." Setting targets, and setting them scientifically, is a complex task, and there is a long way to go in reflecting this complexity in the way that decisions are made.

Even with targets, and the corresponding indicators needed to monitor progress toward those targets, the challenge remains of mapping the policies and programs that are related to the targets. This mapping is easier said than done; many programs do not have clear objectives, or the causal links between a program (say, of school feeding) and the outcomes (say, child undernourishment) are not well established. In many cases, the production functions behind outcomes are not well known. Or the links are clear but the magnitude of the intervention needed is not well known. Process evaluations are now used to verify that projects have clearly stated objectives (too frequently, objectives are lacking) and that they are accomplishing what they are supposed to accomplish. And impact evaluations are being used to assess whether projects are truly effective in reaching the desired outcomes. But using evaluations is not the norm, and neither is it the norm to use the information generated by evaluations to improve program design or to decide whether a program should be eliminated.

The policy discussion has shifted in recent decades. There is much more consensus about the need for macro stability, low inflation, fiscal responsibility, market integration, and openness to trade. The discussion lies more on how to achieve higher quality public interventions, greater efficacy and efficiency in spending, and increased accountability to citizens in the use of public resources. The role of government is as important as ever. We are in a world of good performance at low levels. That is, changes are headed in the right direction, but we are far from doing well. Take monetary poverty. It has fallen dramatically and the percentage of people living on less than $1.25 a day fell 20 points since 1990. But as of 2008, 1.29 billion people were still living on that amount or less. And 2.47 billion people live on less than US$2 a day. Moreover, improvement has been dramatically heterogeneous across and within countries. Living standards have improved for many but have barely changed for many others. So income inequality is still high, and to a great extent it is a reflection of the inequality of opportunity across population groups, inequality in access to basic nutrition among infants, inequality in access to basic quality education among youth, and inequality in access to high productivity jobs among adults. Closing those opportunity gaps requires a state that is more efficient in providing or assuring the provision of services to all. That requires a state that knows what works and what doesn't, and can adjust accordingly. An M&E system that is embedded in the policy decision-making process is the tool that allows governments to learn, decide, and allocate resources.

There is no template for a good M&E system that can be replicated from one country to the other. Models are not possible, feasible, or appropriate. There is a lot of interest in learning from Mexico, Chile, the Republic of Korea, the United Kingdom, Colombia, Australia, and the United States, all countries that have made good progress in different aspects of M&E systems. These countries are the basis of examples provided in this book. But in no case can one country adopt another country's model; the institutional environments of each country define the right structure. Countries have to slowly build internal capacity, and little by little, step by step, can define what the best system is for them. This book is an excellent resource in that process.

Jaime Saavedra-Chanduvi
Director
Poverty Reduction and Equity
The World Bank

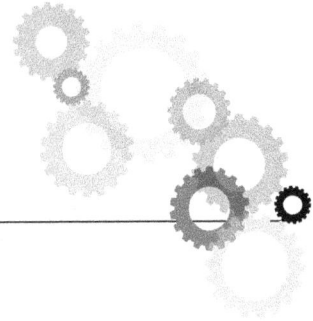

ACKNOWLEDGMENTS

This book has been edited by a team of the Poverty Reduction and Equity Unit (PRMPR): Gladys Lopez-Acevedo (Senior Economist), Philipp Krause (Consultant), and Keith Mackay (Consultant) under the guidance of Jaime Saavedra (Director, PRMPR). It is a compilation based on work previously published as part of the PREM Notes Special Series on the Nuts and Bolts of Monitoring and Evaluation.[1] The editors thank Helena Hwang for her many contributions throughout this project, beginning with the launch of the Nuts and Bolts Series. The editorial work of Madjiguene Seck (Poverty Reduction and Economic Management Network) is gratefully acknowledged. The publication of this book has been supported by the Poverty and Social Impact Analysis (PSIA) Multi-Donor Trust Fund.

Bertha Briceño (Senior Evaluation Specialist, Water and Sanitation Program) and John Newman (Lead Poverty Specialist, Economic Policy and Poverty Sector) served as peer reviewers for the entire volume. Their comments are much appreciated. We are also grateful for the peer review comments on individual chapters received from Richard Allen (Consultant, Public Sector Governance [PRMPS]), Amparo Ballivian (Lead Economist, Poverty, Gender and Equity Group, Latin America and the Caribbean [LCSPP]), Jim Brumby (Sector Manager, PRMPS), Manuel Fernando Castro (Consultant, Communications, Learning and Strategy [IEGCS]), Markus Goldstein (Senior Economist, Development Research Group, Poverty and Inequality), Helena Hwang (Consultant, PRMPR), Indu John-Abraham (Operations Officer, LCSPP), Nora Kaoues (Senior Economist, Delivery and Results Management, Results Secretariat), Nidhi Khattri (Senior Evaluation Officer, IEGCS), Jody Zall Kusek (Adviser, Health, Nutrition and Population), Mariano Lafuente (Public Sector Specialist, Poverty Reduction and Economic Management, Public Sector, Latin America and the Caribbean Region [LCSPS]), Nick Manning (Adviser, PRMPS), Laura Rawlings (Lead

Social Protection Specialist, Social Protection, Human Development Network), Fernando Rojas (Consultant, LCSPS), Jaime Saavedra (Director, PRMPR), Emmanuel Skoufias (Lead Economist, PRMPR), and Vera Wilhelm (Program Manager, Delivery and Results Management, Operations Policy and Country Services).

We would also like to thank Chris Humphrey for his tireless editing, Michael Alwan for his help putting together the final document, as well as Paola Scalabrin, Stuart K. Tucker, Cindy Fisher, and Andrés Menéses from the World Bank's Office of the Publisher.

Note

1. http://go.worldbank.org/CC5UP7ABN0.

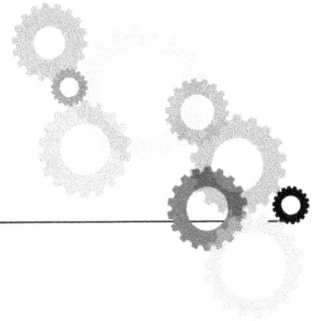

ABOUT THE AUTHORS

Michelle Adato is director of Social and Gender Assessment for the Millennium Challenge Corporation of the U.S. government, which she joined in late 2010. At the time that she wrote this chapter, she was a senior research fellow at the International Food Policy Research Institute (IFPRI). For eight years, she was co-leader of IFPRI's Global and Regional Program on Large-Scale Human Capital Interventions, which specialized in program evaluations using quantitative and qualitative methods. She is the co-editor of two books based on multi-country impact assessments. She has a PhD in Development Sociology from Cornell University and an M.P.A. from Harvard University's John F. Kennedy School of Government.

Michael Bamberger has a PhD in Sociology from the London School of Economics. He worked for 23 years with the World Bank as adviser on monitoring and evaluation to the Urban Development Department, training coordinator for Asia, and senior sociologist in the Gender and Development Department. Since retiring in 2001, he has worked as an evaluation consultant and evaluation trainer with 10 United Nations agencies, the World Bank, the Asian Development Bank, and a number of bilateral development agencies and developing country governments. He has published extensively on evaluation and is on the editorial board of several evaluation journals.

Bertha Briceño works as senior evaluation specialist at the World Bank's Water and Sanitation Program (WSP). Before joining WSP in 2009, she served for three years as director of Colombia's monitoring and evaluation system, SINERGIA. Previously, she worked in the Office of Evaluation of the Inter-American Development Bank, participating in project and country program evaluations. She has also consulted for the International Initiative for Impact Evaluation (3ie). She holds a master's degree in International Development from Harvard Kennedy School.

Manuel Fernando Castro is the executive director of Economia Urbana Ltda., a Latin American consultancy firm that supports government development policy. Castro is also an international consultant for the World Bank and the U.S. Agency for International Development. He was the director of Colombia's results-based management and evaluation system, SINERGIA. During 2008 and 2010, he worked as a senior evaluation officer at the Independent Evaluation Group of the World Bank, providing technical advice in the development of country monitoring and evaluation systems. He has provided support to more than 20 countries, particularly in Latin America and Asia.

Harry P. Hatry is a distinguished fellow and director of the Public Management Program for the Urban Institute in Washington, DC. He has been a leader in developing performance management and performance measurement procedures for federal, state, and local public and private agencies. His book, *Performance Measurement: Getting Results,* Second Edition, is widely used and has been translated into two other languages. He has provided assistance on monitoring and evaluation to the U.S. Departments of Education, Justice, Health and Human Services, and the Environmental Protection Agency, and has participated in projects in Albania, Colombia, Hungary, Indonesia, Pakistan, and Thailand.

Philipp Krause specializes in public administration and budgeting. He is currently the head of research, Budget Strengthening Initiative, at the Overseas Development Institute in London. He has previously worked on public sector issues for the German Technical Cooperation and the World Bank, and has advised governments in Latin America, Africa, Europe, and the Middle East. He has written scholarly articles and reports on public sector reform, budgeting, and fiscal governance, as well as monitoring and evaluation.

Mauricio I. Dussauge Laguna specializes in Comparative Public Administration. He is completing his PhD on "Cross-National Policy Learning and Performance-Based Reforms in Chile and Mexico" at the London School of Economics and Political Science (LSE). A graduate of El Colegio de México and the Maxwell School of Syracuse University, he has written extensively on topics such as administrative reforms, Mexican bureaucratic politics, policy transfer, and performance management. He has taught Public Policy and Administration at the LSE and El Colegio de México. He has worked as a policy analyst and senior executive in the Mexican government, and was a Fulbright Fellow at the U.S. Office of Personnel Management.

Robert Lahey was the founding head of the TBS Centre of Excellence for Evaluation, the Canadian government's evaluation policy center. He has headed evaluation units in a number of departments and agencies over a 32-year career in the Canadian public service. Since establishing his own consulting firm in 2004, he has advised many countries and organizations around the world on building monitoring and evaluation (M&E) capacity appropriate to their circumstances. He has written and presented extensively to the international M&E community. He is a member of Canada's Evaluation Credentialing Board and has been recognized by the Canadian Evaluation Society for his contribution to the theory and practice of evaluation in Canada.

Gladys Lopez-Acevedo is a senior economist in the World Bank Poverty Reduction and Equity Unit in the Poverty Reduction and Economic Management Network. Her research interests include poverty, labor markets, and evaluation, and she has published extensively in these areas in academic and policy journals. Prior to joining the Bank, she held several high-level positions in the government of Mexico, including senior adviser to the vice minister of finance. Lopez-Acevedo was also an associate professor at the Instituto Tecnologico Autonomo de Mexico (ITAM). She holds a BA in Economics from ITAM, and a PhD in Economics from the University of Virginia.

Keith Mackay retired from the World Bank in 2008 and now works as a consultant. He was a lead evaluation officer in the Bank's Independent Evaluation Group, providing technical advice and other support to countries working to strengthen their monitoring and evaluation (M&E) systems as an integral part of sound governance. Before joining the Bank in 1997, he was the manager of Australia's whole-of-government evaluation system. He has written over 60 publications on M&E systems.

Gloria M. Rubio is the former director general of the Social Programs Evaluation and Monitoring Unit at the Ministry of Social Development in Mexico. Prior to joining the ministry, she worked as a research associate at the Public Policy Institute in the Universidad de las Americas in Puebla. She has collaborated with the World Bank as a consultant and staff member in Washington, DC. She holds a master's degree in Public Affairs from the Woodrow Wilson School at Princeton University. Currently, she works as a consultant, providing technical assistance in designing and implementing monitoring and evaluation systems and conducting analytical work on social policy issues.

Jaime Saavedra-Chanduvi is director of the Poverty Reduction and Equity Department at the World Bank. Previously, he was manager of the Poverty and Gender Group in the Latin America and the Caribbean Vice Presidency, also at the World Bank. His major areas of interest include poverty reduction, inequality, labor markets, and social policies. He was executive director and principal researcher at Grupo de Análisis para el

Desarollo (GRADE) a non-partisan think tank based in Lima, and a principal advisor to the Ministry of Labor and Social Promotion in Peru. He has been president of the Executive Committee of the Network on Inequality and Poverty of the Latin America and Caribbean Economic Association (LACEA), IADB, World Bank, and United Nations Development Programme; and a board member at LACEA, the Nutrition Research Institute, and the National Council of Labor in Peru. He has held teaching positions at Pontificia Universidad Católica del Peru and Universidad del Pacífico in Peru, and has been a visiting researcher at the University of Toronto. Saavedra-Chanduvi holds a PhD in Economics from Columbia University and a BA in Economics from the Catholic University of Peru.

Rajiv Sharma has worked in leadership positions in the Indian public sector and has dealt extensively with developmental issues involving poverty alleviation, education, urban development, agriculture, environmental management, and e-governance. Until recently, he worked as director general of the Center for Good Governance, Hyderabad, India.

Geoffrey Shepherd is an economist with a particular interest in institutions and public sector reform. He received his D.Phil. from the University of Sussex, where he also worked from 1978 to 1986 (with appointments in the Sussex European Research Centre, then in the Science Policy Research Unit). He worked for the World Bank in the 1970s, then again from 1986 to 2001 on private sector development and trade issues in many parts of the world and, later, on public sector reform and institutional development issues in Latin America. He now consults for the World Bank.

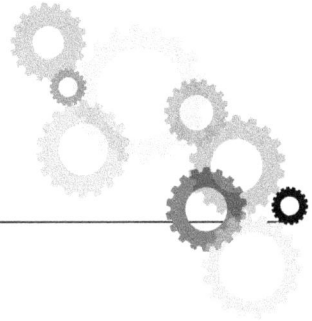

ABBREVIATIONS

ASF	Auditoría Superior de la Federación (Federal Supreme Audit; Mexico)
CONEVAL	Consejo Nacional de Evaluación de la Política de Desarrollo Social (National Council for the Evaluation of Social Development Policies; Mexico)
DAC	Development Assistance Committee (of the OECD)
DEPP	Directorate for Evaluation of Public Policies (Colombia)
DIPRES	Dirección de Presupuesto (Budget Office of the Ministry of Finance; Chile)
DNP	Departamento Nacional de Planeación (National Planning Department; Colombia)
DoF	Department of Finance (Australia)
ICT	information and communication technology
INEGI	Instituto Nacional de Estadística y Geografía (National Statistics Institute; Mexico)
M&E	monitoring and evaluation
MoF	Ministry of Finance (Australia, Chile)
OECD	Organisation for Economic Co-operation and Development
PAE	Programa Anual de Evaluación (Annual Evaluation Plan; Mexico)
SED	Sistema de Evaluación del Desempeño (Performance Evaluation System; Mexico)
SEDESOL	Secretaría de Desarrollo Social (Ministry for Social Development; Mexico)

SFP	Secretaría de la Función Pública (Ministry of Public Management; Mexico)
SHCP	Secretaría de Hacienda y Crédito Público (Ministry of Finance; Mexico)
SIGOB	Sistema de Gestión y Seguimiento a las Metas del Gobierno (Government Goals Monitoring Information System; Colombia)
SIIF	Sistema Integrado de Información Financiera (Integrated Financial Information System; Colombia)
SINERGIA	Sistema Nacional de Evaluación y Resultados de la Gestión Pública (National System for Evaluation and Management for Results; Colombia)

PART I

FRAMEWORK AND PRINCIPLES OF M&E SYSTEMS

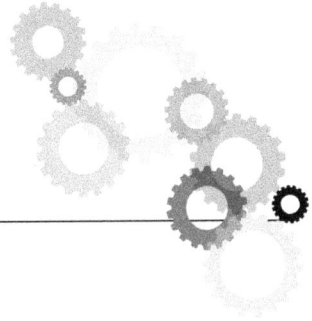

CHAPTER 1

Introduction

Philipp Krause, Keith Mackay, and Gladys Lopez-Acevedo

The Motivation for This Book

Governments around the world face ongoing pressures from citizens to provide more and better services, and to do this under a tight fiscal environment. This provides the context for government efforts to ensure their policies and programs are as effective, and as efficient, as possible. An emphasis on government performance has led a number of governments to create formal systems for monitoring and evaluating their performance—on a regular, planned, and systematic basis—with the objective of improving it. The focus of this book is on these government monitoring and evaluation (M&E) systems: what they comprise, how they are built and managed, and how they can be used to improve government performance.

M&E systems focus on measuring the results produced by government—its outputs, outcomes, and impacts. The M&E system may exist at the level of an individual agency, entire sector, or the government as a whole. M&E can provide unique information about the performance of government policies, programs, and projects—at the national, sector, and sub-national levels. It can identify what works, what does not, and the reasons why. M&E also provides information about the performance of a government, of individual ministries and agencies, and of managers and their staff. Highlighting examples of good practice and poor practice can help improve performance.

Perhaps the best way to understand the potential contribution of M&E to sound government is to view it at different parts of the policy cycle. The early stages of the policy process—analyzing and developing government policy and planning priorities and strategies—all benefit from evidence of what has or has not worked in the past; in other words, evidence-based policy making. Information on the performance of existing government programs and on the expected performance of new programs is important for the next stage of the policy cycle: the allocation of resources in the budget. M&E information, especially evaluation findings that explain past performance, helps to guide government decisions so that the most cost-effective collection of policies and programs can be adopted in the annual budget.

At the next stage in the policy cycle—the implementation and management of activities funded by the budget—M&E helps managers to monitor their activities, including government service delivery and staff management, so that they learn quickly what is working and what is not. Evaluations or reviews can identify the reasons for this good or bad performance. This is the learning function of M&E, often referred to as results-based management. The final stages of the policy cycle include accountability relationships. M&E reveals the extent to which the government has achieved its objectives and thus provides the evidence needed to ensure strong government accountability to outside actors such as the parliament and civil society, and within government between sector ministries and central ministries, among agencies and their sector ministry, and among ministers, managers, and staff. Strong accountability can provide the incentives necessary to improve performance.

There is an increasing body of literature on the experience of countries in building and strengthening their M&E systems,[1] and on the M&E tools and techniques[2] that they use. As it is difficult for non-experts to come to grips with these issues, a main purpose of this book is to synthesize existing knowledge about M&E systems and to provide it in a highly succinct, readily-understandable, and credible manner. This book is not designed to be a manual, however, guidance concerning further reading is also provided.

Another objective is to document new knowledge on M&E systems, such as on issues that may not be well understood so far, for example on how best to use different types of evaluations. The book comprises a collection of individually-authored papers, prepared by leading exponents of M&E and M&E systems. The papers reflect some differences in emphasis and perspective; and there are even some contradictions—typically minor—between some of the papers. Generally speaking, there exists substantial consensus on most of the issues relating to M&E systems.

This book endeavors to expand the frontiers of issues that have been researched and analyzed. However, there are still a number of issues that are still not understood well enough. These include, for example, the extent of utilization of different types of M&E systems, and the ways in which system design helps to determine utilization. Related issues are the cost and the cost-effectiveness of different M&E systems. These and other frontier issues are discussed briefly at the end of this chapter.

The target audiences for this book are busy people who have limited time to come to grips with the nuts and bolts of M&E systems. They include senior decision makers and policy advisers, such as civil servants, members of congress or parliament, academics, and others who might not be familiar with M&E systems but are aware of their potential importance for improving government performance. Another target audience is World Bank and other donor staff working to support client governments to strengthen their M&E systems.

The chapters in this book were originally published as separate briefing papers, available via a World Bank Web site: http://go.worldbank.org/CC5UP7ABN0. Additional papers will be prepared after the publication of this book, and these will be added to the Web site.

Two themes that emerge from this book merit particular notice. First, we highlight the importance of M&E utilization. No M&E system matters without being utilized over a sustained period of time. Second, we highlight the institutional dimension of M&E systems. The current literature has at times been overly focused on the instruments of M&E, neglecting the important institutional choices that determine how exactly an M&E system is run, and for what purpose. We will explore these two themes in a bit more detail below. The remainder of this introduction will then briefly outline the three main sections of this book.

What Is a Successful M&E System: Sustainability and Utilization

Most would agree that a successful M&E system is one where good-quality performance information and evaluation findings are produced and are used intensively at one or more stages of the policy cycle—this is what defines a well-utilized M&E system (see Chapter 2). For this situation to occur, both the supply and the demand of M&E information must be sufficient. The supply side includes attributes such as the quality and reliability of monitoring data, the number and coverage of performance indicators, the types of evaluations conducted and the issues addressed, and the reliability and timeliness of the evaluations. The demand side includes the range of potential users of M&E information—such as ministers, senior officials, policy analysts, program managers, congress or parliament, and civil society—and the extent of their use of this information in the policy cycle.

An important misunderstanding concerning M&E systems is that a supply-driven approach is sufficient: some evaluation advocates appear to believe that if high-quality, rigorous evaluations are conducted their findings and recommendations will almost automatically be used because of their self-evident value. Anyone who has worked at a senior level in government will recognize the fallacy in this belief. In the real world, there are many determinants of government decision making; evaluation findings relating to the effectiveness of policies and programs are only one input to these decisions.

That said, there are many ways to make monitoring information and evaluation findings as useful as possible (see IEG 2004, Chapter 2). Thus for budget decision making, it is helpful to ensure that evaluations have been conducted in a timely manner on a broad range of major spending programs, particularly those with uncertain performance. For decisions about initiating, scaling up, or eliminating programs, credible information about results can be crucial. For ongoing program management, it helps if evaluations have drawn on detailed program information and have focused on important operational issues, with the evaluation input and ownership of the program managers. And for accountability purposes, it helps when M&E information is available for the entire range of government spending, and when it allows simple comparisons over time and between different sectors and programs. Different potential users of M&E information have different needs, and it is difficult for an M&E system to satisfy all of them.

Experience with a broad range of types of public sector reform emphasizes the key role played by incentives (World Bank 1997).[3] Similarly, experience with M&E systems shows that powerful incentives are important on the demand side for achieving a high level of utilization of the information they provide. These include "carrots" (rewards), "sticks" (deterrents), and "sermons" (statements of support). Carrots might include positive encouragement and rewards for using M&E; sticks might include, for example, financial penalties for ministries that fail to implement evaluation recommendations; and sermons might include high-level, ministerial statements of support for M&E (see Mackay 2007, Chapter 11).

This book presents case studies on several countries that have succeeded in achieving high levels of utilization of M&E information, including Australia, Canada, Chile, and Mexico. There is also some discussion of other countries that utilize M&E information heavily, such as Colombia, the United Kingdom, and the United States. Each of these countries has its own, somewhat unique M&E system, and this reflects different historical factors, institutional contexts, key champions of M&E, and the manner in which the M&E system was developed. These country cases yield many insights into success factors that have determined the extent of utilization, as well as into the obstacles facing high levels of utilization. There is a range of evidence concerning the extent of utilization of M&E in these countries. A common feature is that the M&E system has been regarded as highly cost-effective in each country.

Another dimension of a fully "successful" M&E system is its sustainability—its ability to survive changes in government and to endure as a continuing feature of a government's approach to public sector management. Most of the countries that have built an M&E system whose outputs are highly utilized have spent a number of years in progressively improving the system. It takes time to create or strengthen data systems; to train or recruit qualified staff; to plan, manage, and conduct evaluations; and to train officials to use M&E information in their day-to-day work. Australia and Chile were able to create well-functioning M&E systems within four or five years, but Colombia has taken more than a decade.

An M&E system that achieves high levels of utilization but that proves not to be sustainable cannot be regarded as fully successful. Nevertheless, such systems provide valuable lessons for other countries. A good example here is Australia (see Chapter 14). Its M&E system lasted for a decade (1987 to 1997) and was generally considered to be one of the most successful in the world at that time, achieving a high level of utilization of the M&E information that the system produced. But a new government elected in 1996 was hostile to the civil service and it wanted to cut what it regarded as "non-core" government activities; it decided to significantly reduce the central role and functions of the powerful finance ministry that managed not just the M&E system but the entire budget process. This led to the dismantling of the M&E system; that said, a later government elected in 2007 is taking a number of steps to reinvigorate monitoring and evaluation.

Some outside observers have expressed surprise that a successful M&E system might be abolished, arguing that once evidence-based decision making and management have been established within a government, they will have demonstrated their value and will thus survive indefinitely. However, while it takes time and considerable effort to build an M&E system, that success can be undermined quickly. This has occurred when a new government does not place the same premium on having M&E information available to assist its decision making—such as in Australia or the United States after 2008—or where the government wished to reduce the power and influence of a key ministry that managed the M&E system—a risk factor that, arguably, the powerful finance ministry in Chile has faced in recent years. The eventual departure of influential M&E champions is another risk factor for M&E systems.

It might also be hoped that, once an M&E system has been in place for a lengthy period, a measurement-oriented "performance culture" might become established in government ministries, and that this would also persist even if the M&E system itself were to decline or even be abolished. The limited evidence on this does not give grounds for optimism, however. Ministries in Australia devoted considerable attention to M&E and made extensive use of this information during the life of the M&E system. However, after the system ended most ministries ended any substantive involvement in M&E; interestingly, some good-practice ministry "islands" of M&E persisted in later years (Mackay 2011).

One reason that has been suggested to explain this decline in a performance culture is the substantial cuts in the civil service which made it much more difficult to fund what might be regarded as "discretionary," long-term activities such as evaluation and research. Another possible reason is that the heads of ministries, and their ministers, might be disinclined to conduct evaluation: while positive evaluation findings that reveal good performance are always welcome, adverse findings can pose significant political and reputational risks. That said, the persistence of some M&E islands demonstrates that not all ministry heads hold such views.

The Institutional Dimension of M&E

There is a confusing degree of institutional variety to M&E systems, with many countries using different terminologies. In addition, the institutional settings fundamentally differ in terms of the overall leadership and centralization of the system, as well as its day-to-day operation. Commonalities and patterns between countries do exist, even among the unique characteristics of any one country. It is important to be able to assess how institutional incentives shape M&E systems.

Even in cases where most of the day-to-day work of managing evaluations is decentralized through ministries and programs, there is usually one central steering agency in charge of the overall framework of the system. Indeed, a common feature of successful M&E systems is having a capable ministry in charge—a ministry that can design, develop, and manage the system

(Chapter 2). In countries where evaluation systems are well utilized and survive for extended periods of time, this leadership is usually provided by the main users of evaluation information, as they are also the actors with the biggest stake in the success of the evaluation system. The principal stakeholders of this "evaluation agency" provide the steering of the system either directly or they delegate it to a special-purpose agency (a good example is the case of Mexico, see Chapter 12).

Direct steering is most common in countries with unified governments, and where the evaluation system is closely tied to the budget. Here the ministry of finance leads directly, and this delegation of authority via the finance minister is made possible by a strong mandate in budgetary matters, where evaluations are a natural extension of already existing budget systems. The most cited case for such a system is that of Chile (see Chapter 13), where the budget office (DIPRES) within the Ministry of Finance is directly in charge of all key aspects of the evaluation system, including the conduct of evaluations, and the follow-up of decisions on whether to implement evaluation recommendations. In this case, the following key activities are managed internally: (i) the selection and scheduling of evaluations; (ii) the process of identifying appropriate methods and evaluators; (iii) the supervision of the conduct of evaluations; and (iv) their eventual receipt and the follow-up of recommendations and their implementation. For evaluation systems that operate with a government-wide or at least an inter-ministerial mandate, this is an exceptional arrangement. While it allows a very high degree of control over all details of the evaluation work, it also retains a high cost burden at the center. Furthermore, it reduces significantly the potential for sector ministries and other spending units to develop a stake in the system, and thus might endanger its long-term viability.

In Chile, the budget process provides a natural structure to run the evaluation schedule, and gives strong incentives—be it through carrots or sticks—to other actors to provide necessary performance information concerning program operations and performance. The major leadership elements are all set up in-house within the budget office, building on an already very strong mandate that delegates virtually unlimited (by international standards) budgetary authority to the minister of finance.

It is far more common for evaluation agencies to decentralize the implementation of the system. In a decentralized system such as Canada (Chapter 15), the evaluation agency often retains control over the procedural framework and the methodological toolkit, as well as the quality control of the evaluation work. The day-to-day work of carrying out the evaluations themselves is then done by ministries and agencies in coordination with the evaluation agency. Such an arrangement makes it much easier for ministries to develop an interest in the evaluation work and to start utilizing the outputs for their own purposes, as opposed to seeing the evaluations as an externally imposed burden upon their work. Sharing the burden of implementation can also ease the setting up of evaluation systems by distributing the workload more evenly, thereby reducing the need for any one actor to devote large numbers of specialized staff.

Even in cases where a powerful finance ministry is in charge of steering the evaluations, they often find it expedient to involve spending ministries in the implementation, most often because it helps to gain support, but also because it reduces the workload at the central budget office. In Australia between 1987 and 1997 (see Chapter 14), the Department of Finance obliged spending ministries to develop multiannual evaluation plans, endeavored to persuade ministries to evaluate "problem" programs, and used the results of the evaluations as inputs into the budget process. However, the spending ministries were responsible for the conduct of each evaluation; the finance department would offer to help oversee them, although ministries might view this as intrusive.

Indirect steering is a model adopted in countries where either the separation of powers is strong or the evaluation system has multiple strong stakeholders with an interest in the evaluation system's outputs. In this case countries such as Mexico (Chapter 12) have found it useful to delegate the steering of the system to a specially designated technical agency in charge. This allows the evaluation system to function with a higher degree of technical independence and avoid the political conflict that may arise from having the evaluation very closely linked to one particular actor.

The Australian experience following the end of the M&E system—where most ministries conducted few evaluations and where monitoring information was generally of low quality (see Chapter 14)—suggests that a wholly devolutionary approach to M&E is unlikely to be sufficient, both to support evidence-based decision making and even for purposes of internal management. This suggests that some sort of centrally-driven approach is necessary.

Some M&E systems are clearly geared toward a single user and its information needs, while others serve a broader group of stakeholders. Single-user systems are most common where the finance ministry is clearly in charge and the main purpose is to inform budgetary decisions. In these cases it is relatively easy to develop a formal approach to ensure the implementation of evaluation recommendations, because the budget process provides a natural structure into which the evaluation system can be embedded. The budget calendar is already formalized, often in law, and the institutional roles are clearly defined (see Chapter 6).

The implementation of evaluation recommendations, if so desired by the designers of the system, can be organized by linking it to the budget. In Chile, the budget office maintains a record of all recommendations made in evaluations and follows them up annually in the budget negotiations for each program. This, however, is an exceptionally top-down system and far from common elsewhere. Many evaluation systems do not produce formalized sets of recommendations, and often the policy implications from a particular evaluation are far from clear. It is very common even for countries with advanced M&E systems to have a budget process where M&E information is not rigorously linked to budgetary decisions. The most common follow-up arrangement is therefore to make it mandatory for evaluation results to be considered at important decision points in the budget cycle, such as the annual or multiannual negotiations between finance and spending ministries, in budget deliberations in the legislature, and in policy discussions over the adoption of new programs.

The discussion so far has focused on the evaluation side of M&E systems. The monitoring side is also very important. Monitoring data for government programs provides useful "headline" information concerning their performance (see Chapter 8). In addition, such information is usually needed to conduct evaluations; if such information does not exist, or it is not reliable, then it will be necessary to undertake special data collections, and this can be an expensive undertaking. An advantage of monitoring information is that it can provide a broad coverage of government performance, across all ministries and sectors. A disadvantage, however, is that it provides little understanding of the reasons for good or bad performance. Evaluations can provide such understanding, if used in the proper context. An isolated impact evaluation might only say whether an intervention works or not, but not necessarily why. If evaluations of different types and regular monitoring are used in conjunction, it increases the ability of key decision makers to disentangle the difficult causal relationships that underpin government performance.

Government M&E systems typically rely largely or wholly on sector ministries to provide the necessary monitoring information. However, the ministries themselves usually rely on a number of separate, uncoordinated monitoring systems to provide this information. Problems with data harmonization and especially data quality are common. Another common weakness with monitoring systems is an excessive number of performance indicators. The lesson here is that "less is more": it is better to have a small number of reliable and highly used performance indicators than large collections of doubtful quality that—partly as a result of this quality—are seriously underutilized.

It has become a truism of institutional development that reforms must take the context of existing institutions into account. Naturally, systems that fit under the broad umbrella of "M&E" look quite different in different places. Although patterns clearly exist, in each individual country a multitude of formal and informal factors influences whether an M&E function is successfully and sustainably established. Ultimately, M&E as a function of government evolves because important actors find the outputs of M&E instruments useful for the purpose of governing. Sustained demand drives institutionalization, and systematic M&E can sustain such demand. These two elements are mutually reinforcing and mutually dependent. However, if a demand for M&E exists among central government actors, a technically ill-fitted system design might still derail implementation. Similarly, just because an M&E system has been built to resemble a successful model in a superficially similar country, success is not automatic. Hard-to-observe characteristics, such as a lack of sustained demand, can just as easily cause M&E systems to fail. Success and sustainability depend on both the right fit and the right demand.

In this book, we use country examples and case studies as references to illustrate common patterns that are relevant beyond the individual country case. Faced with the complexity of M&E-related reforms, readers will find it easier to access the appropriate information for the challenge at hand by being able to see M&E systems in context. Readers can then pick and choose what they find most appropriate, without necessarily having to read through large amounts of possibly unsuitable material. This volume tries to capture the key ingredients to both in three sections: The framework of M&E; the tools of M&E; and finally M&E systems in context.

Framework and Principles of M&E Systems

The first seven chapters introduce the core set of cross-cutting concepts, definitions, and first steps. This framework of M&E comprises the importance of utilization of M&E instruments when designing and implementing an M&E system (Chapter 2), a typology of different M&E systems (Chapter 3), common implementation challenges, and how to deal with them, especially from a sectoral perspective (Chapter 4), approaches toward conducting M&E diagnoses (Chapter 5), the challenges arising from the links between M&E and budgeting (Chapter 6), and the use of information technology and social accountability tools (Chapter 7).

Following this introduction, Chapter 2 by Keith Mackay outlines the main ways in which M&E findings can be used throughout the policy cycle to improve the performance of government decision making and of government services and programs, including the use of M&E for evidence-based policy making, budgeting, management, and accountability. There are many different types of M&E tools and approaches, each with advantages and limitations. This chapter presents four examples of successful government systems for M&E—in both developed and developing countries—and discusses some of their hard-earned lessons for building M&E systems. These lessons are evidence of what works and what does not in the development and sustainment of successful M&E systems.

Bertha Briceño in Chapter 3 characterizes various types of M&E systems, including examples from three government-based systems in Latin America: Mexico, Colombia, and Chile. The characterization outlined here ranges from completely independent outside bodies, to strongly centralized government systems, to highly decentralized systems. Each type of system has different advantages that result from the interplay of demand and supply forces: on the supply side, actors produce M&E information for a variety of intended purposes; the demand side responds with actual utilization, revealing the real incentives of the system's clients. In addition, strategies are presented to mitigate potential disadvantages of the different types of systems.

M&E systems are frequently designed and implemented based on an initial diagnostic study. Geoffrey Shepherd in Chapter 4 discusses the core issues of how to think about such a diagnosis. There is no one blueprint for preparing an M&E diagnosis: content and presentation depend on the specific context. The chapter illustrates the range of contexts by discussing a number of issues that help explain the differences and illuminates these issues, where possible, by referring to various country studies that have appeared in recent years. They cover six Organisation for Economic Co-operation and Development (OECD) countries—mostly studies that draw "good practice" lessons—and two African and four Latin American countries—a mix of diagnostic and "lessons-of-experience" studies.

Implementing M&E systems is a challenging process. Harry Hatry in Chapter 5 identifies the key steps in designing and implementing an M&E system for ministries and individual government agencies that provide services. These suggestions are intended to apply irrespective of sector. The system might have been ordered or requested by the president or prime minister's office, by a minister, or by any agency head. The design of an M&E system should focus on creating a process that will yield regular outcome data, in addition to data on the organization's outputs that can be used by the designing agency and upper-level officials.

Philipp Krause in Chapter 6 introduces the main issues surrounding M&E as a tool for budgeting—a system usually referred to as performance budgeting. OECD countries that adopt performance budgeting tend to develop a performance-informed budget process, where M&E instruments serve as analytical tools. In this model, performance indicators are integrated into the budget and regular evaluations are scheduled into the budget cycle. Performance indicators and evaluations are institutionally considered during budget formulation. This process can take various forms. Inevitably, the right setup will depend on the specific administrative context. The main design challenge is how to tailor the system to the likely users of M&E information and their position within the budgeting framework. This is a universal concern, irrespective of a country's stage of development.

Rajiv Sharma addresses in Chapter 7 the basic concepts relating to the use of social accountability and information technology to monitor and evaluate public services and other governance processes that affect citizens. With the help of simple though practical examples that use these concepts, Sharma explains how to bring a qualitative change in monitoring and evaluation by making the whole process more citizen centered and outcome oriented. In turn, these practices can help improve the quality of service delivery. The chapter's arguments are illustrated by several examples from India.

Components and Tools of M&E Systems

The second section of the book introduces the most important tools commonly used in M&E, with a focus on practical applications in context. The section covers defining and monitoring results indicators (Chapter 8), different types of evaluations (Chapter 9), how to reconstruct baseline data for ongoing programs (Chapter 10), as well as the importance of mixed-method approaches (Chapter 11). Policy makers and program managers are faced every day with major decisions resulting from insufficient funding, ongoing complaints about service delivery, unmet needs among different population groups, and limited results on the ground.

Developing effective M&E systems requires well-defined formulation and implementation strategies for performance indicators. These strategies vary depending on a country's priority for measuring results and on the scope and pace of its performance management reform objectives, argues Manuel Fernando Castro (Chapter 8). Castro's chapter directly links to the discussion in Chapter 5 of key steps for setting up sectoral monitoring systems and how officials can go about defining good indicators. The extensive literature on performance management indicators contains relatively few references to practical elements of successful government implementation of performance indicator systems. Castro's chapter encapsulates some of the main elements for senior officials to realistically and practically consider when introducing performance indicator and target systems in government to ensure sustainability.

Gloria Rubio in Chapter 9 outlines the menu of evaluation types implemented by developing and OECD countries to tackle a wide range of policy and program management issues. The suitability of each type of evaluation depends on the available time and resources, and on capacity constraints. The chapter emphasizes the importance of a gradual approach when introducing evaluation tools into country-level M&E systems. Different paths may work better for different countries depending on the main purpose of their M&E system, existing institutional capacity, the availability of funds, and external technical assistance.

Every type of evaluation requires the collection of baseline data before the project or program begins. Once the project or program has been underway for some time, an evaluation can compare its performance with the baseline data—using advanced statistical techniques—to provide an estimate of its outcomes and impacts. However, as Michael Bamberger points out in Chapter 10, it is often the case that a baseline study is not conducted, seriously limiting the possibility of producing a rigorous assessment of project outcomes and impacts. This chapter discusses the reasons why baseline studies are often not conducted, even when they are included in the project design and funds have been approved. It also describes strategies that can be used to "reconstruct" baseline data at a later stage in the project or program cycle.

Despite significant methodological advances, the value of monitoring data and of many evaluations is reduced because of an over-reliance on quantitative methods alone, argues Michelle Adato in Chapter 11. The addition of qualitative methods to the M&E toolkit can also inform survey design, identify social and institutional drivers and impacts that are hard to quantify, uncover unanticipated issues, and trace impact pathways. When used together, quantitative and qualitative approaches provide more coherent, reliable, and useful conclusions than do each on their own. Adato's chapter identifies key elements of good mixed-method design and provides examples of these principles applied in several countries.

M&E Systems in Context

The final section of this book illustrates the central themes in a set of country briefings. These show how the different parts of an M&E system interact in a dynamic and challenging environment. The cases were selected to show the diversity in terms of country contexts and regions. Mexico and Chile are both presidential democracies in Latin America, while Australia and Canada are Westminster-style parliamentary systems. In each of these contexts, relatively successful M&E systems evolved and were maintained over extended periods of time.

The cases also show how seemingly quite similar countries sometimes develop very different systems. Although Chile and Mexico have some institutional characteristics in common, they are also different in many ways. Chile has a highly centralized budget process with stable legislative majorities, while Mexico's central government is much more fragmented and the Congress is quite powerful. These differences illustrate that Mexico's and Chile's M&E systems serve different principals, are operated differently, and yet serve their purpose in their respective contexts. These kinds of patterns can be found elsewhere, and understanding them can provide important clues to how best to design an M&E system in any one place.

Fifteen years ago, Mexico, like most countries, had undertaken a few scattered evaluations, but no systematic performance measurement, argues Gloria Rubio in Chapter 12. Political changes in the late 1990s generated an increased demand for transparency and accountability. This led to new legislation and institutions aimed at strengthening independent government oversight through several channels. The development of an M&E system in Mexico can be divided in two stages. The first phase from 2000 to 2006 was characterized by good intentions, but unrealistic expectations and lack of vision concerning the institutional capacity-building required for the new evaluation efforts. After 2007, an increased concern with fiscal matters by the finance ministry, along with the spread of knowledge led by several influential evaluations, led to the emergence of a national evaluation system, which links a dedicated evaluation agency with the ministry of finance, line ministries, and other actors.

According to Mauricio Dussauge Laguna in Chapter 13, the Chilean management control and evaluation system is internationally regarded as a strong example of how M&E can be successfully put into practice. The main M&E tools are centrally coordinated by the Ministry of Finance's Budget Office and promote the use of M&E information in government decision-making processes, particularly those related to the budget. The Chilean experience, covering the period of 1994–2010, provides a highly relevant example of the strengths, benefits, and limitations of M&E design and implementation in a centralized public sector. In many respects the Chilean "model" is highly impressive—in terms of the system's design, evolution, utilization, cost-effectiveness, and discipline. The individual monitoring and evaluation instruments used by the Chilean government tend to be of high quality. Several authors in this volume use examples from Chile to illustrate their points and even hold them up as models of how a particular tool ought to work. For this reason, many other countries in Latin America and other regions look to Chile as providing a model to aspire to or even to emulate. However, Dussauge Laguna discusses various reasons why it could be difficult to attempt to transfer the Chilean model to other countries with different institutional contexts. Even though the technical quality of the Chilean system is very high, as always there are tradeoffs and institutional constraints that reflect the peculiarities of a country's context and legacy.

Countries from all over the world have shown an interest in Australia's experience in creating an M&E system that supports evidence-based decision making and performance-based budgeting, finds Keith Mackay in Chapter 14. The Australian M&E system in existence from 1987 to 1997 was generally considered to be one of the most successful and was driven by the federal Department of Finance. This chapter discusses the genesis, characteristics, and success of this particular system and briefly considers the Australian government's approach to M&E after the system was abolished. The contrast between these two periods provides many valuable insights into success factors and challenges facing successful M&E systems, and into implementing evidence-based decision making more broadly.

Robert Lahey explains in Chapter 15 how performance measurement, monitoring, and evaluation have long been a part of the infrastructure within the federal government in Canada. With over 30 years of formalized evaluation experience in most large federal departments and agencies, many lessons can be gained from this experience, not the least of which is the recognition that the M&E system itself is not static. The Canadian government has a formalized evaluation policy, standards, and guidelines and these have been significantly modified on three occasions over the past three decades. Changes have usually come about due to a public sector reform initiative, such as the introduction of a results orientation to government management, a political issue that may have generated a demand for greater accountability and transparency in government, or a change in emphasis on where and how M&E information should be used in government. This illustrates the manner in which even mature M&E systems need to continue to evolve.

The issues addressed in this book are faced by the growing number of developing countries that are working to improve their performance by creating systems to measure and help them understand their performance. This trend is influenced by OECD countries, most of which give a high priority to four main uses of M&E information at different stages of the policy cycle: to support policy development based on evidence, budgeting, ongoing program and project management, and accountability. Developing countries are also looking to their peers—countries such as Chile, Colombia, and Mexico—that have created reasonably well-performing M&E systems where the monitoring information and evaluation findings that are produced are used intensively.

Frontier Issues

As noted earlier, there are a number of issues that are still not sufficiently well researched and understood. The evidence on utilization of the information produced by M&E systems can best be described as patchy. This is partly because of the number and complexity of the different ways in which monitoring information and evaluation findings can be used at different stages of the policy cycle. The lead M&E agencies in some countries—most notably Chile, but also others such as Australia and the United States at different times—have devoted some effort into tracking the use made of the system's M&E information. Other countries, such as Canada and Colombia, have not done this to any considerable extent, or at least not on a systematic basis. Much more is known about the use made of particular evaluations, particularly of high-profile programs such as the large conditional cash transfer programs in many Latin American countries.

The knowledge gap concerning system utilization is unfortunate, as it reduces the insights that can be gained from the experience of different countries. Such information should be sought keenly by the managers of an M&E system—it is important for them to understand what aspects of the system are effective, which are not, and the reasons why. It is hoped that a later paper in this World Bank series will investigate further the issue of utilization.

Another frontier issue that has not received much attention is the cost of M&E systems. This would seem to be a fundamental issue, not least because it goes to the heart of the cost-effectiveness of an M&E system; its omission is hard to understand. Chile, again, is at the forefront in being able to provide average costs for the various types of evaluation instrument that it uses, and the total cost of the system[4] has been estimated at about US$0.75 million per annum—a very modest amount compared with the total government budget of some US$20 billion per annum. Most government M&E systems cost much more than this amount; indeed, a single, large impact evaluation can cost over US$1 million, although most cost much less than this.

Other issues that merit further research include the timescales for building different kinds of M&E systems. Well-functioning M&E systems were created in Australia and Chile in four or five years, but it has taken over a decade to build such a system in Colombia. The U.S. M&E system—based on the *program assessment rating tool*—was up and running in only a few years, but this was able to draw on the experience and considerable M&E efforts inherited from earlier government administrations (see Mackay 2007).

One final frontier issue flagged here is the extent to which it is realistic to create an M&E system in fragile states. One view—which is unlikely to be shared by everyone—is that M&E systems are sufficiently complex that they should usually only be contemplated by middle income or high income countries; from this perspective, countries with M&E systems such as Tanzania and Uganda would be considered "the exceptions that prove the rule." Another, less restrictive, view is that even low income countries and fragile states can still put in place the basics of a workable monitoring system, often centered on the national statistical institution, and with heavy donor support. The World Bank will soon publish a meta-analysis on M&E in fragile and post-conflict states.

It is hoped that this book will help senior officials and others working to strengthen their government's monitoring and evaluation system. Like other types of public sector management, a considerable amount of time and effort is required to build an M&E system that produces reliable information that is utilized intensively. The growing number of success story countries attest to the value of such effort—they demonstrate that government M&E systems can be highly cost-effective. The chapters in this book and the further reading they suggest will help readers to come to grips with the issues faced in such efforts. We believe that this wealth of experience should prove invaluable.

Notes

1. See for instance: Ospina et al. 2004, May et al. 2006, Mackay 2007, and Lopez-Acevedo et al. 2010. See also www.worldbank.org/lacmonitoringandevaluation and the collection of country case studies at www.worldbank.org/ieg/ecd.
2. A useful overview of M&E tools and techniques is provided by IEG 2004a, Busjeet 2010, and at http://go.worldbank.org/GSD78LQBV0.
3. See World Bank (1997).
4. This figure relates only to the spending of the finance ministry; it excludes the cost to sector ministries of providing monitoring information. See Mackay 2007.

Bibliography

Busjeet, Gita. 2010. *Planning, Monitoring and Evaluation: Methods and Tools for Poverty and Inequality Reduction Programs.* Washington, DC: Poverty Reduction and Economic Management Unit, World Bank.

IEG (Independent Evaluation Group). 2004. *Monitoring and Evaluation: Some Tools, Methods and Approaches.* 2nd Edition. Washington, DC: World Bank.

Lopez-Acevedo, Gladys, Katia Rivera, Lycia Lima, and Helena Hwang, eds. 2010. *Challenges in Monitoring and Evaluation: An Opportunity to Institutionalize M&E Systems*. Washington, DC: World Bank and Inter-American Development Bank.

Mackay, Keith. 2007. *How to Build M&E Systems to Support Better Government*. Washington, DC: World Bank.

———. 2011. "The Australian Government's Performance Framework." World Bank ECD Working Paper 25. World Bank, Washington, DC.

May, Ernesto, David Shand, Keith Mackay, Fernando Rojas, and Jaime Saavedra, eds. 2006. *Towards Institutionalizing Monitoring and Evaluation Systems in Latin America and the Caribbean: Proceedings of a World Bank/Inter-American Development Bank Conference*. Washington, DC: World Bank.

Ospina, Sonia, Nuria Cunill Grau, and Ariel Zaltsman. 2004. "Performance Evaluation, Public Management Improvement and Democractic Accountability: Some Lessons from Latin America." *Public Management Review* 6(2): 230–251.

World Bank. 1997. *World Development Report 1997: The State in a Changing World*. Washington, DC: World Bank.

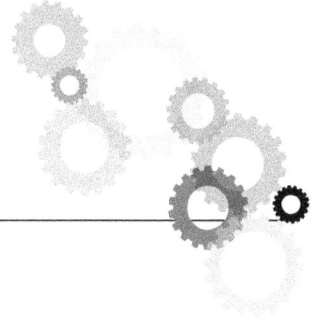

CHAPTER 2

Conceptual Framework for Monitoring and Evaluation

Keith Mackay

A growing number of governments in developing countries around the world are working to improve their performance by creating systems to measure and help them understand the performance of their services and programs. This trend is influenced by the Organisation for Economic Co-operation and Development (OECD) countries, most of which place a high priority on the four main uses of monitoring and evaluation (M&E) findings:

1. Policy development
2. Evidence-based policy making and budgeting
3. Management performance
4. Accountability

The priority for measuring and better managing government performance in middle- and low-income countries is intensified by continuing fiscal and macroeconomic pressures affecting all countries, and by ever-rising

This chapter has benefited from comments by Gladys Lopez-Acevedo, Nidhi Khattri, Jaime Saavedra, and Helena Hwang. The views expressed in this chapter are those of the author.

expectations from ordinary citizens. It is also influenced by the need for citizens, governments, and the international community to make state actions more effective in increasing welfare, reducing poverty, and improving opportunities for all. An additional impetus to focus on performance is the strong expectations of international donors.

This chapter outlines the main ways in which M&E findings can be used throughout the policy cycle to improve the performance of government decision making and of government services and programs, including the use of M&E for evidence-based policy making, budgeting, management, and accountability. Many different types of M&E tools and approaches exist, each with advantages and limitations. This chapter presents four examples of successful government systems for M&E in both developed and developing countries, and discusses some of their hard-earned lessons for building and sustaining successful M&E systems.

Why M&E Systems Improve Government Performance

Government M&E systems focus on measuring the results produced by government—its outputs, outcomes, and impacts. The M&E system may exist at the level of an individual agency, entire sector, or the government as a whole. M&E can provide unique information about the performance of government policies, programs, and projects—at the national, sector, and subnational levels. It can identify what works, what does not, and the reasons why. M&E also provides information about the performance of a government, of individual ministries and agencies, and of managers and their staff. Highlighting examples of good practice and poor practice can help improve performance.

Three defining characteristics of successful M&E systems are:

1. Intensive utilization of the M&E information in one or more stages of the policy cycle
2. Information that meets standards for data quality and evaluation reliability
3. Sustainability, by which the system will survive a change in administration, government ministers, or top officials

Perhaps the best way to understand the potential contribution of M&E to sound government is to view it at different parts of the policy cycle (Figure 2.1). The early stages of the policy process—analyzing and developing government policy and planning priorities and strategies—all benefit from

FIGURE 2.1 The Policy Cycle: Linking Policy, Planning, Budgeting, Management, and M&E

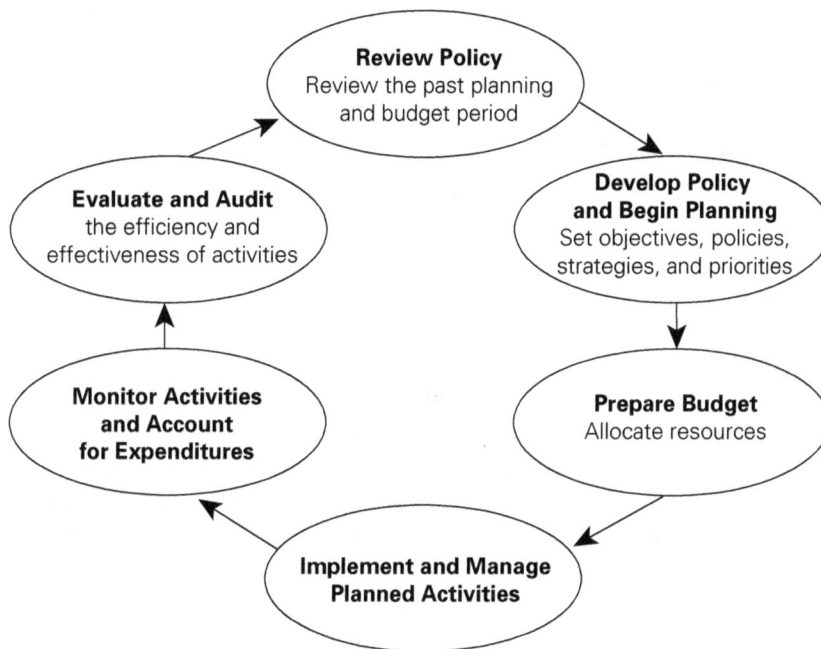

Review Policy
Review the past planning and budget period

Develop Policy and Begin Planning
Set objectives, policies, strategies, and priorities

Evaluate and Audit
the efficiency and effectiveness of activities

Prepare Budget
Allocate resources

Monitor Activities and Account for Expenditures

Implement and Manage Planned Activities

Source: Adapted from World Bank 1998.

evidence of what has or has not worked in the past; in other words, evidence-based policy making. It is an important discipline for governments to consider carefully what they are trying to achieve from their policies, and to plan for them accordingly. Thus it helps to clarify, for each possible program, what success would look like and how the government will know if it has (or has not) been achieved. It also helps to clarify the potential poverty and distributional effects of policies and programs. Setting performance targets and measuring progress toward achieving them is thus an important part of government planning and policy review.

Information on the performance of existing government programs and on the expected performance of new programs is important for the next stage of the policy cycle: the allocation of resources in the budget. M&E information, especially evaluation findings that explain past performance, helps to guide government decisions so that the most cost-effective collection of policies and programs can be adopted in the annual budget.

At the next stage in the policy cycle—the implementation and management of activities funded by the budget—M&E helps managers to monitor their activities, including government service delivery and staff management, so that they learn quickly what is working and what is not in terms of expected outputs, expected outcomes, or even higher level objectives such as increasing welfare. Performance indicators can be used to make cost and performance comparisons among different administrative units, regions, and districts. Ongoing monitoring of these activities—including spending, processes, outputs, outcomes, and impacts—is particularly important. Comparisons made over time can help identify good, bad, and promising practices. Evaluations or reviews can identify the reasons for this good or bad performance. This is the learning function of M&E, often referred to as results-based management.

The final stages of the policy cycle include accountability relationships. M&E reveals the extent to which the government has achieved its objectives and thus provides the evidence needed to ensure strong government accountability to the legislature, to civil society, and to donors. M&E also supports accountability relationships within government between sector ministries and central ministries, among agencies and their sector ministry, and among ministers, managers, and staff. Strong accountability can provide the incentives necessary to improve performance. M&E can also play a role in anticorruption efforts. It can help identify "leakages" in government funding as well as some of the possible manifestations of corruption, such as when government spending is not reflected in the physical quality of infrastructure or in the volume and quality of government services provided.

What Does a Government M&E System Look Like?

Most governments have data systems for measuring their spending, processes, and outputs. But this is not the same as a system to monitor and evaluate the performance of all of its programs. A much smaller number of governments possess such systems. These systems involve the regular, systematic collection and use of M&E information at the level of an individual agency, an entire sector, or for the government as a whole. The focus of these systems is on measuring the results produced by government—its outputs, outcomes, and impacts.

A number of governments have devoted the effort necessary to build high-performing M&E systems. Examples of four countries with well-documented and analyzed M&E systems that are highlighted below are Australia, Chile, Colombia, and the United States (Box 2.1). Canada is another example of a successful government M&E system (Chapter 15); note that while Mexico (Chapter 12) provides a very promising case study, its M&E

BOX 2.1
Four Examples of Successful Government M&E Systems

Australia: The government evaluation system was managed by the Department of Finance (DoF), and it required ministries to evaluate every program every three to five years. The line ministries themselves conducted the evaluations, but they were overviewed by the DoF and other central departments. By 1994, almost 80 percent of new spending proposals in the budget process relied on evaluation findings, usually to a significant degree. About two-thirds of savings options also relied on evaluation findings. DoF officials, who attended the Cabinet meetings that considered these budget proposals, judged that this information was highly influential on the Cabinet's budget decision making. The Australian National Audit Office found that line departments also used this information intensively, particularly to help improve their operational efficiency.

Chile: The Ministry of Finance (MoF) commissions evaluations externally to academics and consulting firms, and it uses standardized terms of reference and methodologies for each type of evaluation. MoF officials use the M&E findings intensively in their budget analysis of the performance of each ministry and agency. The ministry also uses the information to set performance targets for each agency and to impose management improvements on both ministries and agencies. The MoF carefully oversees the

extent to which each ministry implements these management improvements.

Colombia: The National Planning Department manages the government's M&E system, SINERGIA. The system includes information for 500 performance indicators, as well as a number of rapid and impact evaluations. The president has used the information provided by SINERGIA intensively in his monthly management control meetings with each minister and in his weekly town hall meetings in municipalities around the country.

United States: In 2002, the government created the Program Assessment Rating Tool (PART), building on earlier efforts to measure government performance. The performance of all 1,000 government programs have been rated using the PART methodology, and PART ratings are required to be used by departments in their annual budget funding requests to the Office of Management and Budget (OMB). The requests must highlight the PART ratings, the recommendations for improvements in program performance, and performance targets. OMB, in turn, also uses the PART ratings when it prepares the administration's funding requests to the Congress, and to impose performance improvement requirements on departments.

system has not been in existence long enough to demonstrate its extent of success—in terms of the quality of M&E information, the extent of its utilization, and its sustainability (see below).

Each of the four governments utilizes its M&E information intensively. Common features include a powerful central ministry with a leading role in the M&E system (such as the finance or planning ministry), and—as a consequence—an emphasis on using M&E information to support the budget process. What is less well known and documented, however, is how effective these systems have been in supporting the use of M&E information for ongoing program management. Different countries emphasize different M&E tools and techniques. Some place a heavy reliance on monitoring data, others on evaluations and reviews of various kinds. Some countries have extensive (and expensive) M&E systems; others have more streamlined, low-cost systems.

What does a good M&E system look like? The answer to this question depends on country-specific factors, such as government demand for M&E information, the uses to which the information will be put, the availability and quality of existing government data, the abilities of officials and consultants to evaluate and analyze M&E information, and the amount the government is prepared to spend on M&E.

The Three Defining Characteristics of Successful M&E Systems

A "successful" M&E system has three defining characteristics. The first is intensive utilization of the M&E information provided by the system in one or more of the stages of the policy cycle. It may seem trite to argue that M&E information should only be collected if it is going to be used, but most evaluators in governments (and in donor agencies) have a surprisingly poor understanding of the extent to which the M&E information they produce is actually used by others. If M&E information is not being used, then it is important to discover the reasons why. Is it because the M&E information is regarded as being of poor quality, or not timely, or because evaluations have not addressed the most relevant questions concerning program performance? Or is it because the intended users within the government—such as the finance or planning ministries—have neither the skills nor interest in using this information in their work?

Reliable, quality information is another feature of successful M&E systems. Various standards define what constitutes quality monitoring data and evaluations, and these standards can be used to assess the reliability of the information that any M&E system produces. Most government evaluation offices have some sort of quality control mechanism in place. Most, however, do not appear to conduct or commission formal reviews of the quality of their work. Three of the four countries highlighted in Box 2.1 have conducted such reviews: Australia, Chile, and Colombia.

The third characteristic of a successful M&E system is sustainability. This relates to the likelihood that the M&E system will survive a change in administration, government ministers, or top officials. When the utilization of

M&E information is firmly embedded in core government processes, such as the budget cycle, it is likely to be sustained over time. Conversely, when M&E has only a handful of key supporters or is little used, or if it is largely funded by donors rather than by the government itself, then sustainability is less likely.

One question that is often asked is how many countries have successful M&E systems. A related question is how many countries have M&E systems, however successful or not they might be. These are difficult questions to answer. Almost every country in the world possesses ministry systems that produce monitoring information on government spending, processes, and outputs with some degree of regularity. Most countries also have national statistical collections that provide information on country health and education outcomes, among others.[1] Most low-income countries have poverty reduction strategies that require sets of government and country performance indicators; these constitute a form of M&E system. Many countries also conduct evaluations of some sort; these may be government funded or, for low- and middle-income countries, donor funded, and they are often conducted on an ad hoc basis.

While it is a judgment call as to when these M&E arrangements can reasonably be termed an M&E "system," it is likely that there are dozens of countries that possess some kind of whole-of-government M&E system. Among these, the countries that could be judged to be fully or partially successful would probably number in the tens or at most the twenties—including a number of OECD and middle-income countries, with the latter especially in Latin America, and a small number of low-income countries such as Uganda and Tanzania. More precise estimates would require strict and measurable criteria for "success," as well as detailed reviews or diagnoses of each country against these criteria. The country case studies highlighted in this volume provide a sample of M&E systems, and these illustrate a range of issues relating to system architecture, capacity-building efforts, quality, and utilization, among others.

Building a Government M&E System— What to Do and What Not to Do

Many developed and developing countries have accumulated substantial experience in building M&E systems. As with any form of capacity building, a number of hard-earned lessons about what works best and what does not can be drawn from these experiences (discussed more fully in Mackay 2007). Eight key lessons are discussed below.

Lesson 1. First and foremost is the need for substantive government demand for M&E information. Such demand is necessary if a serious effort to build an M&E system is to be started and sustained. A significant effort is required to build an M&E system, including: creating or upgrading data systems, choosing evaluation tools and techniques and adapting them to local circumstances and priorities, training evaluators and developing national evaluation consultants, creating M&E offices inside a lead ministry and probably in some or all sector ministries, training the users of M&E information—mid-level analysts, senior officials in central and sector ministries, and possibly their ministers—and creating a bureaucratic infrastructure to decide which government programs should be evaluated and what issues should be addressed in each evaluation. Frankly, this effort is not worthwhile unless the resulting M&E information is likely to be used intensively.

Lesson 2. Incentives are a key part of the demand side. Strong incentives are needed for M&E to be conducted, and for the information to be used. M&E experts often make a basic mistake by asserting that M&E information is intrinsically "a good thing" and that if the information is made available, then it will automatically be used. This technocratic view that M&E has inherent merit is naïve; M&E information has value only if it is reliable and if it is used intensively.

Intensive, ongoing utilization does not happen by chance. Incentives are needed for M&E information to be used by program managers in their day-to-day work, by budget and planning officials responsible for advising on policy options, or by a legislature responsible for accountability oversight.

Incentives come in three types: carrots, sticks, and sermons.[2] An example of a carrot is the provision of greater autonomy to managers who can demonstrate (through reliable M&E information) that their programs are performing well. An example of a stick is to set challenging (but realistic) performance targets that each ministry and program manager is required to meet. An example of a sermon is a high-level statement of support for M&E, such as from a president or influential minister. Many of these incentives have been applied successfully in building M&E systems in developed and developing countries.

Lesson 3. It helps to start with a diagnosis of what M&E functions already exist in the country—in the government, academia, and the consulting community. A diagnosis should identify the strengths and weaknesses of what exists on both the demand and supply sides. This is really a type of evaluation, and the very process of conducting it provides an opportunity for key stakeholders within the government to become more familiar with M&E and its potential benefits. A diagnosis naturally leads to an action plan to strengthen M&E, which can facilitate a coalition of support from interested sector ministries and the donor community.

Lesson 4. Another dimension of the demand side is the need for a powerful champion, an influential minister or senior official who is able to lead the push to institutionalize M&E, to persuade colleagues about its importance, and to allocate significant resources to creating a government-wide M&E system. Government champions have played pivotal roles in some of the most successful M&E systems.

Reliance on a law, decree, or cabinet decision has much less success institutionalizing M&E systems. Such an approach can help to legitimize an M&E system, particularly in countries where the presence of a legal instrument is viewed as necessary for any government reform to be perceived as worthwhile and to be taken seriously. But a law or decree on its own does not ensure that the considerable efforts required to build an M&E system will be undertaken and maintained.

Lesson 5. Another common feature of successful M&E systems is stewardship by a capable ministry that can design, develop, and manage the system. Thus it helps to have the institutional lead of the M&E system close to the center of a government, such as in the president's office or in the finance or planning ministries.

One role of this institutional leader is to continually review progress in developing the M&E system and to make any necessary adjustments to its action plan. Difficulties and roadblocks are inevitable, so it is important to identify what is working, what is not, and why. Regular progress reviews provide the opportunity to analyze both the demand and supply sides of the M&E system. In fact, most countries with well-performing M&E systems have not actually developed them in a linear manner—that is, starting with a clear understanding of what the system would look like once fully mature and then progressively achieving this vision. Rather, M&E systems are more commonly developed incrementally and even in a piecemeal and opportunistic manner, with some false starts and blind alleys along the way.[3]

Lesson 6. A common mistake once M&E has been embraced enthusiastically is to over-engineer the M&E system. This is often evident in the large number of performance indicators that are collected. Over-engineering can also result in the proliferation of ministry data systems. These are often uncoordinated even within each ministry. The problem is multiplied if there are several government-wide data systems, which may be managed by different central ministries and may well require related (but different) information to be provided by sector ministries and agencies. In Mexico, for example, the social development agency SEDESOL had eight different, uncoordinated management information systems. In Uganda in recent years, the government had to try to coordinate as many as 16 separate sector and subsector systems.

That said, there is real value in building reliable ministry data systems: these provide the raw data on which a government-wide M&E system depends. An audit of data systems and a diagnosis of data capacities can be helpful in this situation because they could provide a basis for rationalizing existing data collections and improving their quality.

Lesson 7. Unsurprisingly, building an M&E system usually includes training for a range of M&E tools, methods, approaches, and concepts. Well-trained officials or consultants who are highly skilled in M&E are needed. Training should provide more than competencies in M&E, however. Senior officials need to understand the strengths and limitations—the relative cost-effectiveness—of various types of M&E tools and techniques. Introductory training can also raise awareness of and demand for M&E information. Training should extend to the use of M&E findings. Budget analysts, poverty analysts, and program managers need to be able to interpret monitoring data to understand trends, data definitions, breaks in data time series, and so forth. They also need to be discriminating consumers—they must be able to tell when an evaluation is reliable or when its methodology or findings are questionable.

Lesson 8. Building an effective M&E system requires a long-term effort, with patience and determination. It takes time to create or strengthen data systems, to recruit and train qualified staff, to plan, conduct, and manage evaluations, and to train staff to use M&E in their day-to-day work, whether that involves program operations or policy analysis and advice. Australia and Chile were able to create well-functioning M&E systems—in terms of the quality, number, and utilization of evaluations—within four or five years, but in Colombia's case, it has taken more than a decade.

Conclusions

A growing number of developing countries are successfully building government M&E systems. They look to the examples of developed countries—especially members of the OECD—but increasingly they are also looking to their peers: countries such as Chile, Colombia, and Mexico. These countries have created well-performing M&E systems the findings of which are used intensively. These countries have demonstrated not only that it is feasible to build a government M&E system, but that the systems are valued highly by the governments.

Hopefully, this introductory chapter and later chapters in this volume will engage the interest of senior officials in developing countries and prompt them to fully investigate whether their government should devote the time and effort to building such a system. The donor community—including the World Bank—stands ready to support them in this work.

Notes

1. The link between government outputs and country outcomes can be very hard to demonstrate in the absence of evaluation findings. This gap has been termed the "missing middle."
2. An extensive list of M&E incentives is provided by Mackay (2007, Chapter 11).
3. Reasons for this are discussed more fully by Mackay (2007).

Bibliography

Independent Evaluation Group (IEG). 2004a. "Influential Evaluations: Evaluations that Improved Performance and Impacts of Development Programs." World Bank, Washington, DC.

———. 2004b. *Monitoring and Evaluation: Some Tools, Methods and Approaches.* 2nd Edition. Washington, DC: World Bank.

Lopez-Acevedo, Gladys, Katia Rivera, Lycia Lima, and Helena Hwang, eds. 2010. *Challenges in Monitoring and Evaluation: An Opportunity to Institutionalize M&E Systems.* Washington, DC: World Bank and Inter-American Development Bank.

Mackay, Keith. 2007. *How to Build M&E Systems to Support Better Government.* Washington, DC: World Bank.

World Bank. 1998. *Public Expenditure Management Handbook.* Washington, DC: World Bank.

World Bank Web Sites

www.worldbank.org/poverty
www.worldbank.org/lacmonitoringandevaluation
www.worldbank.org/ieg/ecd

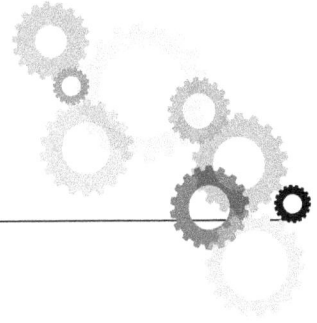

CHAPTER 3

Defining the Type of M&E System: Clients, Intended Uses, and Utilization

Bertha Briceño

This chapter characterizes various types of monitoring and evaluation (M&E) systems, including examples from three government-based systems in Latin America: Mexico, Colombia, and Chile. The systems outlined here range from completely external independent bodies, to strongly centralized government systems, to highly decentralized systems. Each type of system has different advantages that result from the interplay of demand and supply forces on the supply side, actors produce M&E information for a variety of intended purposes, while the demand responds with actual utilization, revealing the incentives of system clients. In addition, strategies are presented to mitigate potential disadvantages of the different types of systems. As countries are in-

This chapter draws extensively upon previous work conducted for the International Initiative for Impact Evaluation (3ie) and the Department for International Development of the United Kingdom (Briceño and Gaarder 2009). The author acknowledges their generous support. For their comments, the author thanks Keith Mackay (Consultant, Poverty Reduction and Equity Unit [PRMPR]), as well as Gladys Lopez-Acevedo (Senior Economist, PRMPR) and Jaime Saavedra (Director, PRMPR). The views expressed in this chapter are those of the author.

creasingly expressing a need for M&E support, this analysis should help champions and task team leaders identify suitable opportunities for their particular context, identify and understand the forces that drive the creation of new M&E units and bodies, and better understand the trade-offs involved.

Who Produces M&E Information and Why

A good starting point is to ask who conducts M&E activities and for what purpose, in order to later draw lessons relevant for the design of new M&E units. Development banks, bilateral aid agencies, independent organizations, academia, and above all governments are closely involved in monitoring and evaluating development programs. Development banks and bilateral aid agencies often use M&E to measure development effectiveness, be accountable to donors and stakeholders, and to demonstrate transparency. Academics—typically through centers affiliated with economics and public policy faculties—conduct rigorous studies with a knowledge-generation focus in the field of development economics.

In general, governments carry out M&E activities as a way to increase program effectiveness and improve resource allocation. Government-based systems typically serve internal clients from the executive branch such as planning and budget offices, central units within ministries or agencies in charge of planning and budget, and in some cases special evaluation units. All of these government units commonly use the M&E system as a tool to improve the efficiency and effectiveness of resource allocation, with a centralized control approach.

Internal clients also include executing or implementing agencies in governments and task team leaders in development banks. They are generally more interested in revising processes, changing and improving practices with a results orientation, generating visibility for projects, and responding to constituencies and managers with concrete information. Efficiency and effectiveness of resource allocation are also main focuses of internal clients from bilateral aid agencies and development banks, such as boards of donors and directors, internal evaluation units, and sector/regional managers.

In terms of external clients of government-related M&E systems, there is potential for use by legislatures and civil society, which are interested in fostering transparency, accountability, and social oversight.[1] On the other hand, M&E activities that development banks and donors carry out have policy makers, client governments, legislative bodies, and constituencies in general as external clients. Table 3.1 presents a simple classification of main clients and their corresponding usage focus.

TABLE 3.1 Hosts of M&E Activities, Clients, and Uses

Governments	**Internal clients**	• Executive: planning/ budget/presidential ministries	• Control/improve efficiency and effectiveness of resource allocation
			• Control implementation of national policies
		• Internal central units in agencies/ministries (planning/budget units)	• Feedback into policy/budget decision making
			• Feedback into planning
		• Managers in implementing agencies/ministries	• Revising processes
			• Improving managerial practices with a results orientation
			• Program management and staff or institutional management
			• Respond to constituencies with concrete information
	External clients	• Multilaterals/donors	• Focus on transparency and accountability
		• Legislature	
		• Civil society	
Development banks, aid agencies, special evaluation bodies	**Internal clients**	• Managers	• Control implementation
		• Task team leaders	• Exposure of innovative programs
			• Visibility of projects with a focus on results
			• Revising processes
			• Improving portfolio programming
			• Improving design of programs
			• Testing innovations
		• Internal evaluation offices	• Control/improve efficiency and effectiveness of resource allocation
		• Governing bodies (board of directors, board of donors)	• Revising processes
			• Focus on transparency and accountability
			• Respond to constituencies with concrete information
	External clients	• Civil society	• Focus on transparency and accountability
		• Policy makers	• Control implementation of national policies
		• Governments	
		• Legislature	
Academia	**Internal clients**	• Academia and scientific communities	• Knowledge generation in economic development
	External clients	• Policy makers, non-governmental organizations, donors, international organizations	• Diffusion of knowledge and advocacy for effective interventions

Source: Author.

Types of M&E Systems and Intended Uses

The majority of the M&E bodies for development programs strive for independence, transparency, autonomy, credibility, usefulness, and ownership, among other qualities.[2] In theory, an ideal M&E system should be independent enough to be externally credible and socially legitimate, but not so independent to lose its relevance. The M&E system should be able to influence policy making by ensuring adoption of recommendations informed by lessons learned, and it should be sustainable over time and through government transitions by responding to the needs of clients and remaining useful to its main stakeholders.

The M&E bodies are different in their nature and predominant incentives. Institutional arrangements range from independent external bodies, to strongly centralized government systems under budget authorities, to highly decentralized government systems. Three government-based systems in Latin America conforming to these three types of institutional arrangements include CONEVAL from Mexico, SINERGIA from Colombia, and DIPRES from Chile (Box 3.1).

Independent, external body: transparency and social oversight emphasis

When transparency, social oversight, and accountability are the main drivers of M&E activities and there is a strong emphasis on independence, creation of external independent bodies is appealing. Location outside the government and independent financing provide for the possibility of freely making assessments and limit improper influence. This high degree of independence ultimately reinforces external credibility.

Examples of these types of M&E bodies include donor and civil society initiatives, independent oversight institutions, and think tanks. Some examples of bodies that fund or carry out M&E activities on their own are Transparency International, the International Initiative for Impact Evaluation (3ie), the Center for Global Development, and the Bogotá Cómo Vamos initiative in Colombia.

The disadvantage of an external body is that it may lack adequate access to information, insight, and contextual knowledge. These bodies often rely on building a strong reputation of independence and non-partisanship to influence policy making. Transparency and accountability might be easier for an independent M&E body, but influencing policy remains a significant challenge.

BOX 3.1

Main Features of Three Government M&E Systems: CONEVAL, SINERGIA, and DIPRES

Mexico: The National Council for the Evaluation of Social Development Policies (Consejo Nacional de Evaluación de la Política de Desarrollo Social, CONEVAL)

CONEVAL was created in 2004 as part of the Social Development Law and financed through a direct budget line in the national budget. CONEVAL was established with a double mission: to measure poverty and to evaluate all social development policies and programs at the federal level. CONEVAL is headed by an executive director and belongs to the executive branch through the social sector, but has technical and managerial autonomy. It is governed by an executive board of six independent academics, the Minister of Social Development, and its own executive director.

In a decentralized setting, CONEVAL sets standards and guidelines for the evaluations of federal government programs that the federal agencies commission themselves. There are approximately 130 federal programs under the mandate of CONEVAL, all of which are required to carry out logframe-type evaluations. In addition, CONEVAL directly oversees about 15 evaluations per year under the Annual Evaluation Plan (*Programa Anual de Evaluación* [PAE]). The PAE is defined jointly by CONEVAL, the Ministry of Finance, and the Public Comptroller's Office.

Colombia: The National System for Evaluation of Public Sector Performance (SINERGIA)

A mandatory government development plan should guide every new administration in Colombia. In this context, Law 152 of 1994 explicitly assigned to the National Planning Department (*Departamento Nacional de Planeación* [DNP]) the mandate to plan, design, and organize a system for evaluation and monitoring of results-based management in the public sector. DNP is a long-standing administrative department organized in technical units or directorates. Within DNP, the Directorate for Evaluation of Public Policies (DEPP) assumed the promotion of the national M&E system, which became known as SINERGIA (*Sistema Nacional de Evaluación y Resultados de la Gestión Pública*). DEPP is one out of ten technical directorates in DNP and is headed by a technical director, reporting directly to DNP's deputy director and general director, who have the status of minister and vice minister, respectively.

DEPP's main activities involve administration of the governmental system of goals (Sigob), which includes goals for every sector and ministry, and management and commissioning of evaluations of major governmental programs. Currently the system includes approximately 600 goal indicators across sectors, and more than 30 evaluations have been completed.

Chile: The Management Control Division (DIPRES)

In Chile, DIPRES is in the budget department of the Ministry of Finance. Within DIPRES, a special unit, the Management Control Division, leads the system for evaluation and management control. Since the early 1990s, the evolution of the management control system has been a longstanding effort of the Chilean government under the strong leadership of successive budget directors.

(continued)

BOX 3.1 *continued*

The overall goal of the unit is to contribute to the efficiency of allocation and utilization of public spending, contributing to better performance, transparency, and accountability. The Management Control Division is one of the four divisions and two subdirectorates that constitute DIPRES.

The head of the Management Control Division reports directly to the budget director under the Minister of Finance. The Budget Directorate is accountable to the Congress. Four areas of work have been developed and reinforced since the early 1990s: evaluation of programs and institutions, instruments for monitoring and supervision, institutional salary incentive mechanisms, and the public management modernization fund.

For the 2010 budget, 150 governmental institutions adopted approximately 1,200 performance indicators, and there are 28 ongoing evaluations of institutions and programs.

Centralized government-owned M&E system: management or control tool

When the M&E system is housed in the government's center (budget, central authority, planning, presidency, or internal control office), it usually serves as a tool for management or for budget control. Under central budget authorities, M&E is often used to control efficiency and/or efficacy of resource use, and as such the M&E body usually enjoys considerable power to enforce the recommendations resulting from M&E assessments. In the extreme enforcement version, the M&E body has direct power over the evaluation agenda and enjoys a prominent position and support from the legislature. This is the case of DIPRES in Chile. Location under the budget authority also provides better integration of M&E into the budgeting and executing stages of the public policy cycle.

On the other hand, when M&E activities are mainly intended to serve as managerial tools, a central coordinating body can be placed outside of direct budget authorities to avoid a "force-fed" approach. The body seeks managerial buy-in and ownership and expects voluntary adoption of recommendations. For this, the M&E body makes significant investments in consultations, in demonstrating the benefits of evaluation as a managerial tool, in capacity-building activities, and in establishing a favorable cultural climate for M&E. Both Colombia's SINERGIA and Mexico's CONEVAL regularly carry out capacity-building and dissemination activities to promote a results-oriented management culture.

Some of the advantages of a centralized M&E agency include:

- More authority to prioritize key programs to be monitored and evaluated when resources are limited
- Ability to pursue recommendations that affect multiple agencies or the whole government
- Ability to pursue standard practices, best practices, and quality methodologies
- Maintaining specialized technical staff for support (which individual agencies may not be able to afford, especially in the beginning when the volume of M&E activities is low)
- More opportunities for generating learning synergies and economies of scale in data collection
- Reducing duplication
- Maintaining an institutional memory of M&E practices

Decentralized government-owned M&E system: full ownership by agencies

In the extreme decentralized version, the agency that runs the program also conducts M&E activities to improve its own performance, rather than reporting to a central entity or authority. The advantages are in-depth contextual knowledge and better access to data and disclosure. Since M&E activities are largely dependent on the quality and availability of internal information produced by the programs and on their willingness and capacity to generate primary data or recover information on beneficiaries, the agency has many incentives to produce and use the best information and use the results internally.

Some disadvantages of the completely decentralized arrangement are less standardization in methodologies and practices leading to more heterogeneous quality and rigor in M&E products, limited coordination across sectors, fewer opportunities for best practice sharing, and the need for maintaining technical expertise. Some may argue that the separation between evaluator and executor is less clear, which may increase the potential for undue interference, but in theory this should not be the case if the use is mainly internal and the true motivation is improving self-performance rather than reporting.

Supporting strategies

Some of the potential risks to different types of M&E systems can be mitigated through various supporting strategies or complementary institutions:

Key alliances. Support from the legislature, fluid communication, and promotion of alliances with government central authorities are common strategies used to overcome weak enforcement powers and to promote adoption of recommendations in reluctant sectors. Examples of these alliances include CONEVAL with the Ministry of Finance and SINERGIA with the presidency. In Organisation for Economic Co-operation and Development countries such as Canada, Australia, the United States, and the Netherlands, support provided by the national audit offices has been considerable: they have helped by reviewing (via efficiency audits) the planning, conduct, and use of M&E in the executive branch, publishing good practice guides, analyzing the quality of department/agency data and data systems, and using their influential and prominent position to advocate the merits of M&E. Alliances with national statistical offices, although not pursued so far, could become important as well.

Financial independence. The ability of the coordinating agency to influence policy, have recommendations adopted, and set an evaluation agenda can be enhanced with strong legal support (CONEVAL), a permanent budget line, or by using the agency's own financial resources to carry out M&E activities (DIPRES). In contrast, when resources for M&E activities come out of the program's budget, have to be earmarked in loans, and in general, depend highly on buy-in and voluntary adoption, then the agency could end up neglecting precisely the programs and sectors most in need of M&E.

External contracting. Contracting out M&E systems to consultants, firms, or research centers and using competitive, open procurement processes increases legitimacy and independence and reduces potential conflict of interest between evaluators and managers. DIPRES in Chile and SINERGIA in Colombia are good examples of systems using external contracting.

Hybrid governance. One example of a highly independent M&E body that still belongs to the government is CONEVAL. Although it pertains to the executive branch through the social sector, it enjoys technical and managerial autonomy greatly supported by a particular governance structure: an executive board of six independent academics, the Minister of Social Development, and its own executive director.

Quality control mechanisms. The higher the buy-in of M&E by the agencies, the better the insight, quality, and completeness of information provided by the programs for M&E. In centralized settings, the M&E body can seek higher quality and more reliable input information from the executing agencies by establishing control mechanisms, such as external verification, audits, or alliances with internal control offices as well as with national auditing and statistics offices.

Public disclosure. The principle of openness refers to making the evaluation process as transparent as possible and the results widely available. Far-reaching laws regarding public information access have been recently introduced in various countries, which indirectly supports the M&E system disclosure ability (such as Chile and Mexico). The risk of lack of autonomy to disclose M&E information when the system is located under an executive authority can be mitigated with other provisions such as a long-standing tradition of public disclosure. SINERGIA's evaluations exemplify limited public disclosure, as well as the absence of a broader public information law.

Academic rigor. Evaluations conducted externally by researchers and academics often undergo additional quality filters established by the academic community. They can also easily support capacity-building activities. Peer reviewing, screening in seminars, and the process of publication all contribute to increased rigor and quality in findings (for example, SINERGIA and CONEVAL). These important advantages may come at the cost of immediate usefulness if dissemination in accessible, non-technical language is neglected. In the extreme, evaluation blends into pure research, and although the generation and use of research has been extensively and formally studied, the essence and rationale behind the two are very different.

Capacity building and standardization. Capacity building and standardization are always important, but become even more so under highly decentralized settings, when a considerable volume of M&E activities is reached or has been mandated, and when agencies devote significant financial and human resources to M&E (CONEVAL).

Revealed Demand: Actual Utilization of M&E Information

The usual yardstick of success for the M&E system is the degree of utilization of the information produced. Utilization can also be thought of as one major determinant of sustainability. The Development Assistance Committee (DAC) principles for evaluations state: "for evaluations to be useful, they must be used" (OECD-DAC 1991). Utilization is a prerequisite for financial sustainability: why fund costly M&E tools or evaluations if they are not used?

TABLE 3.2 Tracking Utilization of M&E Information

Coverage	• Proportion of budget evaluated/ monitored	• Budget of evaluated or monitored programs over total budget amount
		• Number of programs evaluated or monitored over multiyear agenda
		• Number of programs evaluated or monitored over number of programs in programmatic classification of budget
Utilization	• Follow-up of recommendations, commitments, and action plans derived from M&E information	• Number of changes derived from evaluations
		• Number of alerts generated from monitoring
		• Number and list of recommendations adopted
		• Recommendations prioritized and adopted
		• Recommendations implemented/total number of recommendations formulated
	• Transparency/accountability	• No measures associating transparency or accountability with information from M&E systems
	• Improving quality and efficiency of public expenditure and influencing budget allocations	• No applications
		• Changes in budget/resource allocations resulting from utilization of M&E findings by legislature
		• Correlation with changes in budget or other resource allocation
	• Public good/ applied research (for most rigorous studies)	• Scientific production (number of citations and publications)
		• Use of public datasets (citations, derived academic and policy research)

Source: Author.

Defining measures of successful use is not easy.[3] Two dimensions of success are commonly employed (Table 3.2). The first is coverage—the extent of evaluation in relation to a reference value or universe. This is usually the proportion of the budget evaluated, which can in turn be measured as the value of the programs that have been evaluated to the total budget amount, or the number of programs evaluated in relation to a multiyear agenda, or the number of programs in a programmatic classification of the budget. The second dimension is consensus on the need to follow up on recommendations, commitments, and action plans derived from M&E activities. This can include simple measures such as the number of alerts derived from monitoring or number of recommendations from evaluations that are actually adopted to more demanding measures such as the proportion of the recommendations implemented over the total number of recommendations formulated.

No indicators have been clearly established to measure the final goals of M&E systems, namely improvements in the quality and efficiency of public expenditure that can be attributed to the results of the M&E system. However, a small number of reviews of individual evaluations examine the extent of M&E utilization and measure their cost-effectiveness. Such reviews could be conducted on a more systematic basis to help measure an M&E system's overall cost-effectiveness, although cost and the typical delays between conducting an evaluation and measuring its impact would make this problematical.

Measures on other dimensions, such as transparency and perception of accountability by citizens resulting from well-performing M&E systems, have not been explored. If the system is intended to influence budget allocations, further utilization measures could include the change in allocations as a result of utilization by budget offices and the legislature, or more indirectly, correlation measures with changes in resource allocation. The Republic of Korea utilizes a mechanism whereby budget allocations of programs that fail to reach their performance targets by a specific margin are automatically cut. Some attempts to use this measure examine the correlation between evaluation results and the budget of evaluated programs (Kim and Park 2007; Park 2008). For the most rigorous evaluations, usage could also be measured in terms of the standards for scientific production (that is, citations and publications).

One of the strengths of the Chilean system is that it maintains very specific information regarding program changes and it monitors the extent of recommendations derived from evaluations. Since the standardized terms of reference provide for the production of specific recommendations, these recommendations serve as a basis for establishing institutional commitments that are later closely monitored by DIPRES.

The 2008 report by DIPRES is a good example of the use of M&E information: between 2000 and 2008, 174 programs were evaluated. The classification of changes derived from recommendations in five categories is presented in Figure 3.1. Between 1999 and 2007 more than 3,500 commitments were derived from recommendations, around 500 annually in the early years and less since 2006. Out of these, 82 percent were fulfilled, 11 percent were partially fulfilled, and 6 percent have not been fulfilled.

It is generally accepted that DIPRES's M&E information is extensively utilized in budget analysis and decision making, in imposing program adjustments, and for reporting to the legislature and civil society. However, managerial usage or ownership from the head of programs has been limited, given the centrally-driven nature of the system and the perceived absence of incentives for the agencies to engage in their own evaluations (Mackay 2007, 29).

In Mexico, CONEVAL issued in late 2008 a policy to establish general procedures for tracking aspects of improvement derived from the desk re-

FIGURE 3.1 Classification of Changes in Programs 2000–08, DIPRES

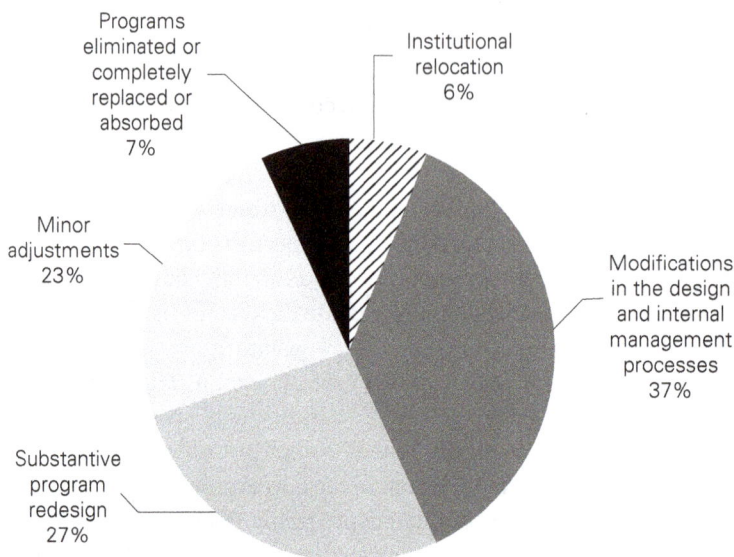

Programs eliminated or completely replaced or absorbed 7%

Institutional relocation 6%

Minor adjustments 23%

Modifications in the design and internal management processes 37%

Substantive program redesign 27%

Source: DIPRES 2008.

view evaluations (*evaluaciones de consistencia*). Aspects to improve are classified according to involvement of different parties: some aspects are under direct control of the program, while others involve various units within an agency, various agencies, or different government levels. In addition, sector agencies themselves classify those aspects as high, medium, or low priority according to their contribution to the program's goal. For the 2008 budget, 101 programs with rapid evaluations were included in the tracking system, with 930 aspects to improve. Out of these, 70 percent were considered to be under direct control of the program (CONEVAL 2008a, 2008b, 2010).

SINERGIA's utilization focus has been on the operations and management of programs, since evaluations are typically conducted with voluntary involvement of sector ministries/agencies, in contrast to the Chilean model. President Álvaro Uribe was a powerful champion of M&E information in Colombia. He demanded intensive use of goals and indicators, especially during his first administration (OECD-DAC 2008). The downside is the limited use by budget authorities and Congress. Recently, the system has also tracked commitments from recommendations derived from each evaluation.

In sum, M&E system utilization assessments have so far included proxies of coverage, client satisfaction surveys (the World Bank's Independent Evaluation Group annual surveys of key stakeholders), evidence on adoption of recommendations and commitments (CONEVAL and DIPRES), and some anecdotal evidence (SINERGIA). Although more work remains to be done, M&E systems utilization is beginning to be addressed more systematically.

Conclusions

M&E capacity building deals with the development of successful M&E systems that are sufficiently independent to be externally credible and socially legitimate, that influence policy making and are sustainable over time, and that respond to the needs of clients and main stakeholders. As more countries consider establishing M&E systems, lessons from other countries' experiences can be extremely useful. Specific circumstances shape the evolution and focus of each system, and no recipe should be exported in a naïve manner to other countries. However, an explicit strategy to support the development of new M&E systems should start by identifying country preferences, clearly defining the clients and main role for the M&E body, and determining how to track performance of the M&E system.

Notes

1. In the Colombian institutional context, social oversight refers to the use of constitutional participatory mechanisms that enable oversight of the state, trust, and efficacy of the entities designed to oversee the state—Congress, *Fiscalia*, or the media—and the accountability mechanisms of those elected in office (Sudarsky 2008).
2. Some examples of principles are the OECD-DAC Quality Standards (2010), the principles of Spain's Evaluation Agency (Ministerio de la Presidencia de España 2010), and the principles of the World Bank–IEG (2010).
3. The World Bank and the Centro Latinoamericano de Administración para el Desarrollo (CLAD) have contributed to the assessment of the systems by actively promoting diagnoses and reviews of system performances in 12 countries (CLAD and World Bank 2008).

Bibliography

Briceño, Bertha, and Marie Gaarder. 2009. *Institutionalizing Evaluation: A Review of International Experience.* International Initiative for Impact Evaluation (3ie) and the U.K. Department for International Development (DFID).

CLAD (Centro Latinoamericano de Administración para el Desarrollo) and World Bank. 2008. "Fortalecimiento de los sistemas de monitoreo y evaluación (M&E) en América Latina y el Caribe, a través del aprendizaje Sur-Sur y del intercambiode conocimientos." http://www.clad.org/investigaciones/investigaciones-concluidas/fortalecimiento-de-los-sistemas-de-monitoreo-y.

CONEVAL. 2008a. "Informe de seguimiento a los aspectos susceptibles de mejora de programas federales 2008." http://medusa.coneval.gob.mx/cmsconeval/rw/resource/coneval/eval_ mon/2733.pdf.

——. 2008b. "Mecanismos para el seguimiento a los aspectos susceptibles de mejora derivados de informes y evaluaciones a los programas federales de la administración pública federal." http://medusa.coneval.gob.mx/cmsconeval/rw/resource/coneval/EVALUACIONES/Mecanismo_seguimiento_291008.pdf?view=true.

——. 2010. "Mecanismos para el seguimiento a los aspectos susceptibles de mejora derivados de informes y evaluaciones a los programas federales de la administración pública federal." www.coneval.gob.mx/contenido/normateca/2339.pdf.

DIPRES. 2008. "Informe de Finanzas Públicas: Proyecto de Ley de Presupuestos del Sector Público para el año 2009." http://www.dipres.cl/572/articles-41339_doc_pdf.pdf.

Kim, John, and Nowook Park. 2007. "Performance Budgeting in Korea." *OECD Journal on Budgeting* 7(4).

Mackay, Keith. 2007. *How to Build M&E Systems to Support Better Government.* Washington, DC: World Bank, IEG.

Ministerio de la Presidencia de España. 2010. "Agencia de Evaluación y Calidad. Principios Rectores y Código Ético." http://www.aeval.es/es/la_agencia/presentacion/principios/.

OECD-DAC (Organisation for Economic Co-operation and Development–Development Assistance Committee). 1991. "Principles for the Evaluation of Development Assistance." Paris. http://www.oecd.org/dataoecd/31/12/2755284.pdf.

——. 2008. *Emerging Good Practice in Managing for Development Results (MfDR) Sourcebook*, Third Edition. Paris. http://www.mfdr.org/sourcebook/.

——. 2010. *Quality Standards for Development Evaluation.* Paris. http://www.oecd.org/dataoecd/55/0/44798177.pdf.

Park, Nowook. 2008. "Does More Information Improve Budget Allocation? Evidence and Lessons from Performance-Oriented Budgeting in Korea." Working Paper presented at the Congress of the International Institute of Public Finance, August, Maastricht, Netherlands.

Sudarsky, John. 2008. "La evolución del capital social en Colombia, 1997–2005." *Bogotá, revista* 747(144).

World Bank, IEG (Independent Evaluation Group). 2004. *Influential Evaluations: Evaluations that Improved Performance and Impacts of Development Programs.* Washington, DC: World Bank.

——. 2010. "Evaluation Methodology Overview." World Bank, Washington, DC. http://web.worldbank.org/external/default/main?theSitePK=1324361&piPK=64252979&pagePK=64253958&menuPK=5039271&contentMDK=20790052.

World Bank Web Site

www.worldbank.org/poverty/nutsandbolts

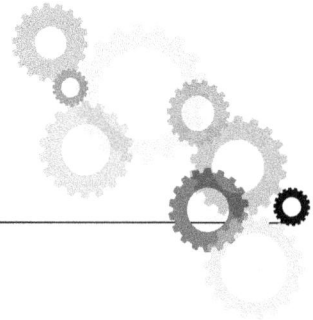

CHAPTER 4

Conducting Diagnoses of M&E Systems and Capacities

Geoffrey Shepherd

Monitoring and evaluation (M&E) systems are one of the important building blocks of a performance-oriented policy cycle in which policy goals are decided on in the public interest and policies are designed and implemented as far as possible in ways that will make them effective, efficient, and consistent. The more that the activities of the policy cycle are based on empirical evidence and analysis (of what has or has not worked elsewhere or is or is not working here), the more likely that policies will be efficient, effective, and in the public interest. As this chapter will argue, the demand for M&E depends on the presence of at least some elements of a performance-oriented policy cycle.

An M&E diagnosis is an analysis of what is and is not working in a country's (or a sector's, or a region's) M&E activities, with recommendations for improving activities and systems. The diagnosis aims to identify needs and to

For their comments, the author thanks Nick Manning (Adviser, Poverty Reduction and Equity, Public Sector Governance Unit), Philipp Krause (Consultant, Poverty Reduction and Equity Unit [PRMPR]), Keith Mackay (Consultant, PRMPR) as well as Gladys Lopez-Acevedo (Senior Economist, PRMPR), and Jaime Saavedra (Director, PRMPR). The views expressed in this chapter are those of the author.

find the combination of institutional arrangement and technical capacities that can address these needs.

- The diagnosis emphasizes an institutional analysis of the factors that drive demand for and supply of M&E. Institutions are the formal and informal rules that shape the behavior of individuals and organizations in society. Where there is little or no demand for better public sector performance, an M&E diagnosis will probably make little sense. But in countries (or sectors or sub-national governments) where there is some demand for better performance, an M&E diagnosis can pave the way. A good M&E diagnosis provides a useful entry point into broader issues of performance management.
- The diagnosis emphasizes technical capacity because without reliable data, good analytical instruments, and solid technical capacity M&E systems will not get results, even where institutions and organizational capacity might favor good M&E practice.

Although the broad questions that an analyst might want to ask for any M&E diagnosis might be similar, country situations differ so much because of varying levels of development and local situations, that the topics addressed, the way the diagnosis is presented, and conclusions and recommendations may look very different. Mexico, for instance, has established important elements of a centralized M&E system and one of the main issues in improving this system is to ensure that the nascent performance-informed budgeting system develops properly (Castro et al. 2009). In Uganda and South Africa, the issue is more one of creating greater coherence among separate systems (Hauge 2003; Engela and Ajam 2010). In the United Kingdom, evaluation is underdeveloped compared to monitoring and the two are relatively unconnected (Talbot 2010).

There is no one blueprint for preparing an M&E diagnosis: content and presentation depend on the specific context. This chapter seeks to illustrate the range of contexts by discussing a number of issues that help explain the differences in context. The chapter illuminates these issues, where possible, by referring to various country studies that have appeared in recent years (see Further Reading below). They cover six OECD countries—mostly studies that draw "good practice" lessons—and two African and four Latin American countries—a mix of diagnostic and "lessons-of-experience" studies.

A Checklist of Topics for a Diagnosis

We start by proposing a checklist of topics to be considered in preparing an M&E diagnosis (Table 4.1). This checklist is broadly based on a number of

TABLE 4.1 A Checklist of Topics to Consider in Preparing an M&E Diagnosis

Block A. The national environment for M&E	
Topic A1	*The national policy and institutional framework:* How are policies made? What role do donors play? Is political power wielded in the public interest? Do policies create a demand for M&E? How decentralized is the country? How has the relevant policy environment evolved over time?
Block B. M&E systems If the study covers multiple M&E systems (government-wide, cross-sector, or within ministries, agencies, audit institutions, or donor projects) then Block B applies separately to each system.	
Topic B1	*Historical development:* How and why did the system develop? Who championed it and who opposed it? What kind of implementation strategy was adopted?
Topic B2	*Objectives* (announced, implicit, or revealed): These can include budget support, support to policy making and/or program improvement, or accountability.
Topic B3	*Processes, tools, and products:* What is produced (indicators and evaluations by type and numbers, and so on)? What are the selection criteria? What is the production cycle? How is the information used (dissemination, reward, sanction, or correction)? How is the quality of the information controlled? What are the tools used to collect, manage, and analyze information and are they appropriate?
Topic B4	*Relationship with other systems:* How are systems interconnected, if at all? Monitoring with evaluation? M&E with the budget? Ministry or sub-national monitoring systems with national systems? Monitoring with information systems? M&E with quality-management systems?
Topic B5	*Institutional architecture:* How do the system's components fit together? How is cooperation (exchange of information, willingness to act on results) achieved within the system? How centralized is the system?
Topic B6	*The organizational characteristics of public agencies that are part of the system:* What is the historical reform/policy-change process? The tasks of the agency? Its resources (budget, incentives, expertise, training, donor support, etc.)? Its sources of authority (the legal framework, roles of stakeholders)? The obstacles it faces (information, coordination problems)?
Topic B7	*Results:* What are the quality, credibility, and accessibility of the products of M&E? What is the impact of these products? Where there are multiple objectives, are there multiple impacts?
Block C. Findings	
Topic C1	*Conclusions and recommendations:* What is working and not working, and why? What reforms are underway? How can things be improved?

Source: Author

M&E country diagnoses and several diagnostic how-to guides that have appeared in the last decade. These diagnoses by no means follow the same outline, but they do tend to cover similar sets of topics. The checklist is designed for a diagnosis at a national level, although adapting a diagnosis to a particular agency or sub-national government would not require any fundamental alteration of the checklist. The chapter then discusses at greater length some of the issues that arise with each topic. This chapter is not intended as a how-to guide so much as a tool to help better understand the issues.

Diagnostic Issues

Topic A1. The national policy and institutional framework

Placing M&E within the public policy cycle. Perhaps the single most important point to be made about an M&E system is that it must be embedded within a broader policy framework that is conducive to M&E. This policy framework must in some sense be performance-oriented—that is, setting performance expectations, monitoring progress, measuring results, and appraising, rewarding, or correcting performance. M&E cannot be considered independently of a performance-oriented policy cycle, where future actions are evidence-based and strategically planned, implementation is monitored, and results are evaluated and then fed back into the planning process. Lack of clarity in objectives and unpredictability in future resources undermine the possibility of such a policy cycle and hence the demand for effective M&E. In short, where elements of performance management are absent, it is hardly likely that M&E can flourish. Thus any M&E diagnosis has to investigate those broader elements of the policy framework that drive, or could drive, investment in M&E.

Recent M&E diagnoses make it clear that performance orientation is central to the successful development of M&E systems. Castro et al. (2009) describe how Mexico's evaluation agency, CONEVAL, sits at the apex of a comprehensive (if not yet fully institutionalized) M&E system that is part of a performance budgeting system. Somewhat similarly, a centralized evaluation system in Chile is integrated within a broader performance management regime (Rojas et al. 2006). By contrast, Matsuda et al. (2006) argue that the poor performance of Brazil's centralized M&E system has to be understood in the context of the problems of that country's planning and budgeting processes. A comparative diagnosis of M&E systems in Australia, Canada, the United Kingdom, and the United States (Lahey 2005) argues that in all four countries public sector reforms involved the devolution of managerial discretion to individual government departments and agencies, as well as a desire to link evaluation and performance information to budget decision making and high-level policy debate. More recent studies for Canada (Lahey 2010), the United Kingdom (Talbot 2010), and Australia (Mackay 2011) tell a similar story of M&E systems embedded within performance-management regimes. In Australia, a new government elected in 1996 and favoring less government partially abandoned an effective evaluation system that had been built up over the previous decade.

In Uganda, the "performance" driver behind M&E reforms was the poverty reduction agenda (Hauge 2003). In Ireland and Spain, the evaluation requirements that accompanied structural aid from the European Union were one of the principal drivers of M&E, but not the only one (Boyle 2005, and Feinstein and Zapico-Goñi 2010). Foreign donors have also been important as initiators of evaluation activities, but these efforts have largely concentrated on donors' own projects. In Uganda, for instance, there has been considerable donor investment in M&E. As a result, Uganda's problem is not the quantity of M&E, but poor quality, poor coordination, and substantial duplication.

M&E in a federal system. M&E diagnoses have mostly covered central governments. But particularly for federal countries, the role of M&E in linking central and sub-national governments is also an important if under-discussed issue. When activities are devolved to sub-national governments, it is usual for federal authorities to retain substantial overall responsibility for policies and results. But this devolution means that the federal authorities lose management control and have greater difficulty in getting information. In other words, what were formerly *outputs* of the federal authorities (i.e., results over which they had substantial control) become *outcomes* (i.e., results to which they contribute, but over which they do not have substantial control). Thus the federal authorities need their own M&E systems to give them managerial control over the discretionary funds they transfer to lower-level governments and fiduciary oversight over sub-national governments' use of their own funds. Federal authorities can additionally promote the quality of local public spending (and national learning) by encouraging sub-national governments to carry out their own M&E.

Talbot (2010) mentions the use of a special-purpose agency in the United Kingdom, the Audit Commission, to provide oversight of local governments. Engela and Ajam (2010) and World Bank (2011) note the importance of M&E in the developing federal systems of South Africa and Brazil.

Topic B1. Historical development

History matters for at least two reasons. First, current events and decisions are "path dependent"—they are conditioned by past events and decisions. Thus national idiosyncrasies explain why M&E systems can look so different from country to country. Second, governments do not institute perfect new management systems overnight; instead, they learn with experience and adjust systems over time.

Thus, national M&E diagnoses put the development of M&E systems, as well as the broader policy framework in which they sit, within a historical narrative. One of the main history-related themes comes from studies of the United Kingdom and Canada (Talbot 2010, and Lahey 2010). Even in such "mature" countries with supposedly advanced forms of performance-oriented management—and in Canada's case, an exemplary, well-integrated M&E system—there is little sense that these countries are approaching a final, ideal M&E system. Instead, the story is of constant adjustments to improve systems. Similarly, a learning process has been at work in the development of M&E systems in Chile, Colombia, Ireland, Mexico, and South Africa. But history can also tell a more cyclical story: in some advanced countries, evaluation lost traction in the 1990s because of budget cuts (Lahey 2005); Australia abandoned its evaluation system in 1997 because of changes in political ideology (Mackay 2011); the United Kingdom apparently abandoned its successful system of Public Service Agreements when a new government took office in 2010.

Topic B2. Objectives

M&E instruments can address a multiplicity of different, often incompatible objectives. It is important to understand these objectives—whether they are announced, implied, or revealed—because different objectives can require different objects of measurement and analyses. Table 4.2 lists five sets of objectives: solving problems in program implementation; accountability within the government; provision of public information (for accountability, legitimation, or public choice); improving program design; and prioritizing (and possibly coordinating) across programs. The table also provides examples of national systems that have been functioning reasonably well.

In many cases, it is difficult to use the same system to respond to different objectives. A comparative study of evaluation systems in Latin America (Ospina, Cunill Grau, and Zaltsman 2004) differentiates between systems for designing better programs and policies ("planning models" in Colombia and Costa Rica) and systems for helping expenditure prioritization ("budget models" in Chile and Uruguay). Canada's M&E system provides an example of a system able to answer effectively to more than one objective (Lahey 2010). Brazil's national M&E system failed, in part, because it took on too many objectives (Matsuda et al. 2006). Engela and Ajam (2010) discuss differences in objectives—and resulting tensions—among different government agencies in South Africa, contrasting a more "linear" program logic at the Treasury (which is concerned with budget prioritization) and a more complex view of how programs work in the sectoral ministries.

Topic B3. Processes, tools, and products

This topic encompasses the technical design of the M&E tools (to collect, manage, and analyze information) and the production system in which they

TABLE 4.2 M&E Objectives: A Taxonomy and Some Examples

1. Solving implementation problems:

Monitoring program execution to detect and correct implementation problems. This is a managerial learning function and is usually incorporated within a management information system (MIS).

- *Brazil:* Monitoring the Growth Acceleration Program.
- *United Kingdom:* Prime Minister's Delivery Unit.

2. Intra-government accountability:

M&E of program execution both within government and between levels of government to ensure that public agents are doing what they have undertaken to do. This is a managerial (internal) accountability function also usually incorporated within an MIS.

- *Brazil:* Compliance and process audits (also providing public information).
- *Canada:* Articulated M&E information used for internal accountability and management and for external accountability (reporting to the center of government and to Parliament).
- *South Africa:* Program of Action (MIS).
- *United Kingdom:* Public Service Agreements (also with elements of public accountability).

3. Providing public information:

Providing information to the legislature and the public to: (i) render external accountability; (ii) provide information that legitimizes a public action; or (iii) provide information that facilitates public choice and voice.

- *Brazil:* Performance evaluation of government programs by the Federal Court of Audit.
- *Brazil:* Program evaluation by Ministry of Social Development to legitimize new programs (also for learning related to program and policy design).
- *Colombia:* System of Programming and Management by Objectives and Results (SIGOB), a monitoring system for legitimation (and also to inform the president of ministry performance).
- *South Africa:* Development Indicators (for accountability).
- *United Kingdom:* Education and health "score-cards" (for consumer choice).

4. Improving program design:

M&E allows governments to learn about the efficiency and effectiveness of individual programs to inform decisions to extend, improve, or eliminate them.

- *Chile:* Government program evaluations by the Budget Office (also for budget decision making).
- *Colombia:* Evaluations of the National System for Evaluation of Public Sector Performance (SINERGIA) (also for policy prioritization).
- *Ireland:* Evaluation for projects of EU structural funds (also for accountability).
- *Mexico:* Program evaluations of the CONEVAL.
- *Spain:* Evaluations of the Spanish Evaluation Agency (AEVAL).

5. Coordinating and prioritizing among programs (particularly in budgeting):

M&E allows governments to learn about efficiency and effectiveness *across* programs. This helps the center of government to: (i) coordinate among programs; and/or (ii) prioritize (cabinet, planning, and budget decisions).

- *Australia:* Evaluation system 1987–97 to help in policy and budget prioritization (but also to improve program performance and render internal accountability).
- *Canada:* Strategic Reviews (budget).
- *Chile:* Comprehensive Spending Reviews (budget).
- *Ireland:* Expenditure Review Initiative (budget).
- *United States:* Program Assessment Rating Tool (PART) (budget).

Source: Author

sit, as well as the scale of the activity (for instance number of reports produced annually or number of indicators). The topic covers:

- *Monitoring:* criteria for selecting indicators; appropriateness, periodicity, timeliness, reliability, and quality control of indicators; methods of collecting, reporting, and disseminating data.
- *Evaluation:* the evaluation cycle; criteria for selecting subjects for evaluation; evaluation techniques (impact, rapid, process evaluations, etc.); training and use of evaluators; dissemination methods.

Evaluation encompasses a broad range of tools, from the informal to the formal and from the impressionistic to the rigorous. There is a range of formal evaluative tools (cost-benefit, cost-effectiveness, impact evaluation) and less formal tools (rapid evaluation, user surveys, and so on). Different tools respond to different needs and the differing availability of information. Needs differ in at least three systematic ways:

- *Different types of problem:* problems differ from one policy area to another. In infrastructure activities, for instance, outputs and outcomes are relatively well understood and measurable, but start-up costs (including choice of technique) can strongly affect efficiency. In social areas, start-up costs are more modest, but desired outcomes, though measurable, are harder to attain since human behavior is more difficult to engineer than bridges. This helps explain why impact evaluation is the gold standard of policy analysis in the social sectors and cost-benefit analysis is the gold standard in infrastructure sectors.
- *Different costs of analysis:* the technically best forms of analysis have costs as well as benefits—they require more information (hence cost more) and they may produce results that come too late.
- *Different objectives:* M&E activities cover a range of objectives, as discussed above.

The diagnostic studies under review differ in the amount of information they provide on production routines. Studies for Chile (Rojas et al. 2006) and Colombia (World Bank, IEG 2007) are examples of diagnoses that provide a reasonable amount of detail on evaluation tools and methodologies.

Topic B4. Relationship with other systems

The idea of M&E as a self-contained system (albeit within larger systems of performance management) is a slippery one. First, monitoring and evaluation can be substantially separated from each other, even though the line between them can be blurred. Talbot (2010) differentiates the United Kingdom's monitoring regime from its evaluation regime. The former has attributes of a fairly tight system driven by an efficiency-oriented philosophy and based on organizations rather than programs. Evaluation activities are quite separate—there are, for instance, two separate professional communities driven by somewhat different considerations (substantive policy more than efficiency), and they are program-based, less developed, and less systemic. In Chile and Colombia, M&E are also largely unintegrated, even though they fall under one "system" and one organization. Canada, seemingly the exception, has been able to substantially integrate the two functions.

Second, it can be difficult to separate a specific set of activities called M&E from other policy-oriented information collecting and analytical activities systematically undertaken within the public administration. M&E, compliance and process auditing, quality management, policy analysis, and information management represent separate communities of practice that substantially overlap but are often poorly connected to each other.

M&E crucially depends on good information and good analysis. The ability of governments to use modern technologies to harness the power of modern information and communications technologies is very important in determining the sophistication of their M&E efforts. For instance, crossing physical and financial data allows program implementation to be tracked with greater accuracy and irregularities to be more easily detected. A country's public information infrastructure is influenced by its resources (software and systems development, data management, and statistical skills) and by public institutions (in particular statistics institutes, but also central ministries and line ministries). Knowledge management also requires analytical skills typically found in government think tanks and research institutes, and non-government bodies such as universities, non-governmental organizations, and consultancy firms.

Few M&E diagnoses have discussed national knowledge management infrastructures. A diagnosis for Brazil (World Bank 2011) gives some examples of how innovative uses of information and communication technology have improved monitoring capabilities in some ministries. A diagnosis for South Africa (Engela and Ajam 2010) also discusses information and data constraints. As government has become larger and more complex in Organisation for Economic Co-operation and Development (OECD) countries, specialized government and non-government agencies have come to play an increasingly important role in the analysis of public policies and programs. In effect, policy advice is becoming a more competitive business (World Bank 2010).

Topic B5. Institutional architecture

The key questions relate to the identification of the components of the system (the participants and their roles) and the mechanisms for securing cooperation between the components. This has been a central topic for most diagnoses. The main themes are the degree of centralization of systems and, associated with this, the incentives that induce players to part with information or to act on the results of M&E. There are as many architectural variants as there are systems.

To start with, the diagnoses describe a variety of systems that go from loose to taut. The M&E "system" characterized by Engela and Ajam (2010) for South Africa is in reality a government-wide policy to coordinate many existing and disparate M&E initiatives. At the other extreme, Rojas et al. (2006) describe a centralized and tightly controlled evaluation system in Chile. Canada, Colombia, Mexico, and Spain also have tightly-defined national M&E systems (in various stages of construction). The United Kingdom has a tightly-defined, well-established system for performance monitoring, not evaluation.

These systems have different modes of coordination and degrees of centralization.

- In Chile and Mexico a central agency carries out the evaluations. Mexico's CONEVAL also helps set the rules for M&E practices in the line secretariats.
- In Canada (somewhat like Australia 1987–97), the center of government sets the rules and provides advice, while the line departments are required to carry out the evaluations, with some degree of liberty about how they organize them. South Africa aspires to a somewhat similar arrangement.
- A peculiarity of the United Kingdom is that, in many sectors, it uses a number of specialized inspectorates, standing at arm's length from their sponsoring departments, to carry out monitoring.
- Finally, there is a growing involvement of supreme audit institutions (SAIs), usually attached to legislatures, in performance evaluation. Brazil and the United Kingdom are good examples: their SAIs have the authority to collect information and require program changes, and they have become an important part of a broader national M&E system.

Topic B6. Characteristics of organizations

Public agencies that are part of a particular M&E system—whether a central agency that runs the system or a line agency that participates in the system—have particular organizational characteristics that determine their own incentives to supply information and to use M&E results. Different agencies in the same government can have quite different capabilities and face quite different incentives. These differences are shaped by the history of the agency, what it does, the resources it can command, and the external factors and pressures that influence its behavior (legal framework, stakeholders, and so on). This topic overlaps with the topics on the national policy and institutional framework and on institutional architecture because all three address different aspects of incentives (see Box 4.1).

The organizational framework is generally not treated in a systematic way in the diagnoses and studies under review, but there is a substantial, if episodic, treatment of related themes.

- Studies on Brazil (World Bank 2011) and South Africa (Engela and Ajam 2010) discuss features that explain differences among ministries as regards their cooperation in M&E systems. Talbot (2010) notes the variability of departmental M&E capacities in the United Kingdom.
- Castro et al. (2009) describe the organizational characteristics of political independence and technical capacity that have made CONEVAL a credible and influential evaluator of social programs in Mexico.
- Lahey (2005) emphasizes the importance of formal, legislated polices in reinforcing the use of evaluation in individual government departments and agencies in Australia, Canada, the United Kingdom, and the United States.
- The obstacles to coordination are discussed in several diagnoses. Cunill Grau (2010) suggests that poor information flow and lack of cooperation among public agencies has forced a centralized approach to M&E systems in Latin America, in contrast to the more decentralized approach in OECD countries. Engela and Ajam (2010) describe the culture of information hoarding in South Africa, as well as other differences among public agencies that impede cooperation.

Topic B7. Results

Clearly, there is not much point to an M&E system, however well-designed and functioning, if it does not get results in terms of goals fulfilled, programs and policies improved, budgets rationalized, or a public better informed. Unfortunately, it is quite difficult to measure such improvements and attribute them to specific causes.

Generally speaking, evidence on results is weak or missing from existing M&E diagnoses. The study on Chile (Rojas et al. 2006) was able, in broad terms, to trace the effect of evaluations on budget decisions. Some studies

BOX 4.1

Looking at Incentives in an M&E Diagnosis

Incentives are the factors that motivate a particular course of action by individuals or organizations. At a macro level, incentives are woven into the institutions that determine governance—do the formal and informal rules impel public officials to act in the public interest or in private interests? At a micro level, incentives take the form of sticks (sanctions for poor performance) or carrots (for instance material rewards) that affect the effort that individuals and organizations make, at the margin, to perform better.

Incentives figure prominently in three of the topics in our checklist.

- *The national policy and institutional framework:* The public interest nature of national policies, the clarity and the binding nature of national policy directives, and the nature of national management rules (especially budget rules) determine the core incentives for countries to pursue M&E. It is thus vital for M&E diagnoses to identify these characteristics. But since they are largely driven by politics, it is often difficult to propose solutions in the context of an M&E diagnosis.

- *M&E system: the institutional architecture:* A specific architecture helps determine a narrower set of incentives for agencies to cooperate (exchange information or take corrective actions based on M&E results) within a circumscribed system. Different systems make different trade-offs between the use of hierarchical authority (in centralized systems) and the appeal to the self-interest of agencies in pursuing M&E (in decentralized systems).

- *M&E system: organizational characteristics:* At the agency/sector level, similar incentive issues arise as for the national policy and institutional framework. At the agency level, politics can also be a driving force shaping incentives, but so too are specific features of the sector, as well as the sticks and carrots of micro incentives. Agency-level incentives may thus be more malleable than national incentives.

cited individual examples of evaluations that were influential. Other studies made judgments about the quality of evaluation reports as an implicit proxy for their expected impact. (Rojas et al. 2006 had experts judge the quality of a sample of program evaluations in Chile; Matsuda et al. 2006 compared the quality of evaluations of the same program independently carried out by the SAI and by ministries.) In the main, most studies had to be content with author inferences based, at best, on knowledge of the system and interviews and focus groups with participants.

Topic C1. Conclusions and recommendations

The conclusions should present the overall strengths and weaknesses of M&E systems and activities, as well as indicate current or planned reforms. Because they provide different models and elucidate the topics we have been discussing, existing diagnoses can help frame these conclusions.

By the same token, existing diagnoses can also provide a useful guide to possible reform options. On the other hand, it follows from the large number of national variables—different historical starting points and national institutional environments, the range of objectives and architectures, and differences between public agencies—that no one model will fit all reform situations. Indeed, realistic recommendations must start from the local realities. Public sector reform is subject to bounded rationality—we do not have enough information to know how to get it all right the first time—and path dependence. Thus one has to build on what is in place and what, under local circumstances, is more likely to work. Guidelines, taxonomies, and checklists can only provide limited help.

Organizing the diagnosis

In addition to the valuable information contained in several existing diagnoses, several guides provide useful advice about diagnostic issues, content, and organization (Box 4.2).

This note makes a few final points about organizing an M&E diagnosis.

- An initial decision has to be made about whether an M&E diagnosis makes sense. In some countries, where there is no drive for performance, there will be no motivation for M&E. In such cases, a more basic examination of the institutional conditions for public-sector reform is required.
- As with any diagnosis of public sector issues, it makes sense to involve the government as far as possible in the design and implementation of a study, both to ensure better access to information and to make it more likely that the study's findings will be taken seriously (see Topic B5 above).
- The scope of the study will need to be defined. Will the study concentrate on a particular system or will it look at M&E activities more generally? Where local governments are important partners in implementing national priorities, it will be important for M&E diagnoses to link central and sub-national government M&E activities.
- How large will the study be? Mackay (1998) (see reference in Box 4.2) makes the point that a feasible diagnosis can range from a small team

Published Guides for M&E Country Diagnosis and Capacity Building

- Boyle, Richard, and D. Lemaire, eds. 1999. *Building Effective Evaluation Capacity: Lessons from Practice.* New Brunswick, NJ: Transaction Publishers.

- Cunill Grau, Nuria, and Sonia Ospina Bozzi, eds. 2003. "Guide for Case Studies." In *Evaluación de resultados para una gestión pública moderna y democrática: experiencias latinoamericanas.* Caracas: CLAD.

- Görgens, Marelize, and Jody Zall Kusek. 2009. *Making Monitoring and Evaluation Systems Work: A Capacity Development Toolkit* Washington, DC: World Bank.

- Kusek, Jody Zall, and Ray C. Rist. 2004. *Ten Steps to a Results-Based Monitoring and Evaluation System.* Washington, DC: World Bank.

- Mackay, Keith. 1998. "A Diagnostic Guide and Action Framework." Evaluation Capacity Development Working Paper Series 6, World Bank, Washington, DC.

- ———. 2007. "The Importance of Country Diagnosis." In *How to Build M&E Systems to Support Better Government.* Independent Evaluation Group. Washington, DC: World Bank.

- World Bank, Independent Evaluation Group. 2007. "Annex C: Terms of Reference for an In-Depth Diagnosis of SINERGIA." In "A Diagnosis of Colombia's National M&E System, SINERGIA." Evaluation Capacity Development Working Paper Series 17, World Bank, Washington, DC.

spending one or two weeks in the field to a large team undertaking—in effect, an impact evaluation. No single diagnosis is likely to cover, in any detail at least, all the topics described in this chapter. Thus, the smaller the study, the more that choices have to be made.

- The better prepared an investigative team is by the time it sets foot in a country, the better the end product is likely to be.
- Finding out about the results of M&E systems is likely to prove the hardest challenge in the field. Interviewing and focus groups must be designed to listen to multiple perspectives—producers and users of M&E, participants and observers, supporters and critics.
- There are different ways to tell a story, and the material must dictate the particular way chosen for any diagnosis. A historical narrative has proven important in many diagnoses. On the other hand, where comparability is

required with other studies, a more instrumental approach might make more sense.

Bibliography

Boyle, Richard. 2005. "Evaluation Capacity Development in the Republic of Ireland." Independent Evaluation Group, ECD Working Paper Series 14. World Bank, Washington, DC.

Castro, Manuel Fernando, Gladys Lopez-Acevedo, Gita Beker Busjeet, and Ximena Fernandez Ordonez. 2009. "Mexico's M&E System: Scaling Up from the Sectoral to the National Level." Independent Evaluation Group, ECD Working Paper Series 20. World Bank, Washington, DC.

Cunill Grau, Nuria. 2010. "Latin American Monitoring and Evaluation Systems and Their Governance." In Gladys Lopez-Acevedo, Katia Rivera, Lycia Lima, and Helena Hwang, eds., *Challenges in Monitoring and Evaluation: An Opportunity to Institutionalize M&E Systems*. Fifth Conference of the Latin America and the Caribbean Monitoring and Evaluation (M&E) Network, World Bank.

Engela, Ronette, and Tania Ajam. 2010. "Implementing a Government-wide Monitoring and Evaluation System in South Africa." Independent Evaluation Group, ECD Working Paper Series 21. World Bank, Washington, DC.

Feinstein, Osvaldo, and Eduardo Zapico-Goñi. 2010. "Evaluation of Government Performance and Public Policies in Spain." Independent Evaluation Group, ECD Working Paper Series 22. World Bank, Washington, DC.

Hauge, Arild O. 2003. "The Development of Monitoring and Evaluation Capacities to Improve Government Performance in Uganda." Operations Evaluation Department, ECD Working Paper Series 10. World Bank, Washington, DC.

Lahey, Robert. 2005. "A Comparative Analysis of Monitoring and Evaluation in Four Selected Countries: Canada, United States, Australia and United Kingdom." World Bank, Washington, DC.

———. 2010. "The Canadian M&E System: Lessons Learned from 30 Years of Development." Independent Evaluation Group, ECD Working Paper Series 23. World Bank, Washington, DC.

Mackay, Keith. 2011. "The Australian Government's Performance Framework." Independent Evaluation Group, ECD Working Paper Series 25. World Bank, Washington, DC.

Matsuda, Yasuhiko, Geoffrey Shepherd, and Juliana Wenceslau. 2006. "Management and Evaluation within the Plano Plurianual: Institutionalization without Impact?" LCSPS, unpublished, November 6. World Bank, Washington, DC.

Ospina, Sonia, Nuria Cunill Grau, and Ariel Zaltsman. 2004. "Performance Evaluation, Public Management Improvement and Democractic Accountability: Some Lessons from Latin America." *Public Management Review* 6(2): 230–51.

Rojas, Fernando, Keith Mackay, Yasuhiko Matsuda, Geoffrey Shepherd, Azul Del Villar, Ariel Zaltsman, and Philipp Krause. 2006. "Chile: Study of Evaluation Program, Impact Evaluations and Evaluations of Government Programs." Report 34589-CL. World Bank, Washington, DC.

Talbot, Colin. 2010. "Performance in Government: The Evolving System of Performance and Evaluation Measurement, Monitoring, and Management in the United Kingdom." Independent Evaluation Group, IEG Working Paper Series 24. World Bank, Washington, DC.

World Bank. 2010. "The Practice of Policy-Making in the OECD: Ideas for Latin America." Public Sector and Governance Unit, Poverty Reduction and Economic Management Department, Latin America and the Caribbean. World Bank, Washington, DC.

———. 2011. "Policy Note: Monitoring and Evaluation in Brazil's Federal Government." LCSPP. World Bank, Washington, DC.

World Bank, Independent Evaluation Group. 2007. "A Diagnosis of Colombia's National M&E System, SINERGIA." ECD Working Paper Series 17. World Bank, Washington, DC.

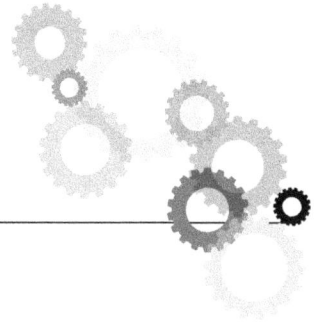

CHAPTER 5

Key Steps to Design and Implement M&E for Individual Country Service Agencies

Harry Hatry

This chapter identifies key steps in designing and implementing a monitoring and evaluation (M&E) system for ministries and individual government agencies that provide services. These suggestions are intended to apply whether the ministry or agency is in health, education, social welfare, environmental protection, transportation, economic development, public safety, or any other sector. M&E development should focus on instilling a process that will yield regular outcome data that can be used by the designing agency and upper-level officials for accountability and management, thereby helping officials improve services to their citizens.

The author thanks Markus Goldstein (Senior Economist, Africa Poverty Reduction and Equity Unit), and Poverty Reduction and Equity Group members Helena Hwang (Consultant), Philipp Krause (Consultant), Gladys Lopez-Acevedo (Senior Economist), Keith Mackay (Consultant), and Jaime Saavedra (Director) for their comments. The views expressed in this chapter are those of the author.

Prerequisites

At least four pre-conditions are vital to successful M&E implementation. First, strong, top-level supporting leaders are needed who are willing to provide the time and resources to initiate the M&E process. Second, the presence of at least some staff and sufficient capacity to undertake basic data collection and analysis is critical. Third, government officials must be willing to use the M&E data to help make resource allocation decisions, and not merely to show that the agency is collecting performance data. Fourth, there should be enough flexibility for agency managers to make changes where the data indicate that changes are needed. If these conditions are absent, the M&E process may be a waste of time.

Basic Steps

A number of basic steps are required for designing and implementing the process, whether at the ministry or agency level.

1. **Establish a committee of key agency personnel to guide and oversee the implementation effort.** The committee should include individuals from within the organization as well as representatives from the offices of the program, budget, planning, information technology, human resources, and an analytical office such as statistics, if one exists, whose work might be expected to relate to M&E. It is also likely to be helpful to include in the committee an "outside" person who can bring a broader perspective, such as someone from a higher-level budget or planning office.

2. **A talented leader should be selected, as well as a small cadre of support personnel** who will be responsible for supporting the implementation of the various administrative and technical elements of the M&E system (under the guidance of the committee).

3. **Consider meeting in the early stages with members of the legislature** to find out what information would be useful to them for annual budget deliberations or other policy or oversight purposes. Similar input should be sought from the national budget office.

4. **Develop a plan and schedule for implementation,** keeping in mind it is likely to take three to five years for full implementation. However, some initial useful performance information can probably be expected to become available by the end of the first year. As part of this step, it is critical to identify who will be needed to undertake each step of implementation. The people selected should be available and committed to providing the time necessary to perform their assignments.

5. Provide training and technical assistance to managers and key professional staff in the basics of M&E. This applies to initial training and training new people as turnover occurs. The training for managers should provide a thorough understanding of what M&E entails and recommendations for using the information. The training for other staff should focus more on the details of how M&E should be conducted so as to make the information obtained both valid and useful. Multilateral and bilateral funding organizations are potential sources of support for these activities.

6. Ask all program managers within the agency to identify a results-focused mission statement for their programs. These statements will necessarily be general, but they should set the tone and direction for the M&E effort in each program.

7. Ask each program within the agency to select a set of outcomes and outcome indicators[1] that will enable the program to monitor progress in achieving the results identified in its mission statement. Programs could establish their own working groups of key personnel to help select appropriate outcomes and outcome indicators.

The M&E working group might also seek input from representatives of the customers served by the program. For example, the program might sponsor meetings (focus groups) with small numbers of clients to help identify outcomes of importance to them. A public welfare agency, for example, might hold such sessions with its clients, a health agency might hold such sessions with patients in health clinics, and an economic development agency might hold such sessions with representatives from businesses.

Outcome indicators should be reviewed at a higher level to ensure that they contain the important performance information needed. For example, a ministry should review the indicators selected by each of its agencies and an agency should review the indicators proposed by each of its programs.

8. Inventory existing databases within the agency to identify the output and outcome information already available (or readily available) that can be used to monitor progress toward the agency's mission. The sources might be inside or outside the agency, such as data already regularly collected by a central planning office. Many, if not most, countries and their agencies already regularly collect outcome data, such as incidence and prevalence of health problems (for example, malaria, tuberculosis, and HIV), road accident fatalities, drinking water and air quality, unemployment rates, school absenteeism and completion rates, or economic development indicators.

9. For each performance indicator candidate, identify the source of the data, collection procedures, and how often the data will be collected and reported. Some outcomes will require new data collection. An indicator should not be considered final until a feasible data collection procedure has been identified. An agency and its programs should not limit itself to considering only outcome indicators for which it currently has data. Depending on the availability of resources, however, the agency may need to defer beginning new data collection procedures until later years. In addition to data obtainable through agency records, two other major data collection options to consider are customer surveys and trained observer ratings.

Surveys of citizens. Surveys are increasingly being used around the world to obtain feedback on outcomes, including the quality of government services. The feedback can be from samples of households or of customers that have been assisted by the agency (such as patients, students, or businesses). These surveys can provide feedback on a variety of program outcomes, including the surveyed person's housing, employment, or health condition status; ratings of various program quality characteristics such as timeliness, accessibility, fairness, and ease of obtaining information on services; frequency of use and reasons for nonuse of the service; and extent of having to make inappropriate payments to obtain service. Citizen surveys can also obtain information on the demographic characteristics of respondents, which helps identify the distributional effects of the program.

Trained observer rating procedures. This option uses personnel to systematically rate physically observable conditions, such as the condition of roads, hospitals, health clinics, school buildings, or other public facilities; proximity of households to sources of drinking water; and the ability of persons with disabilities to undertake basic activities of daily living. Each of these conditions is rated by an observer trained in the use of a well-defined rating scale. The raters visit all, or samples of, the units to be observed. The outcome indicator would be the number and percent of those items rated as being in satisfactory condition. Ratings obtained at regular intervals enable the program to monitor changes in each condition. The procedure has a potentially very useful side benefit of identifying where work is needed and the extent of that need so units with poor ratings can be prioritized for correction as soon as possible.

10. Provide for basic analysis of the performance data. At the ministry or agency level, top-level officials should assign an office to be responsible for examining the data collected, identifying unexpected findings, and reporting these findings to the appropriate officials in time to allow the agency to act on them. The basic analysis for performance monitoring is typically comparisons, including comparing the current reporting period to previous reporting periods, current data to targets, outcomes among different customer groups, and to similar programs in other countries. While more sophisticated statistical analysis would be desirable, this first-level, basic analysis should be highly informative and make the monitoring considerably more useful.

11. Top-level officials in the agency need to emphasize the importance of outcome information, particularly by using the M&E information in decision making. They also need to use information collected on outcomes to identify needed program improvements and training or technical assistance needs, and to draw attention to successful programs. Using M&E data at all levels of the agency, such as planning, budgeting, and program review, highlights the importance of the M&E system.

12. Review monitoring data and data collection procedures periodically. This review is an appropriate time to introduce improved measurements to ensure the continued reliability and credibility of performance measurement. Performance measurement should always be considered to be a work in process.

13. Use M&E information to lay the groundwork for positive incentives to improve the effectiveness of public services. From the beginning, emphasize that achieving good results will be rewarded. Emphasize that a major purpose of M&E information is to help officials and their staff identify what works and what does not.

14. Emphasize the message that outcome information is very useful for benchmarking, but does not provide the background information that tells why. The M&E system should not be used as a blame game. M&E information is often perceived by managers as threatening because it has been used to blame managers for poor outcomes without considering why the outcomes occurred. Outcomes are often affected by factors over which managers have limited or no control. (See Boxes 5.1 and 5.2 for examples of country service agencies that have made considerable progress in most of these steps.)

Making the M&E Process More Useful

Following are six key ways to maximize the usefulness of an M&E process within a service agency.

1. Link key characteristics of the "customers" the agency/program is serving to the outcomes for each customer. Then, report outcome data for each category of customer as well as for all customers. This information can be very useful both for interpreting the data and for identifying what actions are needed.

BOX 5.1

United States National Park Service

The United States National Park Service (NPS) is responsible for 392 park facilities throughout the United States. NPS, as well as all federal programs, is required to provide Congress with annual performance information. The United States Office of Management and Budget left it to each federal program to implement its own performance measurement process. NPS first identified its mission: To preserve the natural and cultural (historical) resources for posterity and to provide those resources for the enjoyment of U.S. citizens.

NPS decided to develop a performance measurement process that would: (1) help identify budget needs and provide justification for funding both individual parks and the park system as a whole; (2) help individual park superintendents manage; and (3) provide fair comparisons across parks.

NPS identified six basic outcome areas to be measured on at least an annual basis: (1) condition of natural resources; (2) condition of cultural/historical sites; (3) park-user satisfaction; (4) condition of non-cultural facilities; (5) safety of park users and employees; and (6) financial management, including park efficiency.

For each outcome area, NPS identified outcome indicators. Measurement of the indicator values has presented some difficult measurement questions, especially given the diversity of the 392 facilities. NPS developed a "scorecard" containing about five key outcome indicators for each of the six outcome areas.

For park-user satisfaction, NPS contracted with a university to develop a process, administered by each park, to annually survey random samples of park users and ask them to assess a number of key park characteristics. Most of the other outcome data for the other five outcome areas are provided by each park.

The scorecard process has evolved over a number of years and is still evolving as measurement procedures have improved. Each park superintendent is annually given its own scorecard results, along with a comparison to the average for all parks and the average of the other parks in its region. Each park can also compare itself to any other parks it believes are similar.

Thus far, the annual process appears to have been more useful for accountability and budgeting than for park management, partly because of the lag time before the scorecard data become available to the parks. However, much of the data can be used by individual parks to identify actions needed throughout the year. For example, the data on safety (accidents, injuries, crimes), feedback from park users, and facility condition data (based on regular inspections) are routinely considered and used for allocating resources. The parks are encouraged to use the scorecard information as part of their justification for funding requests as part of the annual NPS budget process.

The outcome indicators and process have been evolving over the years and will likely continue to be improved as new measurement procedures become available.

For example, program managers in the education, employment, public welfare, housing, and health sectors will find it useful to be able to identify program outcomes by demographic characteristics, such as outcomes by age, gender, income, household size, race/ethnicity, and so forth. This may sug-

BOX 5.2

Mexico's Ministry for Social Development

Mexico's Ministry for Social Development *(Secretaría de Desarrollo Social—SEDESOL)* found that the development of a results-based management system takes time and is a work in progress. In 2007, after earlier piloting a results-based M&E process in four programs, SEDESOL began implementing a more comprehensive process combining results-based monitoring, evaluation, and budgeting. The ministry early on established an office with extensive evaluation capacity, providing a basis for the later results-based process, which included a combination of monthly, quarterly, and annual data reporting.

As of 2009, SEDESOL had 500 indicators. Of these, 112 were linked to results, 170 measured the quantity, efficiency, and quality of the services delivered by programs, and the remaining 218 measured the activities used to produce these products. However, 40 of these indicators were selected by the Ministry of Finance as priority indicators for use in the 2010 budget preparation and subsequent monitoring. The Office of the President also monitors the indicators and goals of sectoral programs such as SEDESOL.

Source: Mexico, Ministry of Finance, and World Bank 2010.

gest the need for program changes for groups that were not sufficiently helped. For programs that do not directly service individual recipients, such as road maintenance and environmental quality programs, breakouts by key characteristics are still very important. For example, data calculated on the number of traffic accidents will be considerably more useful if the outcome data are broken out by characteristics, such as cause of the accident, average daily traffic, and location.

A key problem for many countries, particularly poor countries, is that they may not have M&S systems capable of providing such information. Nevertheless, the programs in such countries should do whatever they can to try to obtain and calculate such breakout data, even if the calculations only can be done manually, and even if they can only focus on outcome breakouts for one or two categories.

2. Set targets for the coming year for each output and outcome indicator. A good time to select targets is during the annual budget process. Setting targets typically starts with the data on the previous years' values for each indicator. These values then can be adjusted for any significant changes expected, such as in funding or personnel. Other considerations are external factors, such as the economy (changing export conditions or new businesses that can increase revenues or reduce unemployment), technology (that could improve service quality), and political changes expected to alter ministry or agency priorities.

Normally the program should propose the targets for its own performance indicators. These targets, however, should be reviewed by upper-level officials to ensure that the targets are neither too easy to meet nor overly high. The danger with targets is that they can become primarily political in nature, making them either much too easy to achieve or unrealistic. Targets are more meaningful when based on previous performance and reasonable expectations of the future.

3. Ask agencies and their programs to provide explanations for unexpected results and indicate plans for correcting any problems noted in the explanations. The ministry or agency might set a threshold, such as requiring explanations for any performance indicator value that differs by more than, for example, 10 percent from the expected target value.

Data on results do not tell what the cause of those results is, or what to do about them. Agencies and their programs should be encouraged to seek explanations for unexpected results and develop plans to correct any problems that are identified. A side benefit of such a provision is that managers may welcome the opportunity to formally provide their explanations, fearing that otherwise they will be blamed unfairly for poor results. This may alleviate the "blame" problem noted earlier.

4. Provide for regular, timely performance reporting for review by ministry, agency, and program officials. For budgeting purposes, only annual performance reports may be needed. However, for managerial purposes, this is too infrequent. Generally, reporting should be done at least quarterly. For some indicators, such as those relating to safety and health, reports are likely to be needed more frequently.

5. Make the report format as understandable, readable, attractive, and informative as possible. Too often performance reports are unclear, uninformative, or filled with unfamiliar terminology. With today's electronic capabilities, even poor countries have access to a variety of report-generating software.

6. Ministry officials, agency officials, and program managers should be encouraged to hold regular "How Are We Doing?" review sessions soon after the latest performance report has been issued. The ministry or agency head meets separately with each major agency program or division to discuss the performance data, identify where the outcomes are going well and not well, and suggest ways to correct poor past results. In subsequent meetings, previous decisions should be followed up on to determine the extent of progress that has been made in correcting previously identified problems.

Incorporating Program Evaluations

The monitoring process described above provides regular measurement of program performance, but it does not tell why the program has been successful or unsuccessful. The explanatory information suggested above provides first-order information on the "whys" and what might be done to improve performance. However, for programs that involve large expenditures and/or are of major importance, more in-depth program evaluation is desirable. In general, program evaluations tend to be expensive and may require long periods of time, perhaps years before the findings are available.

Each year, it is important for the ministry and each agency to establish a schedule of which programs will receive an in-depth evaluation. The choice should depend on criteria such as major uncertainties and lack of information regarding program success, cost of evaluation, time required to complete the evaluation and therefore the timeliness of the findings, and the likelihood that the evaluation will provide useful information for later decisions. For some programs it may not be feasible to obtain the needed information. An initial step is to assess whether these programs are good candidates for evaluation.

It is also critical to select what type of organization will conduct each evaluation. The organization conducting the evaluation should be reasonably independent, if for no other reason than to achieve external credibility for the findings. Few government agencies or ministries are likely to have the in-house capability for such program evaluations. Almost certainly the evaluations will need to be conducted by outside organizations such as universities or specialized, private non-profit or for-profit organizations. Because of evaluation costs, the ministry or agency might seek funding from international multilateral or bilateral funding organizations, particularly for evaluating programs for which the funding organization has provided support.

An important additional step is to ensure that the completed evaluations are professionally reviewed to assess their quality. Most program evaluation reports should be made available to the public. This step itself can help encourage the program evaluators to ensure their work is of reasonable quality.

Uses of M&E Information

M&E information has many uses, including identifying shortfalls in outcomes, thereby enabling service improvement. M&E data can also help to formulate ministry, agency, and program budgets and help to justify budget requests. Program outcome information, whether obtained through regular performance monitoring or from program evaluations, should be linked to program cost information as part of the budget process. The outcomes expected to be achieved by the budget requested should be a major factor in budget decisions.

The information produced by M&E systems is also useful for helping to allocate and prioritize resources throughout the year, such as adjusting the assignment of work or staff to different locations or customer groups based on performance data. For example, outcome indicator data can identify areas most in need of road repairs, emerging health issues, types of housing shortages, traffic accident locations, and locations with the most water or air quality problems.

M&E systems can also develop incentives for agencies and programs based at least in part on success in achieving outcomes. Monetary incentives can be expensive and are not likely to be appropriate for many countries—at least not until considerable experience in M&E has been gained. However, non-monetary incentives can be considered once the M&E process is in place. For example, as noted earlier, recognition awards could be given to agencies or programs that have met or exceeded their targets.

M&E information provides the basis for developing multi-year strategic plans for ministries and agencies. The latest values for key outcome indicators can be used to establish the baselines and subsequent out-year targets. In later years, the annual M&E data on these key outcome indicators can be compared against the targets in the multi-year strategic plan. Such information indicates whether actions are needed to stay on the plan, whether plan revisions are needed, or whether the plan is no longer feasible.

M&E information also helps to communicate with the legislature and citizens. Performance reports that provide data on the ministry's or agency's major outcome indicators are likely to be of considerable interest to legislators and citizens. Such transparency can be helpful in obtaining citizen support for the ministry's and agency's work.

Ministries and their agencies may, understandably, fear that showing bad news (such as worsening outcomes) will only bring them grief from the legislature and public. However, showing only outcomes that look good is likely to undermine credibility. Problems can be alleviated if the ministry or agency provides explanations for poor outcomes and indicates what it plans to do to correct the problem.

Inter-governmental Concerns

Depending on the level of decentralization in the country, a considerable amount of the data may come from local or regional/provincial government bodies. For example, to the extent that education and health services are de-centralized, these lower levels of government should be monitoring the out-comes of these services.

The ministry or agency will likely need to help lower-level governments develop their capacity to operate their own M&E systems. The central min-istry or agency might need to provide guidance, guidelines, and financial support. The national agency will need to check the quality of performance data from lower level governments; this means providing training and tech-nical assistance, but also periodically auditing at least a sample of the data and data collection procedures used by lower levels of government.

Cost of M&E

The added cost will depend considerably on the extent to which each agency program is already collecting reasonably reliable performance data and if the ministry, agency, and program already have personnel that can assist in implementation. Many agency programs are likely to be already tracking a number of outcomes, which can be used as a starting point for the M&E system.

The largest added costs will likely be for any new personnel needed (such as for analysis); training (including start-up, continuing, and replacement training); and for any new data collection procedures (such as the cost of surveys). Household surveys, in particular, will probably need to be adminis-tered by an outside business, university, or the national statistical office. Added costs could also be for a new computer system and technology to pro-cess substantial amounts of data, as well as in-depth program evaluations usually conducted by an outside organization, such as a university or special-ized private firm.

The position of many governments in developed countries that are intro-ducing M&E systems has been that monitoring is a basic management func-tion. The cost of ongoing implementation should, therefore, be primarily covered by the ministry, agency, and the program's own budget. Initial start-up costs are likely to be more of a problem for many ministries and agencies, however, and for these costs funding could be sought from the central government or from donor organizations.

Conclusions

Monitoring and evaluating the results of public services is both common sense and good management. However, performance data obtained from M&E systems do not replace the need for judgments by public officials. M&E information can only serve as one input, albeit a major input, for decision making. Many other factors will also need to be considered.

Implementing M&E successfully and usefully in a ministry or agency requires commitment and leadership from high-level officials in these organizations. And it takes time and special resources. If the organization's climate will not likely permit meaningful use of M&E information, the effort will be a waste of money. However, if the climate is favorable, the ultimate gains should be considerable in improving the organization's services to its citizens.

Note

1. See also Castro's discussion of performance indicators in Chapter 8.

Bibliography

Gorgens, Marelize, and Jody Zall Kusek. 2009. *Making Monitoring and Evaluation Systems Work*. Washington, DC: World Bank.

Hatry, Harry P. 2006. *Performance Measurement: Getting Results*, Second Edition. Washington, DC: Urban Institute.

Kusek, Jody Zall, and Ray C. Rist. 2004. *Ten Steps to a Results-Based Monitoring and Evaluation System*. Washington, DC: World Bank.

Mackay, Keith. 2007. *How to Build M&E Systems to Support Better Government*. Washington, DC: World Bank.

Mexico, Ministry of Finance, and World Bank. 2010. "Mexico Quality of Public Expenditure." Note 11.

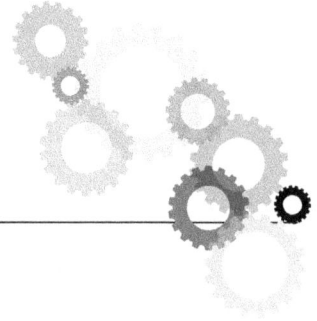

CHAPTER 6

M&E Systems and the Budget

Philipp Krause

Monitoring and evaluation (M&E) are means to multiple ends, such as to improve transparency and accountability or for managerial purposes to reward performance inside ministries and agencies. But a crucial element of running an effective public sector would be missing if M&E were not used to inform the spending of public money. This chapter introduces the main issues surrounding M&E as a tool for budgeting—a system usually referred to as performance budgeting[1]—to help policy makers make strategic decisions about their M&E systems by outlining different design choices and their respective advantages and pitfalls.

Budgeting is said to have three aims: (1) fiscal discipline, (2) allocative efficiency, and (3) operational efficiency. How can M&E help officials involved in the budget process achieve those aims? A traditional ministry of finance usually focuses on enforcing fiscal discipline by tightly controlling spending at the line item level. The German budget, for instance, has around 6,000 line

The author thanks Helena Hwang (Consultant, Poverty Reduction and Equity Group), Mariano Lafuente (Research Analyst, Latin America and Caribbean Public Sector Governance), Nick Manning (Adviser, Public Sector Governance), Gladys Lopez-Acevedo (Senior Economist, Poverty Reduction and Equity Unit [PRMPR]), Keith Mackay (Consultant, PRMPR), and Jaime Saavedra (Director, PRMPR) for their very helpful comments. The views expressed in this chapter are those of the author.

items. This level of detail gives the finance ministry many levers to keep ministerial spending in check. However, it has often been criticized as relatively inflexible and inefficient for budgetary decision making. Budget officials have to spend significant time reviewing small items that have little bearing on important policy decisions, and the system does not facilitate considerations of the results of public spending.

A well-designed M&E system has the potential to overcome some of the shortcomings of traditional budgeting. By defining indicators for public spending outputs and outcomes, governments gain the ability to monitor non-financial performance. By carrying out evaluations that turn performance information into implementable policy recommendations, governments can more efficiently allocate resources to programs with the greatest contribution to its policy priorities. In focusing the effort of public managers on performance, M&E can also contribute to better operational efficiency.

Many Organisation for Economic Co-operation and Development (OECD) countries have introduced some elements of M&E into their budget process over the last three decades. These performance budgeting reforms were often part of other efforts to improve performance in the public sector and to make the budget process more flexible for difficult fiscal climates. Early adopters, such as Australia, New Zealand, and the United Kingdom, pursued their reforms most vigorously in times of fiscal crisis. The main motivation was often not primarily to strengthen spending discipline, but rather to develop the tools that would allow the government to make better use of existing funds.

Many middle-income countries have since taken up the ideas first seen in OECD countries and adapted them to their contexts. In many lower-income countries, the context for introducing M&E into the budget process is quite different. The fight against poverty and the joint push by governments and donors to make progress on the Millennium Development Goals provide a results orientation by default. For lower-income countries, developing a link between the poverty reduction goals in the Poverty Reduction Strategy Paper and the annual budget cycle is a key challenge.

What Are the Different Tools, and How Do They Fit Existing Contexts?

It is very hard to imagine a budget process that does not monitor: even the most basic financial management system tracks the flows of resources. A detailed line item budget is an excellent tool to monitor inputs of money. When using the term M&E, however, "monitoring" means the regular measuring of the outputs of government programs and possibly their outcomes as well.

If M&E are used together for budgetary decisions, a form of performance budgeting emerges (Arizti et al. 2009; Curristine 2007; Shah and Shen 2007).

The most rigid form of M&E is directly linking funding to performance, most commonly outputs. The ministry of finance essentially buys a certain level of performance from spending ministries and only funds what it buys. Formulaic performance budgeting can only be found in a few countries in certain sectors, such as health or education, where outputs can be rigidly standardized. No country has institutionalized such a system for its entire government, because it is both technically and politically almost impossible to automatically tie funding to predefined levels of performance. There is also not much of a role for evaluations in such a system, which is problematic.

Performance information cannot be used to automatically adjust spending—it needs to be interpreted. One might expect programs with negative evaluation results to receive funding cuts; however, politically important programs with negative results might just as well receive funding increases, because failure would be unacceptable and fixing failed programs costs money. Formulaic performance budgeting decreases the scope for informed decision making by public officials.

On the other end of the spectrum, the M&E-budget link can be purely presentational. Sector ministries or the ministry of finance can publish performance data or submit data to the legislature as an appendix to the budget or in the form of performance reports during the budget year. Legislative or executive participants might use these reports in budget negotiations, but there is no requirement to formally consider them.

Presentational performance budgeting can still raise important issues and make budgetary decision makers aware of problems that a traditional line item budget would not uncover. It can also be the result of a budget system where either the finance ministry or the legislature enjoys a large degree of discretion over how they reach their allocative decisions. In many cases, it may be a transitional state, where proper decision-making structures have not yet been set up, or an unintended system where information is produced somewhere in the system, but not used by key budgetary actors.

OECD countries that adopt performance budgeting tend to develop a performance-informed budget process, where M&E instruments serve as analytical tools. In this model, performance indicators are integrated into the budget and regular evaluations are scheduled into the budget cycle. Performance indicators and evaluations are institutionally considered during budget formulation.

This process can take various forms. In the United Kingdom, for instance, the finance ministry uses three-year spending reviews to negotiate spending plans with ministries. The basis of planned expenditures is the "public service agreement," which uses performance indicators to define targets the ministry is supposed to achieve with a given amount of funding over three years. These targets form the core of the interaction between the finance ministry and spending ministries and are meant to capture what a ministry does and to set the agenda for its future achievements. The 1998 spending reviews contained a total of about 600 headline targets; this number was reduced to 110 by the 2004 budget exercise. Inside each ministry, these targets are broken down along results chains into lower-level targets for operational purposes. Ministries have a very high degree of discretion over the internal allocation of funds to achieve their targets. The result is a highly structured, top-down system where performance indicators are very prominently used to inform budgetary decisions.

Many other countries have developed less ambitious ways to use performance indicators, such as by complementing the traditional line items in the budget document with data on ministerial performance. Performance indicators are available as a source of information that can be used for budgetary decisions without laws or regulations prescribing exactly how legislators or budget officials might use them.

A single-minded focus on monitoring performance indicators can be criticized for several reasons. First of all, if indicators are the main sources of information considered for crucial decisions, then incentives grow for public officials to focus on delivering indicators but not necessarily improving the underlying performance. There are numerous examples of public officials trying to "game" indicators to secure funding.[2] Secondly, the supply of performance data can easily outstrip demand. When ministries expect that their performance indicators will shape future funding, they have every reason to develop as many indicators as possible to ensure that every aspect of their work is captured. The result is that much information is produced, but not necessarily used.

In addition, performance indicators alone are not directly actionable. A performance increase of 2 percent can be a substantial success or a deep disappointment when compared to other countries. Numbers can be affected by external factors and changes in funding can influence outcomes with a lag of several years, or very disproportionately, or not at all. It often takes time and specialized policy knowledge to interpret performance information, which are in short supply during the annual budget cycle.

The need to have actionable information is why the combination of monitoring and evaluation is crucial. An evaluation is a systematic review of a program or project that identifies strengths and weaknesses and recommends actions that officials can use for budget formulation. Many policy analysts first think of an evaluation as a rigorous impact analysis that is able to identify the specific contribution of a policy intervention by comparing beneficiaries and non-beneficiaries. Such impact evaluations are indeed used in budgetary decisions and can have a huge impact, particularly for the funding of new policies. The reputation of conditional cash transfer programs, for instance, was in no small part established by the impact evaluations of Mexico's Progresa program in the 1990s. These evaluation results allowed public officials to judge the merit of this innovative policy intervention against other programs with similar aims. However, impact evaluations are not appropriate for all budgetary evaluation needs. Most importantly, they are expensive and take time, usually more than one year.

For a frequent and comprehensive evaluation system, quicker, desk-based evaluations are an important tool. Rather than carrying out original research, a rapid evaluation would rely on the available information that can be provided inexpensively from the evaluated program and other public sources. This can cut costs substantially and reduce research time to a few months—a crucial difference, because they can be made to fit into a single budget cycle. A rapid evaluation can be initiated during budget deliberations, commissioned, and carried out the same year, with the results available to feed into the budget preparation the following year.

For instance, Chile conducted more than 250 rapid evaluations between 1997 and 2010. The evaluation schedule is decided in negotiations between the finance ministry and Congress. Evaluation teams are chosen from a pool of expert consultants. All evaluation recommendations are monitored by the Chilean budget office and revisited annually during budget negotiations. While not comparable to impact evaluations in depth and academic rigor, desk-based evaluations focus on consistency and operational issues and can uncover significant issues relevant to budgetary decisions.

Countries such as the United Kingdom also use comprehensive spending reviews to consider all available M&E data to evaluate spending in one policy area. The U.K. Treasury does not just consider its own M&E data, but also evaluation results commissioned by other government bodies, such as the National Audit Office. Spending reviews are carried out every two to three years.

A traditional line item budget is often criticized for its inefficiency and inability to respond to new policy challenges. Budget officials in the finance ministry as well as legislators have limited time to consider the annual budget. A budget consisting of thousands of individual items makes it possible to closely control where money is being spent. Change, however, is incremental and often limited to distributing the marginal increase from year to year. A combination of soundly measured and regularly monitored performance indicators and accessible evaluations can, in theory, enable budget decision makers to move beyond the limits of incremental budgeting and respond to larger fiscal challenges. But "in theory" is a big caveat, because in practice, M&E only makes a difference if the demand is right.

The Institutional Roles—Who Does What?

M&E is about supply and demand. Unless actors in the budget process demand and use the outputs of M&E, even the most sophisticated tools will have no effect. It is also critically important that budget processes are inherently political in nature. Each phase of the budget process has its technical underpinnings, but ultimately it is about turning political priorities into administrative reality. A country that successfully introduces M&E into the budget process does so because enough actors demand the information that M&E provides.

The finance ministry is the main agency in charge of the budget process and often the appropriate ministry in which to anchor the M&E system. Chile is a good example; the Chilean budget process is possibly the most centralized among OECD countries. The budget director is a key adviser to the president, and the budget process is tightly managed by the budget office (DIPRES). The natural result of such a budget system is that the M&E system is also managed by the budget office. The technical mandate of DIPRES is solidly defined in a legal framework that gives it considerable discretionary scope to change budgeting procedures without new legislation. The budget office controls the schedule and the methodologies, ensures quality, and manages the flow of information between agencies, ministries, itself, and Congress.

Yet even in Chile, the budget office is mostly a compiler, not producer, of information. Evaluations are commissioned by the government, but their implementation relies on a network of universities and other researchers. The indicators that feed into the monitoring system are supplied by agencies and ministries themselves. The main role of the budget office is quality control. The budget office strongly supports the use of M&E information both throughout the executive bureaucracy and for legislative purposes. Yet international studies point out that the budget office remains the principal user and supporter of M&E in Chile. This system has worked very well in Chile over the past 15 years, but it is not the only institutional setup that works. Very few other countries can rely on such a strongly centralized budget process to underpin the introduction of M&E.

The main design challenge is how to tailor the system to the likely users of M&E information and their position within the budgeting framework. This is a universal concern, irrespective of a country's stage of development

BOX 6.1

Mind the Gaps between the Poverty Reduction Strategy and the Budget

A very different challenge arises in the many countries that tried to implement poverty reduction strategies (PRSs) to align country and donor efforts toward reaching the Millennium Development Goals. PRSs are often drafted by planning ministries or special commissions without a central role in the regular budget process. Critics noted that these strategies were geared toward donor audiences and not properly implemented. The format and planning schedule of PRSs did not necessarily fit well into the existing budget process. Countries like Uganda, which was quite successful at using the PRS for planning and budgeting, did so by putting the budget office firmly in charge. The M&E systems that Uganda implemented to feed into the PRS were designed with the budget process in mind.

Source: Wilhelm and Krause (2007).

(Box 6.1). A growing body of literature on fiscal institutions points out that the centralization of the budget process depends on macropolitical factors. The most important factors relate to electoral and party systems and the constitutional separation of powers between the legislature and the executive branch (Hallerberg 2004). They are thus largely beyond the control of technical policy makers. In countries where the right pre-conditions do not exist, other successful models can be viable alternatives to centralization, but only when they take the institutional balance into account. In other words, there is little reason to expect that a highly centralized M&E system will produce good results if the budget system itself is not centralized.

Centralization is most likely in parliamentary systems where either one or a few closely aligned parties form the government. In the United Kingdom, the party with a majority in parliament automatically heads the executive branch as well, which makes for relatively clear lines of accountability within government. If the government has resolved to employ M&E in the budget process and already delegates strong budgetary authority to the finance ministry, then the budget office becomes the main consumer of M&E information. When legislators discuss the draft budget in parliament, their majority will be part of the governing coalition and their policy priorities should be broadly aligned with those of the finance minister.

Many finance ministries make M&E information available to legislators to build legislative support for the M&E system in general and to support controversial budgetary decisions that might be based on M&E data. Legislators have an incentive to consider M&E information, especially when budgetary decisions affect their own constituency. In fact, in many parliamentary systems, the supreme audit office is closely tied to the legislature and often carries out its own evaluations independently of the executive branch. Nevertheless, the budgetary relationship between the budget committee in parliament and the finance ministry is not adversarial.

In presidential countries, the constitutional balance between the legislature and the executive branch plays a crucial role. Chile is a fairly exceptional case in this regard, because the powers of Congress to amend the president's budget proposal are severely limited. On the other end of the continuum lies the United States, where the president's budget can be famously "dead on arrival" if the Congress is controlled by the opposing party. Most presidential systems lie somewhere in between (Box 6.2).

Irrespective of the constitutional or legal powers of the finance ministry, many budget offices find it useful to give agencies and ministries a substantial role in the M&E system. In some countries, a tradition of collegiate cabinet government makes it difficult for the finance ministry to assume tasks without being seen as encroaching on the authority of other ministers to shape the policy in their respective sectors. To push ahead without properly involving sector ministries can imperil the sustainability of reforms, a problem even for successful reformers like Chile.

Generally, finance ministries make their own workload more manageable by delegating parts of M&E to ministries. If ministries operate performance indicators and buy into evaluation results, they can forestall many potential conflicts during budget negotiations with the finance ministry and shape their budget proposals in a way more acceptable to both sides. A strong stake for ministries and agencies also makes it more likely that M&E results are used for operational and managerial purposes within ministries, something that finance ministries might reasonably expect to benefit operational efficiency.

When Australia introduced its evaluation system in 1987, ministries were obliged to develop their own evaluation plans and had to ensure that the entire ministerial portfolio would be evaluated every three to five years. The finance ministry played a key role in quality assurance, but otherwise its main role in the evaluation system was to insist on the use of evaluation results during budget negotiations. Internal surveys carried out by the Australian government in the 1990s found evaluation results to be very influential, particularly in deliberations over new policy initiatives (Mackay 2004).

In weaker administrative environments, it might not be possible to delegate the operation of M&E instruments because of lack of capacity, or be-

BOX 6.2

Not All Presidential Countries Are the Same: The Experience of Mexico

In Mexico, congressional budget powers are considerable. Since 1998, three parties of roughly equal size have shared the legislature. By default, the president's party does not have a legislative majority and thus cannot pass the budget alone. When Mexico moved toward developing M&E capacity in the public sector, it faced a potential impasse. On the one hand, the legislative power of the purse made Congress a legitimate and inevitable consumer of M&E data. The legal framework of budgeting also requires congressional approval for the necessary legal changes to the budget process. Yet if the M&E system was led by the legislature, there would be a strong incentive for the executive bureaucracy not to develop a stake in M&E for fear that the new tools would expose them politically. On the other hand, the Ministry of Finance could not fully centralize M&E authority either, because to do so might jeopardize the credibility of M&E information in Congress. This issue was resolved by vesting much technical expertise and authority over performance monitoring and the evaluation program in an independent technical body called The National Council for the Evaluation of Social Development Policies (CONEVAL). This council maintains close working relations with both Congress and the Ministry of Finance. CONEVAL is in a position to develop a reputation as a producer of credible and useful information and thus ensure that the M&E outputs it supplies are actually used for budgetary decisions in both branches of government.

cause it might compromise their credibility. However, even if the public administration is weak or fragmented, the ultimate measure of success for an M&E system is not the extent to which the ministry of finance operates every aspect of it: M&E is only effective when budget analysts, legislators, and political leaders use the M&E data produced to formulate and negotiate the budget.

Several key factors can severely inhibit the use of M&E for budgetary purposes. A government needs reliable information systems, solid financial management systems, and at least the basic human capacity to generate and process evaluations. It does not, however, need a very systematic and planned M&E system to start with, especially not in countries with lower capacity. Uganda is an example of a country where the creation of a new budget directorate, out of the 1992 merger of the planning and finance ministries, created a big enough unit of professionals to conduct high-level analytical work even though much of the public sector was lagging far behind. Such islands of excellence can make use of performance information from many sources, including from donors, and try to spread their results without relying on a demanding framework that systematically links performance data to the budget process (Kuteesa and others 2009).

How Best to Implement M&E-Budget Links

Institutional change rarely happens because the benefits of change are self-evident. In budgeting, large amounts of money and quite often political futures are at stake, and as long as the budget process works reasonably well, budgetary actors are understandably reluctant to change the institutional setup. Sources of potential resistance against M&E include the finance ministry itself, particularly the budget office. In many finance ministries, budget analysts are very skilled at challenging ministerial budget proposals and successfully trimming down excessive spending. Especially when the introduction of performance information goes hand in hand with dismantling traditional line item controls to "let managers manage," budget analysts might see more danger than gain in reform.

In most OECD countries where finance ministries did take the lead and successfully implemented M&E-oriented reforms, a few factors were usually present:

- Top officials in the finance ministry were convinced that the existing budgetary toolkit was not sufficient for current or looming fiscal challenges. Periods of fiscal austerity, volatile revenues, or crises of confidence in the government's ability to spend wisely often combined to create such a sense of urgency.
- An individual or a group of institutional champions "sold" both the technical and the political benefits of reform to different groups of stakeholders.
- The first two factors eventually combined to make it feasible for ministers and other political leaders to expend the political capital and attention necessary to overcome resistance and adopt the necessary decisions.

Prospective reformers do not have to wait for the next recession and a favorable political climate to attempt setting up an M&E system. In many countries, different budgetary actors successfully experimented with different tools and instruments before the reform climate reached a tipping point and piecemeal change turned into comprehensive reform. In Mexico, the Ministry of Social Development had been working for years on performance indicators, logical frameworks, and evaluations before the finance ministry started to champion reforms on a larger scale. In Chile, reforms accelerated markedly after the country was hit by the effects of the Asian financial crisis. The success of today's comprehensive system benefitted greatly from the experience of a first generation of reforms that some champions within the budget office had implemented. Australia, Sweden, the Netherlands, and the United Kingdom are cases where changes in government prompted dramatic changes over very short periods of time, which were then often followed by many years of fine-tuning.

There does not seem to be a golden rule as to how exactly an M&E function should be anchored within the finance ministry. In several cases, including Mexico and Chile, ministers chose to set up a dedicated M&E unit within the budget office separate from budget analysts. Such a setup ensures that M&E has internal champions charged with promoting the new instruments, yet at the same time it also creates an institutional barrier between M&E and the officials who are in charge of drafting the budget. At the U.K. Treasury and the U.S. Office of Management and Budget (OMB), on the other hand, budget analysts are directly in charge of managing and processing M&E information. OMB's Program Assessment Rating Tool was managed by its individual budget examiners and has been linked closely to the preparation of the executive draft budget. In some cases, officials have noted that such a setup slows down the first implementation of M&E, because budget analysts are so busy running the budget that they find little time to take charge of the new instruments.

Inevitably, the right setup will depend on the specific administrative context. The available evidence, in particular from the United Kingdom, encouragingly suggests that the longer performance budgeting is in use, the more support there is among budget officials. The support seems to grow not only because M&E turns out to be useful as a budgetary instrument, but also because budget analysts come to see M&E work as more policy-oriented and thus more relevant and attractive than the traditional handling of line items.

Key Lessons

Four key lessons emerge from the discussion in this chapter:

- **No single M&E system model works in every country.** Successful introduction of M&E into the budget process has to account for the existing budgetary framework, and very different models have been successful in different countries.
- **M&E is a demand-driven process.** Even the most sophisticated M&E instruments are ultimately ineffective unless public officials actively use them for budgetary decisions.

- **Introducing M&E is a joint effort.** When setting up an M&E system, officials in the finance ministry cannot work in isolation; they need support from ministries and agencies and interest from legislators.
- **Bringing M&E into the budget is a politically sensitive reform.** To use M&E properly for budgeting, established administrative practices need to change, which will require a sustained reform effort and long-term political backing.

Notes

1. For current information on the World Bank's ongoing work on performance budgeting, please refer to the Public Sector Governance Web site: http://go.worldbank.org/SGO4LFRSS0.
2. Among other examples, Hood (2006) reports a U.K. experience: hospital patients waiting in lines of ambulances outside emergency rooms to meet a target for patients to be seen by a doctor within a certain time of admission.

Bibliography

Aritzi, P., M. Lafuente, N. Manning, F. Rojas, and T. Thomas. 2009. "Performance-Informed Budgeting in Latin America: Experiences and Opportunities." LCSPS Working Paper 0309, World Bank, Washington, DC.

Blöndal, J. R., and T. Curristine. 2004. "Budgeting in Chile." *OECD Journal on Budgeting* 4(2): 7–45.

Curristine, T., ed. 2007. *Performance Budgeting in OECD Countries.* Paris: OECD.

Curristine, T., R. Emery, P. Krause, et al. 2009. "OECD Review of Budgeting in Mexico." *OECD Journal on Budgeting* 9(1): 5–136.

Hood, C. 2006. "Gaming in Targetworld: The Targets Approach to Managing British Public Services." *Public Administration Review* 66(4): 515–21.

Krause, P. 2009. "A Leaner, Meaner Guardian? A Qualitative Comparative Analysis of Executive Control over Public Spending." Discussion Paper 22/2009, German Development Institute, Bonn.

Kuteesa, F., E. Tumusiime-Mutebile, A. Whitworth, and T. Williamson. 2009. *Uganda's Economic Reforms: Insider Accounts.* Oxford: Oxford University Press.

Hallerberg, M. 2004. *Domestic Budgets in a United Europe: Fiscal Governance from the End of Bretton Woods to EMU.* Ithaca: Cornell University Press.

Mackay, K. 2004. "Two Generations of Performance Evaluation and Management System in Australia." ECD Working Paper Series 11, World Bank Operations Evaluations Department, Washington, DC.

Shah, A. and C. Shen. 2007. "A Primer on Performance Budgeting." In *Budgeting and Budgetary Institutions*, ed. A. Shah. Washington, DC: World Bank Institute.

Wilhelm, V., and P. Krause, eds. 2007. *Minding the Gaps: Integrating Poverty Reduction Strategies and Budgets for Domestic Accountability.* Washington, DC: World Bank.

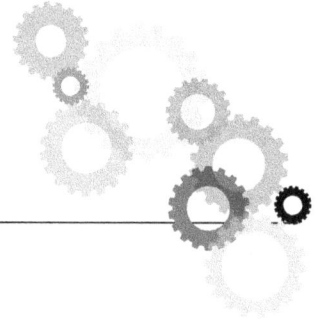

CHAPTER 7

Use of Social Accountability Tools and Information Technologies in Monitoring and Evaluation

Rajiv Sharma

This chapter reviews the basic concepts relating to the use of social accountability and information technology to monitor and evaluate public services and other governance processes that affect citizens. The chapter employs simple though practical examples to explain how to qualitatively change monitoring and evaluation (M&E) to make the process more citizen-centered and outcome-oriented. In turn, these practices can help improve the quality of service delivery. The chapter also discusses a few country-specific initiatives from India and elsewhere to support the arguments.

For their comments, the author thanks Jody Zall Kusek (Adviser, Health, Nutrition, and Population Unit), and the following members of the Poverty Reduction and Equity Group: Helena Hwang (Consultant), Philipp Krause (Consultant), Gladys Lopez-Acevedo (Senior Economist), Keith Mackay (Consultant), and Jaime Saavedra (Director). The views expressed in this chapter are those of the author.

FIGURE 7.1 Integrated Strategy to Use Social Accountability and ICT Tools for M&E

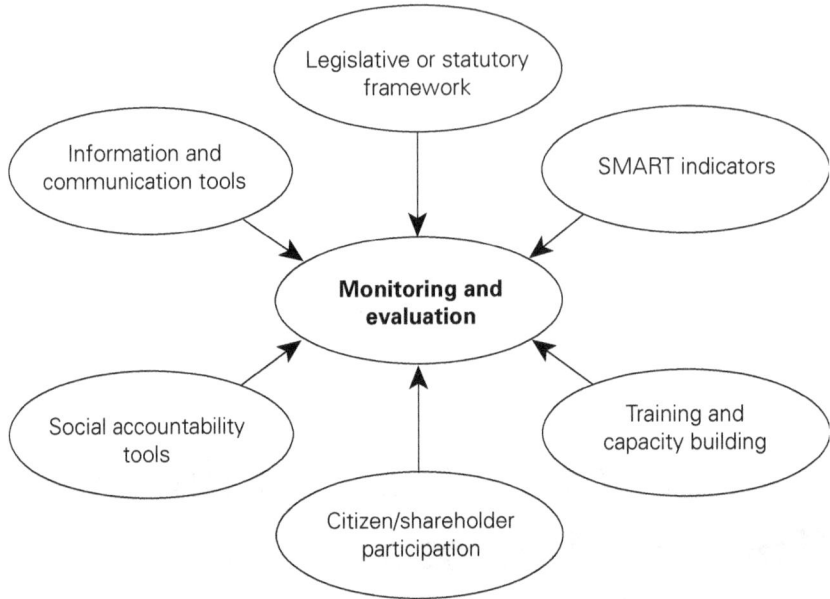

Source: Author's illustration.

In a broad sense, social accountability is a process used to hold the government—through its public officials—accountable to the citizenry. Accountability is promoted with a participatory approach that engages civil society, citizens, and different stakeholders. Social accountability includes a "broad range of actions and mechanisms" that can be used to hold government officials accountable to the citizens (Malena, Forster, and Singh 2004).

Traditional M&E systems typically involve developing and monitoring certain key performance indicators. The service or process is then evaluated in terms of its intended outcome(s). A well-rounded M&E system would take into account the concerns of all stakeholders—those on the demand side as well as those on the supply side. The intense engagement of citizens and civil society improves the quality of monitoring and the accuracy of evaluation by moving beyond a biased and one-sided approach to giving information about various performance indicators.

This chapter does not capture all the critical factors that determine the success of each social accountability tool. It focuses instead on examples of the use of information and communication technology (ICT) tools in combination. Figure 7.1 presents a schematic description of an integrated strategy to use social accountability and ICT tools to improve M&E, based on citizen participation and an appropriate set of specific, measurable, achievable, relevant, and time-bound (SMART) indicators to measure outcomes.

Social Accountability Tools

Social accountability tools involve a step-by-step procedure that ensures civic engagement and promotes citizen participation by revealing their perspectives and priorities regarding what they expect from the services rendered by public officials or state agencies. The tools are usually simple and replicable. The use of ICT improves access to information and transparency, particularly when information is provided in the public domain. Easy access to information for civil society, citizens, and other stakeholders also helps in evaluating a process or a public service in a manner that is people-centric and addresses their concerns and priorities.

Social accountability mechanisms can be employed to help society obtain access to the process of governance in a participatory way. Mechanisms such as right-to-information movements, citizen advisory boards and vigilance committees, public interest litigation, public hearings, or citizens' charters create space for pro-active citizen and civil society engagement with the state. Other social accountability tools designed specifically for the purpose of receiving citizen inputs include social audits, participatory budgeting and expenditure tracking, community or citizen score cards, independent budget analysis, and participatory performance monitoring.[1] These tools are intended to improve citizen participation in formulating public policy and to promote active involvement in the monitoring and evaluation of government processes, including those that have a bearing on service delivery, management of public assets, and financial and physical resources. The tools usually have a specific methodology designed to improve transparency in "government-to-citizen" engagement. Information technologies help improve citizens' participation as stakeholders in the accountability mechanism and develop their confidence in the service delivery apparatus.

The joint use of technology and social accountability tools can serve as a framework to provide better access for poor and vulnerable people because it substantially reduces discretion and subjectivity on the part of state actors and bureaucracy. However, community and other stakeholders' awareness and capacity to participate in this process must be improved to ensure the success of social accountability initiatives.

This strategy requires simultaneous efforts to train and build capacity of stakeholders and to establish a legal framework. Using legislation in combination with the other components discussed here to enforce social accountability is necessary. In general, the integrated strategy described in this chapter is not only useful in ensuring the effectiveness of M&E; it also provides a favorable environment for good governance.

Information Technology for Social Accountability Tools—General Issues

Social accountability tools can be created or improved using an information technology platform. A number of technology options are available to enable citizens and civil society to interact with government agencies and other state-sponsored institutions. Examples include Web sites and portals, video conferencing, telecenters, citizen service centers, electronic kiosks, touch screens, mobile phone-based services using short messages, interactive voice recording, and hand-held devices such as personal digital assistants. Use of smart cards and mobile automated teller machines has also been very effective in improving service delivery and accountability in remote areas, particularly for citizen transactions involving social welfare benefits or government employment program wage payments.[2]

Arroyo and Sirker (2005) note that Web sites are commonly used in several different ways, including preventive (for example, curbing corruption and reducing discretion), informative (giving useful details of various projects to enhance transparency), or punitive (for instance, publicizing the names of corrupt public officials who are punished). The Cristal Web Site launched in Argentina is a good example of a site that widely informs citizens about the activities of government agencies.

E-governance strategy

It is important to have a long-term strategy to provide a holistic environment for electronic enablement of vital government-to-citizen service as well as adequate infrastructure and connectivity to offer easy access to citizens, civil society, and other stakeholders. This requires the preparation of national and sub-national plans for uploading public services onto an e-governance platform. The success of these services will depend on how easy it is for the common citizen to access them.

An appropriate strategy should address issues of technology, infrastructure, reengineering of government processes, capacity building, and change management. The United Nations has developed an e-governance readiness index for comparing different countries. The latest concept also considers how strong the inclusiveness of e-governance is in a given country. It asks whether the national government publishes information on items under consideration, whether there are ways for the public to engage in consultations with policy makers, government officials, and one another, and whether citizens can influence decisions directly (for example, by voting online or by mobile telephone).

Capacity building

Capacity building and change management are important issues in the use of social accountability and ICT tools for M&E. The absence of these elements affects the sustainability of new practices. Building awareness in the community and equipping people with skills necessary to monitor and assess the quality of services is crucial.

There is very limited evidence of systematic and sustained training and capacity-building programs to prepare stakeholders to use social accountability tools. Available examples are mostly in specific projects where stakeholder feedback may be built into the project design and where stakeholders develop basic skills to use the accountability tools.

Use of Web sites to post learning material is very common, for example SASANET (see Figure 7.2) and similar initiatives through the Affiliated Network for Social Accountability.[3] Web-based training in the use of India's Right to Information Act has recently been initiated through an e-learning program.[4] This initiative has targeted both civil society on the demand side and government officials on the supply side. Through different modules, this e-learning course has the following basic features:

- It is Web-enabled.
- It provides an online learning platform with a virtual classroom and both start and end dates.
- Modules are designed with graded difficulty levels, beginning with simple content.
- Learners may ask questions that are answered by mentors through the virtual classroom and discussion forum.
- At the end of the course, the system administers a test comprising a set of questions randomly selected from a question bank. Learners who pass the test are awarded a certificate by the government. This certificate recognizes the effort put in by the participant.

This useful e-learning tool has the potential to solve the problem of training and capacity building for millions of people who need to understand the basics of using India's Right to Information Act. It uses easily accessible means to disseminate knowledge on the technical details of using a legal pro-

FIGURE 7.2 Web Site for Capacity Building

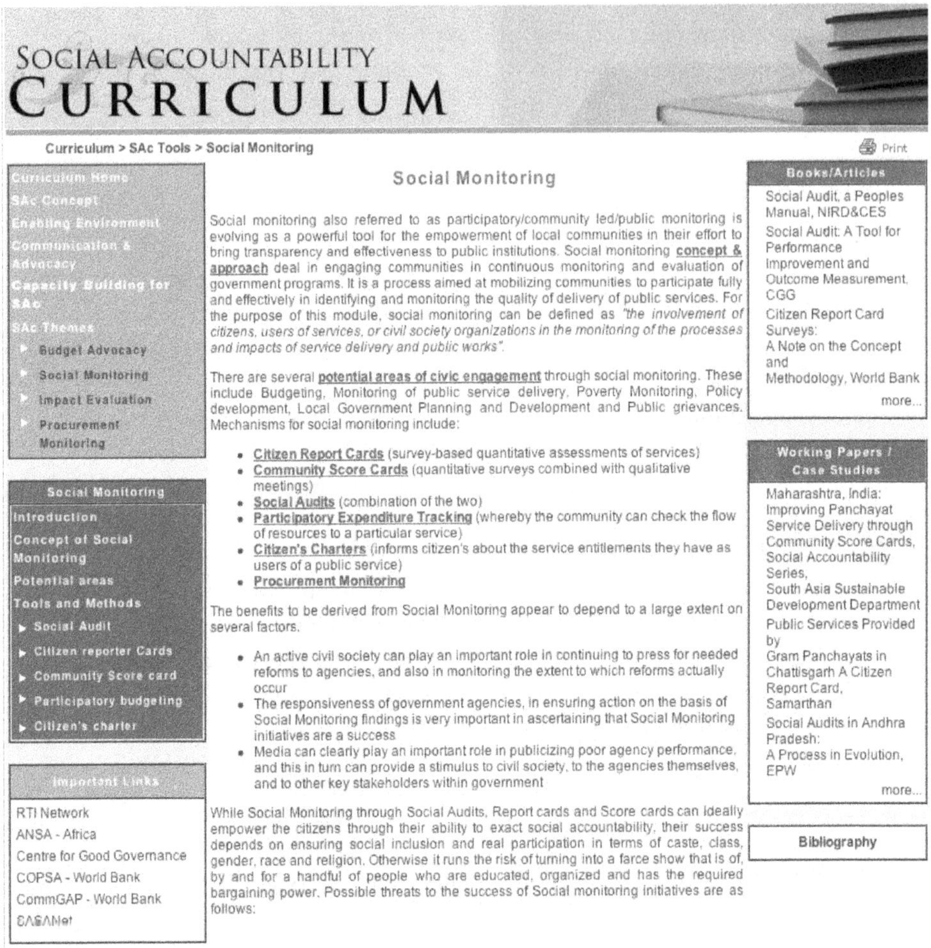

SOCIAL ACCOUNTABILITY
CURRICULUM

Curriculum > SAc Tools > Social Monitoring   Print

Curriculum Home
SAc Concept
Enabling Environment
Communication & Advocacy
Capacity Building for SAc
SAc Themes
  ▸ Budget Advocacy
  ▸ Social Monitoring
  ▸ Impact Evaluation
  ▸ Procurement Monitoring

Social Monitoring
Introduction
Concept of Social Monitoring
Potential areas
Tools and Methods
  ▸ Social Audit
  ▸ Citizen reporter Cards
  ▸ Community Score card
  ▸ Participatory budgeting
  ▸ Citizen's charter

Important Links
RTI Network
ANSA - Africa
Centre for Good Governance
COPSA - World Bank
CommGAP - World Bank
SASANet

Social Monitoring

Social monitoring also referred to as participatory/community led/public monitoring is evolving as a powerful tool for the empowerment of local communities in their effort to bring transparency and effectiveness to public institutions. Social monitoring **concept & approach** deal in engaging communities in continuous monitoring and evaluation of government programs. It is a process aimed at mobilizing communities to participate fully and effectively in identifying and monitoring the quality of delivery of public services. For the purpose of this module, social monitoring can be defined as *"the involvement of citizens, users of services, or civil society organizations in the monitoring of the processes and impacts of service delivery and public works".*

There are several **potential areas of civic engagement** through social monitoring. These include Budgeting, Monitoring of public service delivery, Poverty Monitoring, Policy development, Local Government Planning and Development and Public grievances. Mechanisms for social monitoring include:

- **Citizen Report Cards** (survey-based quantitative assessments of services)
- **Community Score Cards** (quantitative surveys combined with qualitative meetings)
- **Social Audits** (combination of the two)
- **Participatory Expenditure Tracking** (whereby the community can check the flow of resources to a particular service)
- **Citizen's Charters** (informs citizen's about the service entitlements they have as users of a public service)
- **Procurement Monitoring**

The benefits to be derived from Social Monitoring appear to depend to a large extent on several factors.

- An active civil society can play an important role in continuing to press for needed reforms to agencies, and also in monitoring the extent to which reforms actually occur
- The responsiveness of government agencies, in ensuring action on the basis of Social Monitoring findings is very important in ascertaining that Social Monitoring initiatives are a success
- Media can clearly play an important role in publicizing poor agency performance, and this in turn can provide a stimulus to civil society, to the agencies themselves, and to other key stakeholders within government

While Social Monitoring through Social Audits, Report cards and Score cards can ideally empower the citizens through their ability to exact social accountability, their success depends on ensuring social inclusion and real participation in terms of caste, class, gender, race and religion. Otherwise it runs the risk of turning into a farce show that is of, by and for a handful of people who are educated, organized and has the required bargaining power. Possible threats to the success of Social monitoring initiatives are as follows:

Books/Articles
Social Audit, a Peoples Manual, NIRD&CES
Social Audit: A Tool for Performance Improvement and Outcome Measurement, CGG
Citizen Report Card Surveys:
A Note on the Concept and Methodology, World Bank
more...

Working Papers / Case Studies
Maharashtra, India: Improving Panchayat Service Delivery through Community Score Cards, Social Accountability Series,
South Asia Sustainable Development Department Public Services Provided by
Gram Panchayats in Chattisgarh A Citizen Report Card, Samarthan
Social Audits in Andhra Pradesh:
A Process in Evolution, EPW
more...

Bibliography

Source: http://www.sasanet.org.

cess. It is running well, and user feedback on the technology and the course content is very positive (Figure 7.3).

Benchmarking service standards

An essential ingredient for the success of social accountability initiatives is a benchmark for service standards and a measurable and verifiable set of indicators to monitor and evaluate the services provided. Setting the benchmarking standards should involve all stakeholders—citizens, civil society,

FIGURE 7.3 User Feedback on the Right-to-Information Online Certificate Course

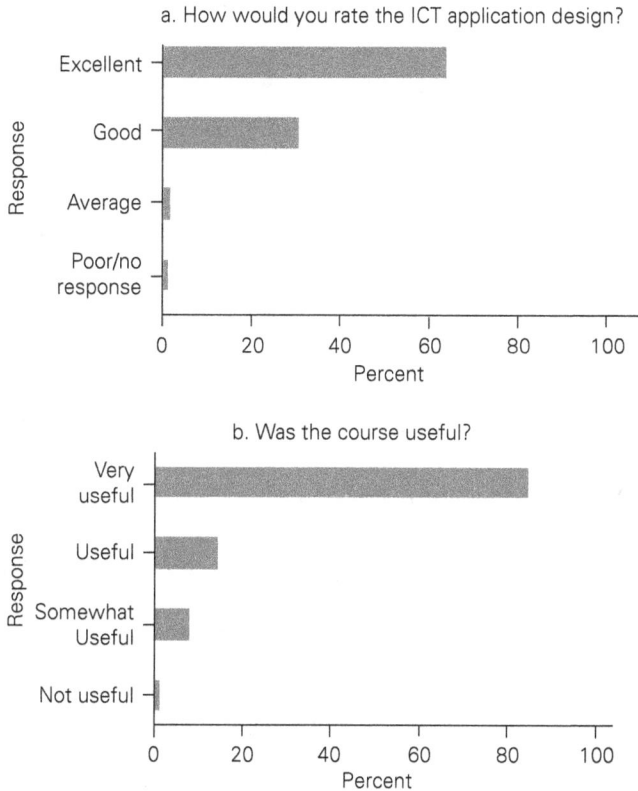

a. How would you rate the ICT application design?

b. Was the course useful?

Source: Author's illustration.
Note: Number of respondents = 1,329.

government officials, and politicians. ICT helps by enabling a smooth flow of information for the use of all stakeholders.

One way to implement this concept is to provide standards in citizens' charters—official documents published by government departments and service providers stating their commitment to citizens regarding standards of service. These charters guarantee a minimum level of service available to the citizen. In case of a breach of this commitment, citizens have a mechanism with which to raise a grievance and get it redressed through a prescribed process.

The Charter Mark national standard of the United Kingdom provides benchmarking for services furnished by the public sector. The Malcolm Baldrige National Quality Improvement Act, signed in the United States in 1987, is another example of service standards.

The use of citizen report cards in assessing public services in Bangalore, India, is a well-documented initiative. The Public Affairs Center, a nongovernmental organization, rated citizen satisfaction with various public services, based on two surveys taken in 1994 and 1999. The services covered were housing, municipal services, water and sewerage, electricity, driving licenses, telephones, banking, and health care. The 1999 survey found that, after five years, overall satisfaction with the services improved from 9 percent to 34 percent (with figures varying for each agency). These findings were widely published and an assessment of the impact of citizen report cards on the performance of public agencies gave a number of insights into the related processes. Though the information provided by the report cards was significant, how that information was eventually used to improve the systems and services depended on many diverse factors, such as responsive leadership, available resources, and the institutional environment of the agency concerned (Ravindra 2004). However, the report cards helped in benchmarking and comparing the feedback from users to articulate those issues in the public domain that triggered the change (Balakrishnan 2006).

There is evidence of increasing use of citizen report cards, despite the initial reluctance of state agencies. This tool is now a permanent feature in Bogotá, Colombia, as part of the CómoVamos project. Report cards were also used in Peru to evaluate nutrition, education, health, and employment programs (Fiszbein 2005). The Ukraine People's Voice project used citizen report cards to benchmark service standards and gather people's opinions of these services, with a goal of improving service delivery in Ukrainian cities.[5] This approach also involved building the capacity of citizens' groups and officials to have meaningful interaction with each other. Citizens and officials were also trained in technical issues, like the design and execution of surveys to monitor service delivery, which were conducted after a proper needs assessment. It should be possible in the future to construct report cards with Web-based surveys to gather the opinions of service users who use the Internet frequently.

Examples of Successful ICT Use for Social Accountability

The following paragraphs discuss several successful examples of social accountability tools utilizing ICT platforms. For more information, refer to the SASANET Web site developed by the Center for Good Governance in India.[6]

Germany uses an interactive forum provided by a Web site to promote a participatory approach in preparing and evaluating citizens' budgets in many cities—for example, Bergheim, Cologne, and the Lichtenberg district of Berlin.[7] The four-stage process involves disseminating information, initiating dialogue, decision making in the council, and communicating decisions to the citizens. These Web sites also allow a "town dialogue" by which the public may freely exchange views on policy issues. One recent example was an online dialogue concerning the new use of Berlin's Tempelhof Airport. These initiatives seem to have positive results: the local council in Lichtenberg borough passed 37 of the 42 proposed amendments to the budget or to policy issues, and the local administration's accountability to the people of the city appears to have been enhanced (Caddy, Peixoto, and McNeil 2007, pp. 72–75).

The Republic of Korea has an online system to open up administrative procedures to public scrutiny and ensure transparency. It also uses an anti-corruption index constructed through public opinion gathered from people who have actually submitted civic applications (Caddy, Peixoto, and McNeil 2007, pp. 98–101). Positive opinion about the behavior of civil servants increased from 54 percent in 1998 to 71 percent in 1999. In the five years following the first survey in 1999, the anti-corruption index has been consistently improving. This example shows how ICT platforms can improve transparency by disseminating government information and how e-governance can enforce social accountability through improved citizen-government dialogue.

India has made extensive use of ICT to foster public accountability. For example, Karnataka reported that the proportion of citizens paying bribes to get copies of land records declined from 33.8 percent to 0.7 percent after these services were computerized (Bhatnagar 2009). An ambitious national program to provide supplementary wage employment to rural poor people, mandated under the Mahatma Gandhi National Rural Employment Guarantee Act of India, 2005 (MGNREGA), has an open-access Web site that provides complete information (including the wage entitlement) to more than 52 million poor rural households that were provided employment by the government. This drastically reduces the chances of corruption because all the information is in the public domain and may be easily accessed by civil society or any watchdog mechanism. The success of the MGNREGA lies in using a multipronged approach like the one shown in Figure 7.4. MGNREGA also uses social audits and intensive ICT to improve program functioning and targeting, as well as a robust grievance redress system with a central helpline.

FIGURE 7.4 Social Accountability and ICT in the MGNREGA

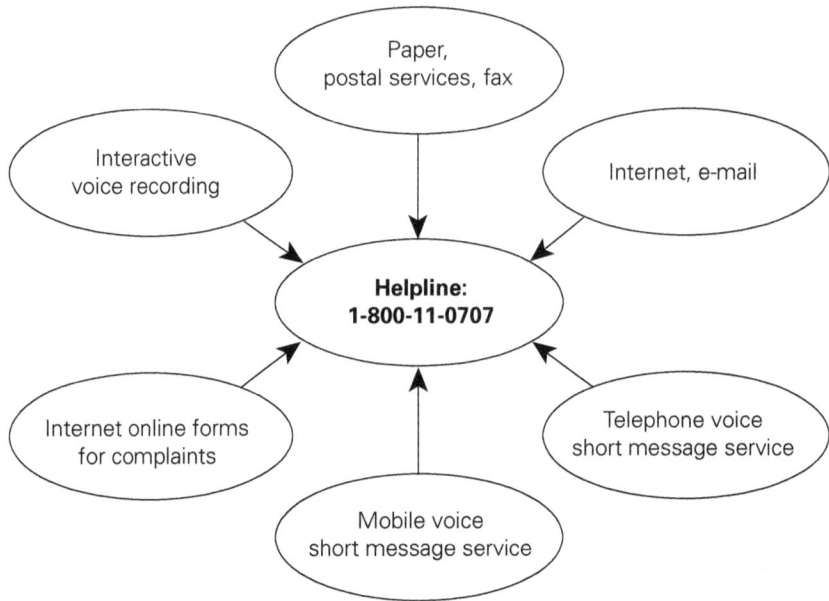

Source: www.nrega.net/ict/new_initiatives.

An evaluation of MGNREGA was done in the Indian state of Andhra Pradesh, and the responses of the wage earners enrolled in the program are shown in Figure 7.5.[8] A multi-pronged approach—including sustained awareness campaigns, capacity building for target groups, introduction of accountability mechanisms, a social audit and public hearing, and the constant involvement of civil society, higher-level bureaucracy, and the political executive brought very positive results. More than US$2 million in misappropriated funds were recovered, and about 500 charges were filed under criminal law and administrative procedures in the state.[9]

An important lesson to be taken from India's MGNREGA scheme is that in addition to using ICT, it helps if the social accountability tools have a legal or a formal position in official evaluation. The contribution of civil society and non-governmental organizations in an M&E exercise may be very useful in bringing about improvements in the services if the agencies providing these services recognize the importance of the input as useful feedback on which to base corrective action. Otherwise, there is a danger that civil society groups will be marginalized and their assessment ignored by the state bureaucracy.

Transparency in government has been legislated in the following countries:

FIGURE 7.5 **Responses of Wage Earners under the MGNREGA, Andhra Pradesh**

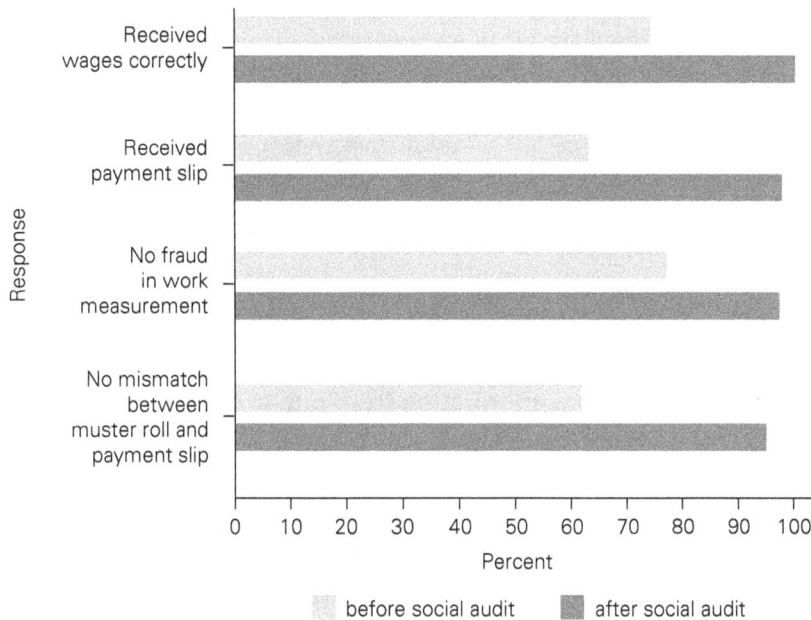

Source: Adapted from http://www.rd.ap.gov.in/SAuditStanding_Under_the_Arch-_V3.pdf.

- Australia—Federal Freedom of Information Act (1982)
- Canada—Access to Information Act (1983)
- France—Law on Access to Administrative Documents (1978)
- Germany—Freedom of Information Act (1999)
- Japan—Law Concerning Access to Information Held by Administrative Organs (1999)
- United States—Freedom of Information Act (1966) and the Openness Promotes Effectiveness in Our National Government Act (OPEN Government Act, 2007)
- India's Community Participation Laws and the Right to Information Act (2005) and the Jawaharlal Nehru National Urban Renewal Mission,[10] which requires states to enact community participation laws

ICT and social accountability in subsidized housing for poor people in India

India has a very large housing program involving subsidies for construction of houses for the poor. An Internet portal for social accountability in the housing program supporting this program in the state of Andhra Pradesh has a database of more than 6.5 million houses. This Web site brings transparency, making the diversion or embezzlement of funds difficult. The Web site[11] has a facility to upload photographs of a building site before house construction begins and at various stages of completion. All managerial processes, including a management information system, are maintained online. It is also very useful for conducting a social audit and preparing report cards or community scorecards, because all information is available on the Internet. This information can be verified easily by members of civil society or any independent agency wishing to compare the situation on the ground with what is reported on the Web site.

Call center for seeking information from public offices

An ICT-enabled call center known as Jankari, run by a non-governmental organization in the Indian state of Bihar, has contributed to improved social accountability, as evidenced by the number of requests filed under the Right to Information Act. This center is a simple facility through which even illiterate citizens can make a phone call and explain the information they require. Their needs are deciphered by the facilitator in the call center and are converted into a formal application for getting relevant information from government records. This information can help enforce accountability and redress grievances for people adversely affected by access to government welfare programs, subsidized housing programs for the poor, public distribution systems, and the like. Figure 7.6 shows how the number of requests for information under the Right to Information Act has risen steadily over the last three years through the Jankari call center.

Quality improvements in government schools in Delhi, India

An initiative to improve accountability in government schools in the National Capital Territory of Delhi included training school officials in the use of information technology and providing a public interface to enhance accountability. The hallmark of this program was to provide e-governance in the management of schools and to give citizens direct online access to all relevant officers, including the minister of education. A feedback system was in place for citizens and parents to communicate with the department to ask questions or give suggestions. The attendance report of both teaching and non-teaching staff was kept in the public domain, with online recording of inspection reports by superior officers. These interventions showed a substantial reduction in the performance gap that had existed between government and private

FIGURE 7.6 Bihar State: Number of Callers Requesting Information

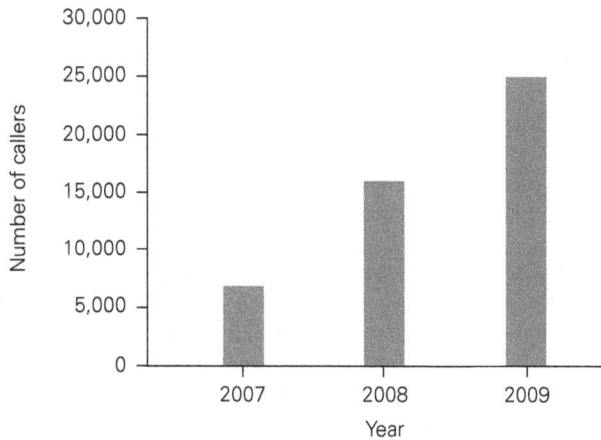

Source: Author's illustration.

schools, and the pass rate percentage increased from 40 percent in 2001 to 77 percent in 2007 (Kundra and Kumar 2008). It is difficult to attribute the positive changes in the government school system in Delhi to a possibly enhanced level of social accountability alone because there must have been all-round attempts at comprehensive systemic improvement simultaneously. But the importance of nurturing a culture of social accountability by skillful use of e-governance cannot be ignored in any such attempt at managing change in service delivery systems.

Conclusions

ICT has a definite role in the design and implementation of M&E systems for social accountability. Evidence is growing that even in case of pro-poor service delivery from public agencies, the level of transparency in state-run programs increases substantially with the use of these tools. Information technology facilitates the free flow of information, and its positive role in establishing a robust dialogue between the citizens and the agencies of the state cannot be disputed. This improves the effectiveness of social accountability tools in promoting the reliability and effectiveness of M&E systems. The capacity of civil society and of public officials should be strengthened to leverage the use of information technology in social accountability, with the final aim of raising the standards of evaluation for better service delivery.

Notes

1. See http://go.worldbank.org/GIILYME1Y0.
2. See i4d (Information for Development), 2006, http://www.i4donline.net.
3. See http://www.ansa-africa.net.
4. The Indian government's Department of Personnel and Training initiated capacity building for government workers and members of civil society that focuses on use of the Right to Information Act through this e-learning course. This was designed by the Center for Good Governance, Hyderabad, India. Each session runs for two weeks, and 7,000 participants have used the program since 2009.
5. The project's report card program is funded by the World Bank, the Canadian International Development Agency, the Open Society Institute, and the Canadian Bureau of International Education. It was initiated in March 1997. Details may be found at http://www.undp.org/oslocentre/do cs08/sofia/Case%20 Study%201-%20Citizens%20 Report%20Cards%20Ukraine%20FINAL.pdf.
6. SASANET stands for South Asia Social Accountability Network. Its Web site (http://www.sasanet.org) was developed by the Centre for Good Governance, Hyderabad, India, with support from the World Bank Institute. It provides information on tools such as procurement monitoring, Citizen Report Card, e-procurement, and participatory budgeting.
7. A citizen's budget is the outcome of a statutory process of participation in which a citizen may submit his or her proposals for expenditure to the city government. The proposal can be debated and ranked using the Internet.
8. The evaluation is available at: http://www.rd.ap.gov.in/SAudit/Standing_Under_the_Arch-_V3.pdf.
9. The information is based on the author's personal discussions with the officials of the Rural Development Department.
10. The Jawaharlal Nehru National Urban Renewal Mission is a flagship program of the Indian government intended to accelerate urban development.
11. http://housing.cgg.gov.in/phase3/BenShow.do?ben_id=091292421P3979523.

Bibliography

Arroyo, Dennis, and Karen Sirker. 2005. "Stocktaking of Social Accountability Initiatives in the Asia and Pacific Region." Community Empowerment and Social Inclusion Learning Program, World Bank Institute, Washington, DC.

Balakrishnan, Suresh. 2006. "Making Service Delivery Reforms Work: The Bangalore Experience." In *Reinventing Public Service Delivery in India: Selected Case Studies*, ed. Vikram K. Chand, pp. 157–85. Thousand Oaks, CA: Sage Publications.

Bhatnagar, Subhash. 2009. *Unlocking E-Government Potential: Concepts, Cases and Practical Insights*. New Delhi, India: Sage Publications India.

Caddy, Joanne, Tiago Peixoto, and Mary McNeil. 2007. "Beyond Public Scrutiny: Stocktaking of Social Accountability in OECD Countries." World Bank Institute Working Paper. World Bank, Washington, DC.

Fiszbein, Ariel, ed. 2005. "Citizens, Politicians, and Providers: The Latin American Experience with Service Delivery Reform." Washington, DC: World Bank.

Kundra, Gitanjali K., and Ashok Kumar. 2008. "Radical Improvement in Delhi Government School System." In *Roofless Towers: A Compilation of Award-Winning Initiatives,* ed. Department of Administrative Reforms and Public Grievances. New Delhi, India: Unicorn Books.

Malena, Carmen, Reiner Forster, and Janmejay Singh. 2004. "Social Accountability: An Introduction to the Concept and Emerging Practice." Social Development Paper 76. World Bank, Washington, DC.

Ravindra, Adikeshavalu. 2004. "An Assessment of the Impact of Bangalore Citizen Report Cards on the Performance of Public Agencies." Evaluation Capacity Development Working Paper 12. Operations Evaluation Department, World Bank, Washington, DC.

PART II

COMPONENTS
AND TOOLS
OF M&E SYSTEMS

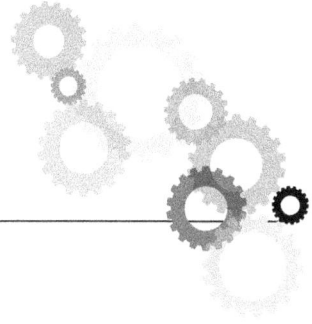

CHAPTER 8

Defining and Using Performance Indicators and Targets in Government M&E Systems

Manuel Fernando Castro

Developing effective national monitoring and evaluation (M&E) systems and/or performance budgeting initiatives requires well-defined formulation and implementation strategies for setting up performance indicators. These strategies vary depending on a country's priority for measuring results and on the scope and pace of its performance management reform objectives. Some countries have followed an incremental method for developing indicators, that is, progressively, at strategically selected programs/sectors (for example, Canada, the United Kingdom, and Colombia), while others have taken a comprehensive, "big bang" approach by defining indicators for all existing programs and sectors at once (for example, Mexico and the Repub-

For their comments, the author thanks Indu John-Abraham (Operations Officer, Poverty, Gender and Equity Unit, Latin America and the Caribbean Region), and the following members of the Poverty Reduction and Equity Group: Philipp Krause (Consultant), Gladys Lopez-Acevedo (Senior Economist), Keith Mackay (Consultant), and Jaime Saavedra (Director). The views expressed in this chapter are those of the author.

lic of Korea). In both cases, countries need to continuously work on their indicators to improve their quality and thus ensure that indicators can meaningfully inform government processes.

There is a large body of literature on performance management indicators. However, the literature contains relatively few references to practical elements of successful government implementation of performance indicator systems. This chapter encapsulates some of the main elements for senior officials to realistically and practically consider when introducing performance indicator and target systems in government and to ensure sustainability. The first section highlights a number of technical elements regarding the formulation of indicators, the importance of institutional arrangements and procedures for consultation and political validation, and the role of indicators in linking funding to results. The second section briefly notes the information challenges associated with developing performance indicators. The third section focuses on country examples of performance indicator systems, with particular emphasis on the United Kingdom and Colombia. The fourth section identifies specific success factors for improving the relevance and utilization of indicators in government. The final section concludes by emphasizing the importance of quality data and processes and the necessity of tailoring performance indicator systems to match available resources and capacities.

Technical Aspects of Performance Indicators

Performance measurement is an essential part of a broader process often referred to as results-based management or managing for results, the objective of which is to improve efficiency, effectiveness, and accountability in government. This process involves the use of performance indicators to assess the degree to which intended results are being achieved. But for indicators to be relevant, timely, and of sufficient quality to facilitate better government decisions, a number of technical elements need to be considered in their selection and for the processes through which they are defined and used. These elements are discussed in more detail in the following sections.

Goals, outcomes, and outputs

At the national level, the task of setting performance indicators must differentiate between high (macro) and low (micro) levels of results in the government's implementation chain. The high level refers to the external influence of all programs and includes impacts, outcomes, and outputs, which are pri-

FIGURE 8.1 Performance Indicators and the Results Chain

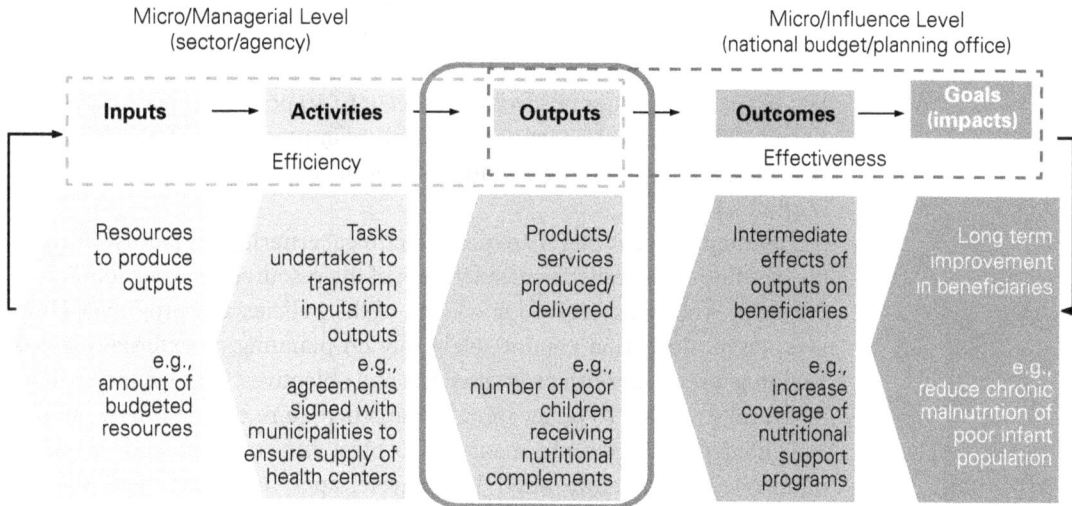

Micro/Managerial Level (sector/agency) — Micro/Influence Level (national budget/planning office)

Inputs	→	Activities	→	Outputs	→	Outcomes	→	Goals (impacts)

Efficiency — Effectiveness

| Resources to produce outputs | Tasks undertaken to transform inputs into outputs | Products/ services produced/ delivered | Intermediate effects of outputs on beneficiaries | Long term improvement in beneficiaries |
| e.g., amount of budgeted resources | e.g., agreements signed with municipalities to ensure supply of health centers | e.g., number of poor children receiving nutritional complements | e.g., increase coverage of nutritional support programs | e.g., reduce chronic malnutrition of poor infant population |

Source: Author

marily of interest to national planning and budget officers. The low level alludes to internal program management and involves outputs, activities, and inputs, which are mostly of concern to the sector and agency budget and program officials. Both sides of the results chain are crucial for measuring performance, and outputs are the "bridge" between the high and low sides of the government's implementation chain (Figure 8.1).

At the agency level, establishing a sequenced results chain for all programs starts with the identification of goals or high-level outcomes, which are medium to long term (4–15 years)—as for example, reducing infant mortality. To identify what agencies expect to achieve with their budgets and to measure their performance with indicators, managers and their M&E officers must therefore have good knowledge of where the agencies are going and what their fundamental business lines are. Then they can identify outcomes and outputs that are linked with the agency goals. This will allow officers to know what successful spending looks like while providing clear and simple statements of what each program and agency aims to do.

Defining targets and setting performance indicators[1]

From their goals, agencies can derive shorter-range targets (1–4 years) that define the expected effects from budget allocations. In essence, targets are quantifiable orders of a given variable for a specific period of time. High-level targets help improve effectiveness, and low-level targets address efficiency. One technique for defining targets is translating outcomes and outputs into positive results-oriented statements that, starting from a baseline level, identify a path and destination (for example, increase coverage of nutritional support programs from 35 percent to 40 percent of poor people between 2008 and 2010). Targets must capture improvements for a single output or outcome, assuming a finite number of required inputs and activities (Figure 8.1).

Defining relevant targets requires technical criteria for identifying credible baseline data, realistic consideration of the resources and capacities necessary, as well as extensive knowledge of the policies and programs. However, target definition cannot solely rely on planning or external experts. Defining targets, as with program goals and objectives, is much more than a technical exercise. To be meaningful, targets require ownership by internal stakeholders (for example, managers, central ministry staff, and/or budget officials), and therefore other key players, apart from technical officials, should also participate in their definition. Defining targets for all the variables involved in resource allocations can be complex and time consuming, but it is important. Targets hold governments accountable and exert external pressure over ministry and agency performance. Lastly, for targets to be relevant and credible, agencies must not be able to modify them at will, and once a target has been achieved, agencies must maintain that standard.

Each target should be accompanied by a performance indicator—a quantitative or qualitative expression of a program or policy that offers a consistent way to measure progress toward the stated targets and goals. Performance indicators reflect changes in variables connected to an intervention, and they should facilitate a timely and cost-effective measuring and monitoring of results. They allow managers and program and budget officials to track progress all the way down the causal results chain, from impacts at the top to inputs at the bottom.

Performance indicators, in contrast, are not necessarily dependent on targets. They can facilitate measuring and monitoring government results in a timely, standardized, and cost-effective manner even in the absence of a benchmark, but to be relevant, indicators need to be of good quality. The results literature contains various acronyms to help officials set good indicators through a set of technical criteria (see Box 8.1 for examples).

In practice, methodological considerations may apply differently to particular contexts. For instance, in the early stages of implementing an M&E system, it might be necessary to allow for a trade-off between the need for performance information and a slightly uneven quality and larger number of indicators. Such a trade-off may imply a process of "improving by measuring," allowing suboptimal indicators while the process progressively improves. Deciding what level of trade-off is acceptable requires good technical judgment. There are no perfect indicators. In many cases it is necessary to use indirect or proxy indicators—for example, when data are not available or cannot be collected at regular intervals, or when information gathering is too costly. Understanding the likely cost of gathering and analyzing data is crucial to sustain performance M&E efforts. Quite often agencies tend to select indicators without previously identifying the sources of information and confirming availability. But indicators are also frequently defined according to readily available information, regardless of how crucial and cost-effective it could be to collect new data for more appropriately measuring performance on a longer-term basis.

Finally, experience shows that developing performance targets can be more difficult than formulating indicators. In particular, the challenge of setting targets for the entire range of government performance can be quite significant. Targets, more than indicators, can create a complex series of undesirable and unintended side effects in government processes and "culture" (for example, in the morale and motivation of the civil service). Reducing the risk of perverse effects requires important knowledge of underlying incentives. Accordingly, the decision to move from indicators to target setting should be taken with care. The development of targets and indicators should also be thought of as two different stages in the evolution and institutionalization of M&E and performance management systems.

Linking funding to results with performance indicators

The robustness of performance management and M&E systems depends on the strength of the links between funding and results. One way of establishing those links is to standardize costs for outputs provided on a unit basis (for example, patients treated in health centers or students enrolled in secondary education). Another is to identify broader quantitative connections between the level of outcome achieved and certain annual or multiannual budget allocations (for example, increases in coverage of water and sanitation).[2] Both approaches seek to serve the same purpose, however, the former is more complex and not always feasible, because it is usually more of a normative proposition rather than a real possibility for the whole budget. The latter is more likely, but is more a way to better inform the budget, which is the dominant factor in funding decisions for only a few cases. In any case, establishing such links demands an enormous amount of technical judgment and significant operational work, because it must be done individually for each budget item and program category.[3]

The differing characteristics of government outputs and outcomes can therefore make it complicated to link some allocations to performance, such as when the unit costs of a service vary considerably. A key technical step for linking funding to results using indicators is establishing a program classification to allow the budget to be read in terms of the results it expects to achieve. In practice, such a classification implies having some form of program budgeting in place. Program categories need to be a by-product of the whole process of defining budget outcomes, outputs, targets, and indicators for each agency—preferably by national budget and program officials working together.

The traditional financial classification, based primarily on global appropriations for inputs (for example, wages and salaries) or organizational units (for example, ministries or agencies), can say little about whether resources have achieved their targets or could produce higher benefits. A program classification helps establish a logical sequence between the program outcomes and outputs and the aggregated agency, sector, or policy results. With such a classification, the budget process can be seen more as a choice among different priorities than as a list of budgetary items. The technical challenge is to ensure that program categories capture the various allocative choices that governments face. When successfully implemented, this exercise can serve the purposes of both accountability (as ex post reporting information) and budget preparation (as ex ante information). But if it is to be effective, the whole budget process needs to be in a program format (for example, ministries' requests, legal appropriations, or evaluation of allocations), at least as a complement to the traditional financial format. Again, some form of program budgeting is thus necessary to achieve sound linkages between program-based performance indicators and funding allocations.

Program costing, the other essential technique for linking funding to results using performance indicators, provides information that traditional financial and accounting systems cannot offer. However, costing can be difficult as well. On the one hand, government outcomes and outputs are not necessarily expressed in standard units. Outcomes, in particular, are often affected by external factors, such as crime, unemployment, or poverty. On the other hand, even outputs can be contingent on many services, such as the military or fire service. Sophisticated methods, such as activity-based costing, which segments organizational units and programs into discrete, quantifiable activities to estimate unitary costs and measurable productivity units (for example, number of hours work compared to units produced), reflect only some of these complexities. Consequently, it is often necessary to use complementary solutions to inform the budget—for example, performance evaluations.

Consultation on and validation of indicators

The single most important characteristic of a strong M&E system is use of the information produced. Low or inadequate use of performance information in management and particularly budgeting is often a problem for many indicator systems. Quite frequently this situation signals not only problems with performance data availability and quality, but also the existence of challenges with political consultation or a lack of buy-in of the performance indicators and the types of information produced.

Lack of consultation and validation are often signs of a weak institutional environment, which tends to result in indicator "inflation"—too many indicators but a very low rate of utilization—which in turn deteriorates their quality. Officials in such environments tend to perceive that information is not a problem; for them, information may in fact be abundant, while for others (the producers), underutilization of the information they produce provides a very weak incentive to take data and indicators seriously. A vicious circle of overproduction, underutilization, lack of validation, and quality deterioration then takes place. It can therefore be useful to conduct surveys of data use (who is using/is willing to use what performance information, for what purposes, and how) before embarking on a large-scale effort to define performance indicators.

Further, if performance measures are to inform ministry budgets or to be used for public accountability of results, both line ministers and central budget officials need to be closely involved and agree on what will be measured and how. High-level officials need to agree on both goals and indicators, especially since the budget and public accountability are fundamentally political processes with complex and varied implications. For instance, on the one hand, budget decisions are made between competing uses that reflect not only policy but also governments' political commitments. On the other hand, external accountability can eventually alter political perceptions about the government's performance in the legislature or with the general public. Accordingly, when defining targets and indicators, program categories, and their links with measurable results, governments must also standardize and institutionalize procedures to ensure broad ownership and validation of their indicators and targets. Consultation procedures also help both central budget and line ministries by limiting discretion and reducing incentives for setting targets and indicators of low relevance, while making palpable the political risk associated with bad performance.

Performance Information

Measuring the results of government, including budget allocations, presents its own set of information challenges. First, collecting information on performance indicators is not easy. For example, output indicators are mainly based on administrative records (day-to-day data produced by programs on their own), which can be very weak in many developing countries. Outcome indicators, on the other hand, often rely more on statistical estimations (discrete observations obtained through survey approximations), which in many countries are not collected regularly enough to inform critical government decisions. In such weak institutional environments, national statistics offices should be considered a valuable resource.

Second, performance information needs analysis. Even if good information exists, it cannot be considered performance information until it is processed and organized in a structured, accessible, and timely manner. Utilization strongly relies on sound analysis rather than on the existence of large volumes of indicators. The challenge is, therefore, who should conduct such analysis and how, so that the information can be digestible and useful for decision makers. Because this analysis can be demanding and time consuming, it requires a technical unit made up of sufficient capable professionals who specialize in conducting regular assessments and reporting performance information within the government.

Third, performance information is different from financial information. Therefore, performance budgeting is possible only if the ministry of finance has competence in policy analysis and assessment of the information to be reported from line ministries and evaluation bodies. Again, program classifications of the budget can help identify links between performance and financial allocations.

Fourth, experience shows that it takes time and practice to develop quality and timely performance information, which in turn requires direct knowledge of the specific policies and programs to identify with precision what will be measured.

Performance Indicators and Monitoring Systems

To ensure efficient collection, management, and reporting of monitoring information on performance indicators, countries need to develop sound indicator monitoring systems. Most budget systems collect financial data, particularly for budgeting control purposes (for example, commitments and payments). However, results-based monitoring requires the integration of financial and performance information; therefore the interaction between different institutional spheres and the potential interoperation among national statistical systems, program information systems, and national financial information systems are vital. Further, monitoring systems can be used not only to describe how a program is performing, but also to help explain why it performs one way or another. In addition, having such systems in place reduces the need for expensive and one-off information collection processes for individual program evaluation.

Choosing the type of monitoring system to implement depends strongly on the specific purposes for which the government intends to use the performance information. That purpose may be associated with the need to inform the budget process and improve efficiency in the provision of public services—for example, the United Kingdom's Public Service Agreements System. Alternatively, systems might also be directed toward monitoring the aggregate results of government to facilitate public accountability, such as Colombia's Government Goals Monitoring Information System (*Sistema de Gestión y Seguimiento a las Metas del Gobierno*. In these two systems, performance indicators serve "central" government purposes, and, to some extent, both governments have found it necessary to establish centralized requirements for producing performance information. Some of these central requirements relate to the methods and procedures for collection, validation, access, reporting, and use of performance indicators and targets, with a focus on ensuring the reliability and suitability of the information for the government's own purposes.

Unfortunately, there is no formula for the development of monitoring systems. Further, there is little evidence regarding the extent to which financial information systems can serve the purposes of performance information management. This seems to be an area with a shortage of good practices from which to learn, particularly in relation to systems capable of consolidating aggregate information on public sector performance.

Two notable exceptions, due to their emphasis on a target-setting approach, are the United Kingdom and Colombia cases referred to earlier. In these two countries, indicator systems have significantly benefited from a custom-made and common sense approach with a strong emphasis on gradual refinement, rather than investing substantial resources in sophisticated information technology developments (Box 8.2).

Two additional country examples of performance information systems are Finland and Chile. Finland developed the Netra Reporting System, which since 2004 functions as a publicly accessible Internet application that integrates financial and performance information. Netra seeks to inform decision making and accountability through predefined reports on service delivery and expenditures for different government levels and users.[4] Chile uses a Web application to transmit performance information from ministries and agencies to the budget office of the Ministry of Finance; however, this application is not publicly accessible.

It should be noted that in all of these cases, countries have from the outset had to devote considerable time and technical effort to define the roles and responsibilities of different agencies, as well as establish standardized processes and requirements for the production, management, access, use, and quality controls of indicator information.

Success Factors in Defining Performance Indicators

A wide range of issues need to be considered in the development of performance indicators to support government M&E systems, or performance management more broadly. There are a number of country lessons or success factors that can help improve the relevance and utilization of performance indicators in government; this section discusses six of the most important success factors.

BOX 8.2

Two Country Examples of Performance Monitoring Systems

United Kingdom: In 1998, the British government introduced the Public Service Agreements System (PSAS), a national system of explicit and measurable performance targets and indicators defined for each ministry and linked to the budget process for which the government is accountable. The performance information underpinning public service agreement (PSA) targets provides the basis for monitoring what is working and what is not, helps ensure that good practice is spread and rewarded, and enables poor performance to be addressed. In 1998, there were more than 300 PSAs with indicators, primarily input and output based. The number has since progressively been reduced to around 30 (2008), with an average of six indicators each, mainly outcome based.

PSAs are set every three years as part of the government's Comprehensive Spending Review (CSR) process. PSAs define government priorities and objectives for the next three-year period, while CSRs set fixed departmental expenditure limits within which departments must meet their objectives. PSAs comprise a fixed set of indicators intended to provide a focus for delivering improved services and to help determine whether targets are met. PSAs are also intended to represent "contracts" or "promises" about the services that government will deliver to the public in return for taxation received, as well as commitments by central government departments to deliver on the government's overall objectives in return for appropriate funding.

The use of information technology tools as part of PSAs has provided opportunities to measure and manage performance data, for example, through electronic record management and the interoperation of systems, particularly at the ministry level. The use of Web-based functionalities has created new opportunities for empowering citizens, in particular by providing them with better real-time data on government priorities and results at each department's Web site. PSA targets are disclosed at the Treasury, the Prime Minister's Office, and each department's Web page. Through departmental Web sites, citizens can use this information for public accountability purposes for politicians and executive officials at all levels of government (local, provincial, and central).

Colombia: Starting in 2002, Colombia developed the Government Goals Monitoring Information System (*Sistema de Gestión y Seguimiento a las Metas del Gobierno*—SIGOB), which uses a logical structure to consolidate and manage goals and indicators for all national government programs, including strategies for achieving the president's priorities and the strategic objectives of the National Development Plan (NDP). SIGOB is an institutional arrangement and a technology platform that allows monitoring of performance indicators in real time, providing readings of government performance from different perspectives (for example, four-year NDP objectives; cross-cutting strategies, such as poverty reduction, agency performance, and presidential priorities; or long-term goals such as the Millennium Development Goals).

To ensure the quality and timeliness of information, indicators and targets are: i) defined with the participation of the technical teams from the

(continued)

BOX 8.2 *continued*

National Planning Department and line agencies responsible for overseeing and implementing sectoral and national programs; ii) validated with the sector ministers and agency directors; and iii) discussed with and approved by the president in the Council of Ministers. Once these internal processes are set, targets and indicators are made public through printed documents and through the SIGOB Web site, to which citizens have open access. Responsible program officials ("goal managers") in ministries, whose names are publicly displayed in the system to foster information reporting accountability, report results electronically via the system.

SIGOB consolidates performance indicators and facilitates public consultation, widely disseminating the results of government programs. The system interoperates with the Integrated Financial Information System (*Sistema Integrado de Información Financiera*), allowing the level of appropriation and budget execution associated with the objectives and goals to be tracked. The presidency and the National Planning Department regularly check the information and conduct managerial oversight meetings with the ministers and directors of institutions to identify progress and define courses of action to resolve implementation problems that may affect target achievements. SIGOB currently has 626 indicators: 104 on impacts (16 percent), 371 on outcomes (60 percent), and 151 on outputs (24 percent). Based on reported information, SIGOB facilitates the preparation of monthly, quarterly, and annual reports on government progress, including the *Annual Report of the President to Congress*.

Sources: Institute for Government (2008); Castro (2009).

Success factor 1. There is no perfect system of indicators. In developing performance measures, governments have benefited enormously from considering the fact that indicators have practical limits on the degree to which they can capture a precise picture of performance. Not only do good indicators rely on information that is often not available, but some dimensions of performance are very difficult to measure (for example, output quality). Further, contextual factors can importantly influence final results, and indicators cannot eliminate or adjust these factors. This is one of the reasons governments need to consider using evaluations as a complementary tool to enhance the information base for performance management.

Success factor 2. Clearly define from the outset what for and how government officials intend to use performance indicators. For example, if indicators are to provide information for program managers at the micro dimension of the implementation chain, or for central budgeting purposes at the macro dimension, then the type of indicators and their requirements can be very different. For the first case, comparative or summary measures might not be so important for informing on the details of a program, while for the second case these measures can have huge benefits for enhancing the scope and perspective of performance.

Success factor 3. Avoid complex performance indicator systems. In several country cases, a critical factor of success has been the adoption of a simple yet very careful approach to the development of performance indicators and monitoring systems. A number of experiences have shown that spending enormous amounts of money to develop sophisticated technological systems does not necessarily guarantee that the indicator base meets technical standards of quality and ensures utilization of performance data. A customized and common sense approach can be far more important. This approach would consider the necessary institutional arrangements, respond to the specific performance measurement needs of key users, and ensure that information sources are available, reliable, and have adequate baseline measurement. The information management model behind the performance indicators base is the real backbone of a system.

Success factor 4. Develop formal quality controls for indicators. Countries have different approaches to developing their performance indicators base. What is common to all countries, however, is the need to ensure that information sources and data flows emerging from indicators can be credible enough to ensure utilization by different users. To that end, countries should be aware that indicators need continuous revision and improvement, and that an indicator base is not a one-shot effort. Experience shows that it requires practice, and that it is necessary to devote time and various attempts to develop indicators that really capture the desired data. Accordingly, formal processes for technical formulation and review, incentives linking indicators to budgeting and planning processes, public access to the indicator base and information sources, and periodic external audits have all proved effective in controlling the quality of indicators and their information base.

Success factor 5. Avoid starting out with an unmanageable number of indicators. Governments do not need to measure everything, at least not all at once. To be useful, performance indicators need to be readily digestible to decision makers, who normally have great restrictions on their time. A couple of good indicators can be more useful than a comprehensive inventory of hundreds of indicators. Controlling inflation of the indicator base is necessary to ensure a manageable indicator system and control indicator quality. Countries should be aware, however, that reducing the size of the indicator base can be technically and politically complex because it implies not only the development of a robust strategic planning process, but a clear sense of the political priorities of the government.

Success factor 6. Differentiate between performance indicator systems and target-setting regimes. Both indicators and targets are key elements of an M&E system or of a performance management model. However, setting performance indicators should not be interpreted as having targets associated with each of them. To be meaningful, targets depend on an underlying measure, but performance indicators do not necessarily need to have associated targets to be useful. The process of defining targets, for which a government will be accountable and against which managerial controls will be exerted, requires a certain level of M&E institutionalization and good performance management practices.

Conclusions

Developing indicators and target systems is not simply a matter of compiling a comprehensive list of algorithms and benchmarks with a series of correspondent reference values. Rather, it implies an elaborated, systematic professional judgment that in turn requires robust strategic planning, important knowledge of the government's priorities and program base, intensive technical and operational work, and a significant understanding of the wide range of incentives, explicit or implicit, that can influence good or bad performance in government.

It is also important to understand that the process of developing indicators is normally a gradual one, which may allow suboptimal versions in the early stages of a system, particularly if their quality and quantity is to improve progressively over time (for example, by sectors or specific agencies). Therefore it will be paramount for a country not only to define the purpose and scope of a system right from the start, but also to establish the institutional setting that will guarantee sustainability, technical adaptability, and political backing for the process so that the effort remains functional and relevant over time.

In terms of indicator utility, experience shows that it might be more important to have good quality information on a fairly small number of simple measures rather than a set of complex algorithms with limited information. It is important that the information feeding the indicators be of good quality, because the results generated will be of the same quality. Strengthening the quality of information should be a continuous process within the government organization, and one for which protocols, technical standards, sound administrative procedures, and adequate technological tools will be required. Ensuring public access to information, making the benefits of having timely and quality information visible to public managers, and establishing meaningful incentives are also key requirements.

It is not a simple task to formulate, manage, and continuously monitor a country system of performance indicators, but, as detailed in this chapter, it is important and worth undertaking, particularly if a country really wants to improve the efficiency and effectiveness of its public service delivery. Over the last decade, there has been growing interest and greater political priority for goal setting, performance indicators, and targets in developing countries, particularly in the poorest ones. This interest and priority are increasingly being translated into the content of poverty reduction strategies and global development agendas. Governments should, however, consider many issues before deciding to embark on a large-scale formulation of performance indicators, and even more so in the case of targets. How far to go with respect to the introduction of indicators will depend on the specific capacity challenges faced by each country. These challenges can be considerable, particularly in countries with limited managerial and policy analysis capabilities.

Notes

1. See also Hatry's discussion of setting up monitoring systems at the agency level in Chapter 5.
2. The British Public Service Agreements System is an example, outcome targets are linked to the multiyear budgeting process (see Robinson 2007).
3. This is especially the case when the exercise is first carried out, but the burden can significantly be reduced over time with practice, particularly if technology is efficiently used to make the process automatic.
4. See the Finnish State Internet Reporting (www.netra.fi).

Bibliography

Castro, M. F. 2009. *Insider Insights: Building a Results-Based Management and Evaluation System in Colombia*. Washington, DC: World Bank/IEG.

Drucker, P. 1954. *The Practice of Management*. United Kingdom: Harper & Row Publishers.

Gash, T., M. Hallsworth, Sharif Ismail, and Akash Paun. 2009. *Performance Art: Enabling Better Management of Public Services in the UK*. Institute for Government, London. www.instituteforgovernment.org.uk/projects/performance.

Hatry, H. 1999. *Performance Measurement: Getting Results*. Washington, DC: Urban Institute Press.

Institute for Government. 2008. *Performance Art: Enabling Better Management of Public Services*. London: Institute for Government.

Mackay, K. 2007. *How to Build M&E Systems to Support Better Government*. Washington, DC: World Bank /IEG.

OECD (Organisation for Economic Co-operation and Development). 2007. "Integrating and Using Performance Information in the Budget Process." In *Performance Budgeting in OECD Countries*, chapter 4. Paris: OECD. http://www.oecd.org/document/38/0,3343,en_2649_ 34119_39921702_1_1_1_1,00.html.

Robinson, M. 2007. "Performance Information Foundations." In *Performance Budgeting: Linking Funding and Results*, ed. M. Robinson. Washington, DC: IMF.

Schiavo-Campo, S., and D. Tommasi, 1999. *Managing Government Expenditure*. United Kingdom: Anybook Ltd.

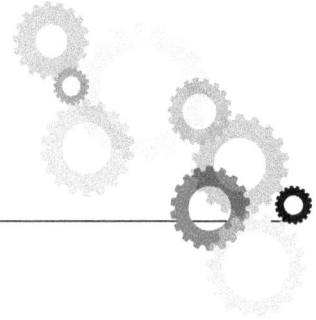

CHAPTER 9

Key Choices for a Menu of Evaluations

Gloria M. Rubio

Every day, policy makers and program managers face major decisions resulting from insufficient funding, complaints about service delivery, unmet needs among different population groups, and limited results on the ground. A menu of evaluation types has been implemented by developing and developed countries to tackle a wide range of policy and program management issues, while taking into account time, resources, and capacity constraints. International experience highlights the importance of a gradual approach when introducing evaluation tools into country-level monitoring and evaluation (M&E) systems. Different paths may work better for different countries depending on the main purpose of their M&E system, existing institutional capacity, the availability of funds, and external technical assistance.

Policy makers and program managers tackle questions such as how to allocate resources across different interventions or program components,

For their comments, the author thanks Manuel Fernando Castro (Consultant, IEGCS), and the following members of the Poverty Reduction and Equity Group: Philipp Krause (Consultant), Gladys Lopez-Acevedo (Senior Economist), Keith Mackay (Consultant), and Jaime Saavedra (Director). The views expressed in this chapter are those of the author.

whether to add a new program or reform an existing one, how to choose between alternative service delivery mechanisms, or how to improve program operations. Any decision, even one favoring the status quo, entails some kind of assessment weighing different courses of action. The extent to which these assessments are systematic and grounded in empirical evidence influences the chances of making a decision based on accurate information and being able to take advantage of opportunities to improve policy interventions.

Evaluation is the systematic collection and analysis of information to provide relevant feedback for decision making and policy formulation. A menu of evaluation types addresses a wide range of policy and program management questions. This chapter discusses the policy relevance, application, and requirements of different evaluation types to facilitate the selection of a mix of evaluation tools depending on the information and feedback needs for decision making at any given moment in the lifespan of an intervention, while also accounting for time, resource, and capacity constraints. International experience illustrates uses of different evaluation tools across countries and over time.

Key Considerations in Selecting an Evaluation Tool

Evaluations are valuable when properly conducted and focused on their intended purpose. Hence, the selection of the right evaluation tool is critical. Choosing an evaluation tool, or combination of tools, depends on two main considerations. First, it depends on what information is needed to make major decisions. For example, is the evaluation prompted by the need to have overall performance information across programs to decide how to allocate resources? Or is it motivated by the need to have information on a particular program operation to identify bottlenecks that hinder adequate service delivery? Policy and program management issues and concerns drive the need for the evaluation, and in turn, point to the selection of a particular set of evaluation tools.

The second consideration in selecting an evaluation tool is the availability of resources to conduct the evaluation. The menu of evaluation tools includes different alternatives in terms of costs, duration, and capacity requirements. For example, some evaluations tools provide rapid feedback at relatively lower costs, while others require a longer implementation period, and their costs vary accordingly. Although there are usually trade-offs between evaluation depth and rigor and resource requirements, the selection of an evaluation type allows some flexibility in accommodating particular circumstances.

Key questions to ask before deciding on an evaluation tool, or combination of tools, include:

1. What is the purpose of the evaluation—that is, what decision will be informed by the evaluation?
2. What kinds of information are needed to make the decision? At what stage in the life of the program will the evaluation be conducted? These questions are closely related—information needs may vary depending on the program life stage. For example, a program that has just been planned would require an ex ante cost-benefit analysis to inform the decision on whether or not to implement it. Alternatively, a newly implemented program would benefit from information on how well operational procedures are followed, and whether any adjustments are necessary for successful program operation.
3. How quickly or (unexpectedly) is the information needed? Sometimes evaluations are planned well in advance and results are expected in due course, giving maximum flexibility in evaluation tool choice. In other cases, the selection of an evaluation tool is influenced by the time frame of information demands from a particular policy process, such as budget preparation. In many cases, however, information needs arise suddenly, triggered by events that demand a quick response, such as a macroeconomic crisis or reform opportunity.
4. Who is the audience for the evaluation information? Some evaluations may be demanded internally within the organization by program managers or policy makers in the ministry. Others may be externally required by the ministry of finance, legislature, or a donor organization. Internal and external information needs may be different, leading to different evaluation types.
5. What resources (financial and human) are available to conduct the evaluation? Evaluation scope and tools should be aligned with available resources. In some cases, an experienced team may be in charge of evaluations with an earmarked budget. However, in most cases, resources devoted to evaluation are limited or non-existent and institutional capacity is just developing.

Three Major Types of Program Evaluation

Once the key questions above have been answered, an evaluation tool or tools can be selected. Evaluations can be classified in several ways and some categories may overlap. For example, evaluations can be grouped according to the analytical paradigm (rationalist, pluralistic, participative, and so forth), purpose (formative versus summative), content (goals, process, outcomes/impact), time perspective (ex ante versus ex post), or the evaluator (internal versus external). Using a content-based classification, this section discusses three major types of program evaluation.[1] Table 9.1 summarizes the policy relevance, application, and requirements of each type of evaluation.

TABLE 9.1 Main Evaluation Types

	Goal-based evaluations	Process-based evaluations	Impact evaluations
What are the main questions answered by this type of evaluation?	• Do policies or programs have clear objectives? • Is the program/policy design appropriate to achieve the objectives? • To what extent have policy/program objectives been achieved?	• What are the actual steps and activities involved in delivering a product or service? How close are they to agreed operation? Are they efficient? • Are there adequate resources (money, equipment, facilities, training, and so forth) and systems (financial, management information, and so forth) in place? • Are program participants receiving quality products and services?	• How have participants' well-being changed as a result of the program/policy? • Are there any unintended consequences, positive or negative, on program participants? • Are program/policy costs justified in terms of welfare impact?
When can this evaluation be conducted?	• It may be conducted at early stages of program/policy implementation, for mid-term review, or at project completion	• It may be conducted at any time, once or regularly, to check that implementation is on the right track, or when there are specific operational concerns	• They are most effective when applied selectively to answer strategic policy questions or to assess innovative pilot interventions testing a new, unproven, but promising approach
What data collection and analysis are required?	• Desk review of existing documents, possibly complemented by monitoring data analysis, interviews, and field visits	• A mix of interviews with program staff and clients, user and facility surveys, record review, direct observation • focus groups and analysis of monitoring data	• Statistical and econometric analysis of survey and administrative data, ideally combined with qualitative data analysis

TABLE 9.1 *continued*

	Goal-based evaluations	Process-based evaluations	Impact evaluations
What skills are needed?	• Policy and program analysis, possibly simple quantitative methods	• Process analysis, quantitative and qualitative methods	• Statistical and econometric analysis, possibly qualitative methods
How long does it take?	• 1– 3 months	• 1–6 months	• At least 6 months (retrospective evaluation) • At least 12–18 months (prospective evaluation)
What are the costs?	• Generally low	• Low to medium	• Medium to high
What are some examples of this type of evaluation?	• Mexico: Performance Specific Evaluation • World Bank: Project Performance Assessment	• Process evaluations • Spot checks • Operational audits	• See suggested Web sites at the end of the chapter
Additional comments		• Large variation in depth and breadth	• Time duration and costs depend on outcomes of interest and data availability

Source: Author.

Goal- or objective-based evaluations

Goal-based evaluations assess the clarity of a program's objectives and its progress in achieving these objectives. Questions asked by this type of evaluation include:

1. How were program objectives established? Was the process effective and are the resulting objectives clear and appropriate?
2. Is there a sound theory of change behind the program design?
3. Are program inputs, activities, and outputs aligned with the objectives or outcomes (internal consistency)?
4. Are there sound performance indicators to assess the program's progress in achieving its objectives?
5. What is the status of the program's progress toward achieving the objectives?
6. Will the goals be achieved according to the timelines specified in the program implementation or operations plan? If not, why?
7. Do personnel have adequate resources (money, equipment, facilities, training, and so forth) to achieve the goals?

8. Do priorities need to be changed to ensure focus on achieving the goals?
9. Should any goals be added or removed? Why?

This type of evaluation may be conducted at any time during program implementation. In early stages it could provide useful feedback on program design, such as early warnings on a lack of clear objectives or inconsistencies between resources, activities, and objectives. It may also be a useful tool for a mid-term progress review or project completion assessment. This type of evaluation is usually based on a desk review of program or project documentation and may be complemented by analyzing monitoring data (if available). In some cases, this evaluation includes interviews with program staff to better understand the goal-setting process and the enabling or hindering factors behind observed progress. These are generally low-cost evaluations that can be completed in a short period of time.

Examples of this type of evaluation include:

- *Mexico, Design Evaluations*: This evaluation analyzes new program design, including the link to national development objectives, internal consistency, alignment between program log frame and operation rules, and potential synergy or duplicity with other programs. It relies on a desk review of program documentation, including the log frame.[2]
- *Mexico, Performance-Specific Evaluation*: This evaluation assesses social program progress in meeting objectives and annual targets based on a desk review of the Performance Evaluation System (SED) data. These evaluations are conducted annually for about 120 different programs and cost on average US$5,500.[3]
- *World Bank, Independent Evaluation Group, Project Performance Assessment*: These assessments evaluate the relevance of project objectives, whether goals are being met, efficiency, results sustainability, and institutional development impact. They are generally conducted at the end of the project by reviewing project documentation, visiting the borrowing country, and interviewing staff and government officials.[4]

Process-based evaluations

Process-based evaluations are aimed at understanding how a program works. What are the actual steps and activities involved in delivering a good or a service? How close are they to agreed operation? Is program operation efficient? Numerous questions might be asked in a process-based evaluation, including:

1. Is the program being implemented according to design?

2. Are operational procedures appropriate to ensure the timely delivery of quality products or services?
3. What is the level of compliance with the operations manual?
4. Are there adequate resources (money, equipment, facilities, training, and so forth) to ensure the timely delivery of quality products or services?
5. Are there adequate systems (human resources, financial, management information, and so forth) in place to support program operations?
6. Are program clients receiving quality products and services?
7. What is the general process that program clients go through with the product or program? Are program clients satisfied with the processes and services?
8. Are there any operational bottlenecks?
9. Is the program reaching the intended population? Are program outreach activities adequate to ensure the desired level of target population participation?

This type of evaluation is useful in a variety of circumstances. For example, process-based evaluations are helpful to obtain early warnings of operational difficulties in newly implemented programs or components, particularly among those involving complex procedures. It may also be conducted at regular intervals to check that operations remain on track and follow established procedures, or at any time when there are staff or client complaints about service delivery. Furthermore, there may be fears of inefficiency in long-existing programs that warrant a process-based evaluation.

Process-based evaluation tools vary considerably in depth and breadth, and thus in required costs and time. They range from qualitative assessments in a few program sites to user or facilities surveys involving representative samples. Process-based evaluations use a combination of data collection and analysis methods including interviews with program staff and clients, user and facility surveys, focus groups, direct observation, record review, and analysis of monitoring data.

Impact evaluations

An impact evaluation assesses if a program is producing the intended outcomes through providing relevant, quality outputs and services to the targeted population. Outcomes are changes in well-being experienced by individuals as a result of participating in the program. They are different from program outputs, which are measured by the number of goods or services delivered or the number of people served. Outcomes involve beneficial transformations in participants' knowledge, attitudes, values, skills, behaviors, condition, or status. Intended outcomes vary depending on program objectives and design, for example, increased literacy, improved nutrition, decreased disease incidence, and so on. The main questions asked in an impact evaluation are:

1. Does the program or policy have the desired effects on individuals, households, or institutions?
2. Are these effects attributable to the program or would they have occurred anyway?
3. Are there any unintended consequences, positive or negative, on program participants?
4. Are program costs justified in terms of its welfare impact?
5. When there are various program implementation alternatives, which one is the most cost-effective?

Impact evaluations are useful to inform a range of policy decisions, from scaling up effective interventions to adjusting program design to curtailing unpromising interventions. In addition, they help generate evidence on which approach is more effective in reaching a particular objective when comparing different programs or different intervention options within a program.

Impact evaluations rely on quantitative methods (statistics and econometrics), but can be complemented with qualitative analysis. Compared to other evaluation types, impact evaluations require more time, technical skills, and are costlier. Hence, they are most effective when applied selectively to answer strategic policy questions or to assess innovative pilot interventions testing a new, unproven, but promising approach. Although the impact evaluation process can start very early in a program life, results are not usually available until after several months of program implementation. Different outcomes of interest require varying exposure and maturation times for measurement. For example, changes in household consumption can be measured after six months of program implementation, but changes in nutrition outcomes require a longer period.

Impact evaluation results combined with program cost analysis create an additional evaluation tool. Cost-effectiveness analysis compares the relative performance of two or more programs or program alternatives in achieving a common outcome. Once impact and cost information are available across a variety of programs, cost-effectiveness analysis will allow policy makers to make informed decisions on which intervention to invest in.

Resources for impact evaluations include:

- The *World Bank Impact Evaluation* Web site, which includes methodological and implementation guidelines for conducting impact evalua-

BOX 9.1

Another Analytical Tool

Cost-benefit analysis is a widely used tool to assess the desirability of a particular intervention. It answers questions such as whether a new airport should be built or a highway expanded. It compares the present value of the proposed intervention's benefits and costs. It is typically conducted ex ante and involves calculating intervention benefits in monetary terms and detailed cost estimates. It can be conducted at a high or low level of rigor, and costs vary accordingly. Examples of agencies using this technique include the Departments of Transportation in the United Kingdom, the United States, Canada, and the European Union.

tions as well as a database of evaluations of World Bank-supported interventions.

- The *Poverty Action Lab at MIT*, which promotes the use of randomized evaluations to answer questions critical to poverty alleviation by providing methodological guidance, a randomized evaluations database, and policy lessons from cost-effectiveness analysis.

In addition to the three types of evaluation discussed here, other analytical tools and approaches are widely used. Box 9.1 briefly discusses cost-benefit analysis and Box 9.2 provides an overview of participatory evaluation.

Selecting a Mix of Evaluation Tools: International Experience

A number of M&E systems at the country level use a combination of evaluation tools. The combinations vary across countries and have evolved over time. Country experiences show that the selection of an evaluation tool responds to differences in the driving principles of their M&E systems: transparency and accountability, policy and spending effectiveness and efficiency, or improved program management. The type of tool selected also reflects myriad country conditions, such as institutional capacity, resource availability, and institutional arrangements. Most countries have followed an incremental approach in the use of evaluation tools, starting relatively simple and increasing in complexity and comprehensiveness over time.

In Chile, for example, the Budget Department (*Dirección de Presupuestos—*DIPRES) at the Ministry of Finance is in charge of the Management Evalua-

BOX 9.2

A Participatory Approach to Evaluation

Goal-, process-, and outcome-based evaluations can be conducted using a participatory approach. This entails:

A process of self-assessment, collective knowledge production, and cooperative action in which the stakeholders in a development intervention participate substantively in the identification of the evaluation issues, the design of the evaluation, the collection and analysis of data, and the action taken as a result of the evaluation findings (Jackson and Kassam 1998).

Participatory evaluation emphasizes the voices and decisions of program participants when analyzing implementation difficulties or program effects, or when information is needed on stakeholders' knowledge of program goals or their views of progress.

Participatory evaluation usually employs rapid appraisal techniques, which are simpler, quicker, and less costly than other conventional data collection methods. This evaluation tool relies on qualitative and quantitative research techniques. Qualitative methods used include community evaluation committees, community workshops, self-directed focus groups, popular theater, community radio, transect walks, and wealth ranking, among others. Quantitative methods include short surveys. The choice of methods depends on local conditions, skills, and interests of various stakeholders.

Source: Jackson and Kassam 1998.

tion and Control System. Its main emphasis is to promote the efficient allocation of public spending, and it uses various M&E tools that were gradually added between 1994 and 2002. DIPRES made a conscious decision to start simple by incorporating the monitoring of performance indicators into the budget process. In 1997, DIPRES began conducting a relatively low-cost and rapid evaluation known as the Government Program Evaluation (Box 9.3). Since then, these evaluations have been consistently used to inform the budget process. In 2001, impact evaluations were added to the Chilean M&E system. Programs are selected for an impact evaluation if they involve a substantial amount of public resources and there is no evidence from previous evaluations of their final outcome. DIPRES and Congress jointly decide which programs should be evaluated each year.

In Mexico, the M&E system stems from an increasing demand for transparency and accountability coupled with the demonstration effect of the im-

BOX 9.3

Overall Performance Evaluation

This tool is a combination of the three types of evaluations discussed earlier—goal-, process-, and outcome-based evaluations. A number of countries have incorporated this tool in their M&E system because it enables a rapid assessment of program performance through a desk review of program or project documentation, existing evaluations, and monitoring data. Using standardized evaluation criteria, overall performance evaluations can be compared across different programs and used for benchmarking.

This evaluation may be conducted at any time during the life of an intervention, although some assessment topics may have to be adapted for recently implemented programs. The main strengths of this evaluation are its short time requirement—three to five months—and relatively low cost. Its main disadvantages compared to more rigorous approaches are the weaker empirical evidence on which it is based and the typically very limited statistical or econometric techniques used for data analysis.

A number of countries include overall performance evaluations in their M&E systems:

Chile, Government Program Evaluations: Their purpose is to assess program design, operation, and results to inform the budget alloca-

tion process. They are based on a desk review of program documentation and staff interviews.

United States, Program Assessment Rating Tool: Although it is no longer used in the United States, this tool served as a model for overall performance evaluations in countries such as Colombia and Mexico. This tool was used to evaluate a program's purpose, design, planning, management, results, and accountability to determine its overall effectiveness. Every year, 20 percent of agency programs were evaluated and all programs were evaluated at least once every five years.

Colombia, Executive Evaluations: They provide feedback for mid-term program adjustment by analyzing programs' design, inputs, operation, results, organizational structure, strategic planning, and monitoring and evaluation.

Mexico, Consistency and Results Evaluation: At the beginning of the new government administration, all federal government programs had an overall performance evaluation. This served as a baseline performance measurement and helped identify the strengths and weaknesses across programs and sectors.

---

pact evaluation of the conditional cash transfer program PROGRESA.[5] Starting in 2000, the Appropriations Bill required an annual external evaluation for all federal programs subject to rules of operation. At the time, evaluation guidelines did not distinguish between different types of evaluations. However, every year external evaluations were expected to answer questions ranging from compliance with operation rules to impact to cost benefits. This was an overwhelming demand given the nascent evaluation institutional capacity, both from the demand (ministries) and the supply side (universities and research institutions). In 2007, the newly created National Evaluation Council (*Consejo Nacional de Evaluación*—CONEVAL), the Ministry of Finance (*Secretaría de Hacienda y Crédito Público*—SHCP), and the Ministry of Public Management (*Secretaría de la Función Pública*—SFP) jointly issued a revised set of guidelines including a set of evaluation tools and the criteria for tool application. The guidelines established the publication of an Annual Program Evaluation that specifies which programs are required to have a particular type of evaluation, depending on their strategic relevance, particular policy interest, and previous evaluation results. The selection of programs and evaluation tools is made jointly by CONEVAL, SHCP, and SFP. Ministries can also propose additional evaluations to support policy or management decisions or to get specific program performance information.

Colombia's M&E system, SINERGIA, was launched in 1994. Its main focus is on national planning and accountability. SINERGIA's two main components consist of a system of performance indicators that tracks progress against the National Development Plan goals and an agenda of rigorous impact evaluations. The evaluation component did not become operational until 2002. Technical assistance and funding from donors allowed Colombia to opt for a more complex and costlier evaluation tool. Recently Colombia incorporated a lower cost and more rapid alternative known as Executive Evaluations (Box 9.3).

Key Lessons

Using the appropriate tool, evaluations can help address a number of different management issues. The appropriate evaluation tool depends on the intended use of the evaluation findings, budget and time availability, and capacity constraints. There are usually trade-offs between evaluation depth and rigor and resource requirements. Goal-based evaluations are quick and low cost, but tend to have data limitations and less rigorous analysis. By contrast, impact evaluations are more rigorous, but require considerable technical expertise, take longer to yield results, and cost more. Moreover, it is important to realize that any particular type of evaluation can be conducted at a higher or lower analytical level, and thus costs vary accordingly.

Another important lesson is that evaluations are not a once-in-a-lifetime exercise, nor does the use of one evaluation type exclude the rest. Policy and program information needs are continuous and change over time, so can the evaluation tool. Moreover, evaluation tools are complements rather than substitutes. When they are combined, they provide an even deeper understanding of program and policy strengths and weaknesses. For example, whereas impact evaluations can produce reliable estimates of the causal effects of a program, they are not typically designed to provide insights into program implementation. Monitoring data and process evaluations are needed to track program implementation and examine questions of process that are critical to informing and interpreting the results from impact evaluations.

International experience highlights the importance of gradually incorporating evaluation tools into country-level M&E systems. Countries will require different evaluation tools depending on the main purpose of their M&E system, existing institutional capacity, and the availability of funds and external technical assistance. In some cases, using less complex evaluation tools, but ensuring that they are properly applied and providing consistent feedback, may be an appropriate strategy to build an M&E system. In other cases, a few properly conducted and highly relevant impact evaluations with large demonstration effects may be a good way to motivate a shift toward results-based management.

Finally, as important as it is to select the right mix of evaluation tools, it is also important that evaluation results are used to inform policy and program decision making. Decision making that is informed and supported by reliable and systematic evaluations is more likely to lead to the success of policy and program interventions.

Notes

1. Other types of evaluations focus on other levels of the public sector, including organizations and sectors that are not considered in this chapter.
2. For more information on Mexico's design evaluations, see http://www.coneval. gob.mx/coneval2/htmls/ evaluacion_monitoreo/HomeEvalMonitoreo. jsp?categorias=EVAL_MON,EVAL_MON-diseno.
3. For more information on Mexico's performance-specific evaluation, see http:// www.coneval.gob.mx/.
4. For more information on the World Bank's Project Performance Assessments, see http://web.worldbank.org/external/default/main?startPoint=0&startDate= 2008%2F01%2F01&theSitePK=1324361&piPK=64254724&pagePK=64254514& menuPK=64253143.
5. PROGRESA, now called Oportunidades, is a conditional cash transfer program launched in 1997 as an innovative pilot intervention to reduce poverty through human capital investment. The program impact evaluation became a role model for other social development interventions in Mexico.

Bibliography

Departamento Nacional de Planeación. 2008. *Evaluación Ejecutiva Lineamientos Metodológicos*. República de Colombia.

División de Control de Gestión. 2009. *Metodología Evaluación de Impacto*. Gobierno de Chile, Ministerio de Hacienda, Dirección de Presupuestos.

Gertler, Paul J., Sebastian Martinez, Patrick Premand, Laura B. Rawlings, and Christel M. J. Vermeersch. 2010. *Impact Evaluation in Practice*. Washington, DC: World Bank.

Jackson, Edward T., and Yusuf Kassam, eds. 1998. *Knowledge Shared: Participatory Evaluation in Development Cooperation*. Kumarian Press.

McNamara, Carter. 2006. *Field Guide to Nonprofit Program Design, Marketing and Evaluation*, 4th Edition. Minneapolis, Minnesota: Authenticity Consulting, LLC.

Zaltsman, Ariel. 2006. "Experience with Institutionalizing Monitoring and Evaluation in Five Latin American Countries: Argentina, Chile, Colombia, Costa Rica, and Uruguay." ECD Working Paper Series 16, Independent Evaluation Group. World Bank, Washington, DC.

Web Sites

Chile, DIPRES: http://www.dipres.cl/572/propertyvalue-15697.html
Colombia, SINERGIA: http://sinergia.dnp.gov.co/PortalDNP/
Mexico, CONEVAL: http://www.coneval.gob.mx/

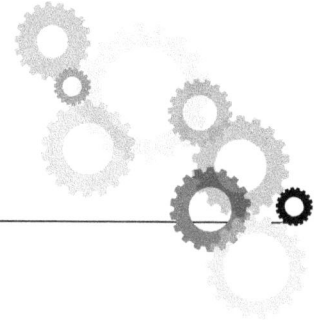

CHAPTER 10

Reconstructing Baseline Data for Impact Evaluation and Results Measurement

Michael Bamberger

Many international development agencies and some national governments base future budget planning and policy decisions on a systematic assessment of the projects and programs in which they have already invested. Results are assessed through mid-term reviews (MTRs), implementation completion reports (ICRs), or through more rigorous impact evaluations (IE), all of which require the collection of baseline data before the project or program begins. The baseline is compared with the MTR, ICR, or the post-test IE measurement to estimate changes in the indicators used to measure performance, outcomes, or impacts. However, a baseline study is often not conducted, seriously limiting the possibility of producing a rigorous assessment of project outcomes and impacts. This chapter discusses the reasons why baseline studies are often not conducted, even when they are included in the

The author wishes to thank these colleagues from the Poverty Reduction and Equity Group: Jaime Saavedra (Director), Gladys Lopez-Acevedo (Senior Economist), Keith Mackay (Consultant), Emmanuel Skoufias (Lead Economist), Philipp Krause (Consultant), and Helena Hwang (Consultant) for comments. The views expressed in this chapter are those of the author.

project design and funds have been approved, and describes strategies that can be used to "reconstruct" baseline data at a later stage in the project or program cycle.

Baseline Data—Important but Often Not Collected

Baseline data can come from the project's monitoring and evaluation (M&E) system, rapid assessment studies, surveys commissioned at the start and end of the project, or from secondary data sources. Whatever the source, the availability of appropriate baseline data is always critical for performance evaluation, as it is impossible to measure changes without reliable data on the situation before the intervention began. Despite the importance of collecting good baseline data, there are a number of reasons why they are frequently not collected, and this chapter presents a range of strategies that can be used for "reconstructing" baseline data when they are not available.

The strategies for reconstructing baseline data apply to both discrete projects and broader programs (the term "interventions" is used here to cover both), although they must sometimes be adapted to the special characteristics of each. Projects often introduce new M&E systems customized to the project's specific data needs, but often with significant start-up delays, which can be problematic for collecting baseline data. In contrast, ongoing programs can often build on existing M&E and other data collection systems, and can also have access to secondary data and sampling frames, although these systems are often not sufficient for evaluation and tend to be difficult to change. Non-governmental organizations (NGOs), important development players in many countries, may face different issues with respect to baseline data for their activities.

Although most interventions plan to collect baseline data for results monitoring and possibly impact evaluation, often data are not collected or collection is delayed until the intervention has been under way for some time. The reasons may include a lack of awareness of the importance of baseline data, lack of financial resources, or limited technical expertise. Even when management recognizes its importance, administrative procedures (for example, recruiting and training M&E staff, purchasing computers, or commissioning consultants) may create long delays before baseline data can be collected.

M&E systems collect baseline information on indicators for measuring program outputs and outcomes for the target population. Impact evaluations collect similar information, but from both beneficiaries and a comparison group. Information is also collected on the social and economic characteristics of individuals, groups, or communities, on contextual factors such as local economic conditions, and on political and organizational factors that might explain variations in outcomes and impacts among different project locations.

The World Bank and other development agencies incorporate this information into a results-based M&E system. Kusek and Rist (2004) describe a 10-step system for implementing a results-based M&E system, three of which involve creating a baseline:

Step 2: Agreeing on the outcomes to monitor and evaluate
Step 3: Selecting key indicators to monitor outcomes and performance
Step 4: Collecting baseline data

Operational Implications of Collecting Baseline Data

Even when an agency is strongly committed to setting up an M&E system to generate the baseline data required for results-based management and impact evaluation, there are often other pressing staffing, organizational, and financial matters, so there will often be considerable delays before the M&E systems are operational. The following measures can increase the likelihood that the M&E systems will be in place from the time of program launch:

- Define funding arrangements that avoid long delays in contracting monitoring unit staff and commissioning evaluation consultants.
- Begin recruiting M&E staff before intervention launch.
- Arrange for M&E staff to receive basic training before intervention launch.
- Recruit an experienced M&E staffer early on.

Having staff on board who are familiar with the practical and technical problems faced when trying to reconstruct baseline data can avoid many of the problems that typically occur when generalist task managers attempt to handle these problems themselves.

An agency can enhance its ability to generate baseline data in a number of ways. Using evaluation funds to contract additional administrative staff may remove bottlenecks and facilitate good quality data collection. In other cases, baseline data on target households, communities, or organizations such as schools, health clinics, or agricultural cooperatives may not be organized or archived in a way that facilitates identification of a comparable sample one or two years later for repeat interviews. Discussions with agency staff at the planning stage could ensure that valuable data, such as application forms that include socioeconomic data on households or communities applying to participate in a project or program or feasibility studies for the selection of roads to be built or upgraded, are not discarded once beneficiaries have been selected or the sites for road improvements chosen. Effective coordination with agency staff is critical.

M&E systems compare progress at different points over the life of the project, and baseline data for these comparisons must be collected throughout the life of the project. So it is important to ensure that M&E systems continue to provide good quality data.

National sample surveys conducted at least once a year on topics such as income and expenditure, access to health or education, or agricultural production provide very valuable baseline data for results-based management and impact evaluation.[1] Household income and expenditure surveys have proved very valuable. If these surveys can be used in the evaluation of several different development programs, they become very cost-effective and they also can provide a larger and methodologically more rigorous comparison group sample than an individual evaluation could afford. Regularly repeated surveys provide a very valuable longitudinal database that can control for seasonal variation and economic cycles.

The value of these surveys for results-based management and impact evaluation can be greatly enhanced if they are planned with this purpose in mind and in coordination with the agencies and donors who may use the surveys to generate baseline data and comparison groups. Some of the ways to enhance their utility include:

- Ensure that the sample is sufficiently large and has a sufficiently broad regional coverage to generate sub-samples covering particular target populations with sufficient statistical power to be used for major program evaluations.
- Include, in consultation with social sector agencies, core information on topics such as school enrollment, access to health services, and participation in major development programs. This facilitates selecting samples of participants and comparison groups for impact evaluations.
- Include one or more special modules in each round of the survey to cover the needs of a particular evaluation that is being planned.
- Document the master sampling frame to facilitate its use for selecting samples for particular evaluations.

Many of these approaches can only be considered for large and expensive evaluations or for studying issues that are of high priority to government agencies and/or donors. Also, national statistics offices are typically overburdened, so they can only be expected to help out when the program is particularly important or when special funding can be arranged to cover the costs of additional staff for data collection or analysis.

Strategies for Reconstructing Baseline Data

This section presents some practical strategies for estimating ("reconstructing") conditions of the project, and sometimes also the comparison group, at the time the intervention is launched. Most of these are economical, relatively simple to apply, and do not require too great an investment of time.

Timing of the baseline

Evaluations, often implicitly, assume that an intervention only starts to produce impacts after it officially begins, but, in fact, changes may occur long before this. For example, once it is known that roads, water supply, or other services are to be provided to certain communities, speculators may begin to buy land and families may start to make improvements to their property. If the baseline is not conducted until the official program launch, many of these important changes may not be captured. Using techniques such as recall or key informant interviews to capture information on these early changes should be considered.

Using secondary data to reconstruct the baseline

Many documentary sources can provide information on the beneficiary population or comparison groups around the time the intervention began. Censuses covering areas such as population, agriculture, industry, education, and environment may be available. Other useful sources are household socioeconomic surveys, the largest of which are the Living Standards Measurement Study, which have been conducted in at least 35 countries.[2] When surveys are repeated periodically, it may be possible to find a reference point close to the intervention launch date. However, while many surveys have a large enough sample to generate a comparison group, the samples are often too small or do not contain sufficiently detailed information to generate a sample of the beneficiary population (particularly when this population is relatively small).

Using Secondary Sources to Reconstruct Baseline Data

The evaluation of the Nicaragua Emergency Social Investment Fund used the 1998 Living Standards Measurement Study, conducted five years earlier, to identify baseline project and comparison communities for each project component (water supply and sanitation, health, education, etc.). Propensity scores were then used to improve the match of the two samples (Pradhan and Rawlings 2002).

The World Bank's Operations Evaluation Department (OED, now the Independent Evaluations Group) evaluated the impacts of the Bangladesh Integrated Nutrition Project using three separate secondary data sets to reconstruct the baseline and to monitor implementation progress. Each survey had strengths and weaknesses, some having more information on project implementation while others had more demographic and nutrition information. The study created a new comparison group using propensity score matching. Combining the data sources reduced bias and strengthened the validity of the impact estimates (OED 2005).

Ministries of education, health, and agriculture, among others, publish annual reports that can provide baseline reference data, and they can sometimes provide information on particular schools, health centers, or other facilities in the target areas. Donor agencies, NGOs, and universities also conduct studies providing useful reference data. Birth and death certificates can be used to examine life expectancy, family size, and common causes of death, while legal documents relating to marriage and divorce can provide information on, for example, the property rights of women. Mass media also provide information on issues concerning local schools, clinics, public transport, and so forth that can provide background information on conditions at the start of the intervention. Box 10.1 presents two examples where secondary data were used to reconstruct baseline data for matched project and comparison groups using propensity score matching.

A number of factors affect the utility and validity of secondary data sources: the data cover the wrong reference period, key information is missing, information was not collected from the right people (for example, only the household head was interviewed), the sample does not cover the whole population of interest or is too small, or the information is not reliable or complete. These factors must always be assessed before utilizing any of these sources.

BOX 10.2

Using Project Administrative Data to Reconstruct the Baseline

A recent post-test multi-donor evaluation of the Nepal "Education for All" project used the project's Education Management Information System to obtain gender-disaggregated data on school enrollment, repetition, and academic test scores at the start of the program and at various key milestones during implementation.

The evaluation of the poverty impacts of the World Bank–financed Vietnam Rural Roads project used administrative data collected at the canton level to understand the selection criteria used to determine where roads would be built and to monitor the quality and speed of construction (Van de Walle 2009).

The evaluation of the feeder roads component of the Eritrea Community Development Fund used planning and feasibility studies commissioned by the implementing agency to obtain socio-economic baseline data on the communities affected by the roads.

Using administrative data from the intervention

Many interventions collect monitoring and other kinds of administrative data that could be used to estimate baseline conditions for the target population (Box 10.2). Examples include socioeconomic data in the application forms of people, communities, or organizations applying to participate or receive benefits, planning and feasibility studies, monitoring reports, and administrative records providing information such as changes in project eligibility criteria or the services provided to particular beneficiaries. Sometimes the application forms for people not accepted can provide a comparison group of non-participants.

While administrative data are a potentially valuable source of baseline data, the data are often not available in a convenient format for analysis. Often the evaluator must work closely with program staff to ensure that administrative data are collected and filed in a usable format (discussed later in this chapter). Often when the evaluator discovers that the expected administrative records have vanished or are not organized in a usable format, staff respond that they were not told that the information would be required for a future evaluation. Better coordination between the evaluators and program staff can ensure that the information is available.

Recall

Recall techniques ask individuals or groups to provide information on their social or economic conditions, access to services, or the conditions of their community at a particular point in time (for example, project launch) or over a particular period of time. Recall is used in poverty analysis, demography, and income expenditure surveys (Deaton and Grosh 2000) to elicit information on behavior (for example, contraceptive usage or fertility) or economic status (household income or expenditure). Several comparative studies (for example, Deaton and Grosh 2000; Belli, Stafford, and Alwin 2009) have concluded that recall, when carefully designed and implemented, can be a useful estimating tool with predictable and, to some extent, controllable errors, and a potentially valuable way to reconstruct baseline data.

Recall can be applied through questions in surveys and individual or group interviews (Box 10.3). In addition to collecting numerical data such as income or farm prices, recall can also be used to obtain estimates of major changes in the welfare conditions of the household, such as which children attended a school outside the village before the village school opened and the travel time and costs of getting there. Families can also provide information on questions such as access to health facilities and where they previously obtained water and how much it cost.

BOX 10.3

Using Recall to Reconstruct Baselines

An evaluation of the gender impacts of a World Bank–financed rural roads project in Bangladesh asked women to recall the situation of their family before the upgrading of the roads and to compare this with their current situation on 20 indicators of economic status, access to water, quality of housing, and consumption of basic items. The differences were used to estimate project impact (unpublished study funded through the World Bank Gender and Transport Initiative 2000).

An evaluation of the impacts of the village school construction component of the Eritrea Community Development Fund asked families to recall which of their children had attended school before the school was built in their village, how far the children had to travel, and the means and cost of transport. Families were able to clearly recall all of this information, and in the opinion of the researchers the information was reliable because the respondents had no incentives to distort their answers (unpublished consultant report).

Recall always involves a risk of bias due to memory or distortion. Unintentional distortion occurs when, for example, people romanticize the past ("when I was young there was much less crime in the community") or unintentionally adjust their response to what they think the researcher wants to hear. Intentional distortion occurs when, for example, families are reluctant to admit that their children had not been attending school, or they might underestimate how much they spend on water to convince planners they are too poor to pay the water charges proposed in a new project. The reliability of recall data also depends on the nature of the outcome variable being studied. For example, families will usually be able to recall major events such as a death in the family or enrollment of a child in school, but it may be more difficult to obtain reliable responses on nutrition questions or changes in the frequency of diarrhea or other very common ailments.

A challenge in using recall is the absence of studies providing guidelines for estimating or adjusting for systematic bias. The most detailed research on this question was conducted on the recall of expenditures in national household income and expenditure surveys and studies on fertility. The income and expenditure studies identified some consistent biases that can be used to adjust estimates: "telescoping," that is, reporting major expenditures as being more recent than they actually were, and underestimating small expenditures. Also, men and the better off of both sexes are more likely to report that they have been sick than women and poorer people. Other areas where research on the validity and reliability of recall is available include substance abuse, adolescent health research, assessment of stressful events, and time use. Belli, Stafford, and Alwin (2009) report that the reliability of recall is significantly enhanced when using the calendar method of life course research (in which topics of interest are linked to critical events in the life course of the subject: birth, death, marriage, enrollment in school, and changing employment) compared to conventional recall questions in a structured questionnaire.

Recall can sometimes provide better self-assessment estimates of behavioral changes and knowledge (for example, child care and nutrition, leadership skills) than pre- and post-test comparisons. People often overestimate their behavioral skills or knowledge before entering a program because they do not understand the tasks being studied or the required skills. After completing the program, they may have a better understanding of these behaviors and provide a better assessment of their previous level of competency or knowledge and how much these have changed (Pratt, McGuigan, and Katzeva 2000).

BOX 10.4

Store Owners as Key Informants on Economic Trends in the Community

In the author's work on the evaluation of urban housing programs in Latin America, local storekeepers were a valuable source of information on changes in the economic conditions of the community. For example, an increase in the demand for meat was an indicator that households had more disposable income. Most stores provide credit and the level of default was another good indicator of changing community fortunes. Storekeepers have a good memory for trends in the sales of key items over long periods of time.

Key informants

Key informants (Box 10.4) can provide knowledge and experience on a particular agency and the population it serves, an organization (such as a trade union, women's group, or a gang), or a social group (mothers with young children, sex workers, or landless farmers). For example, when evaluating a program to increase secondary school enrollment, key informants could include school directors, teachers and other school personnel, parents of children who do and do not attend school, students, and religious leaders.

Key informants combine "factual" information with a particular point of view, and it is important to select informants with differing perspectives. For example, low-income and higher-income parents may have different opinions on programs to increase school enrollment, as may those from different ethnic or religious groups.

Group interview techniques for reconstructing baseline data

Focus groups are used in market research and program evaluation to obtain information on socioeconomic characteristics, attitudes, and behaviors of groups that share common attributes (Krueger and Casey 2000). Groups, usually with five to eight persons, are selected to cover different economic strata, as well as people who have and have not participated in the project or who received different services. The group moderator goes systematically through a checklist of questions making sure that each person responds to every question. For the purposes of reconstructing baseline data, participants could be asked to provide information on, for example, conditions of their household, group, community, or agricultural production at some point in the past.

When properly designed and implemented, **focus groups** ensure that all key sectors are sampled and that responses provide a representative snapshot of each group. However, readers of evaluation reports should be aware that focus groups are often used in development evaluation as a fast and economical way to obtain general information on the opinions of the target population, with very little attention to participant selection or ensuring balanced participation in the discussion. Market research companies make extensive use of focus groups, developing sampling frames to select samples with the socioeconomic characteristics required by different clients. If funds are available, contracting a market research company to design and implement focus groups for a program evaluation could be considered.

Participatory assessment techniques (PRAs), originally meaning "participatory rural appraisal," is now used as a generic term for all participatory studies in which communities or groups report on their conditions, problems, and changes over time. Groups can provide estimates on things such as the volume and quality of water, crop production and sales, travel time and costs, and time use. PRAs are widely used with poor rural and urban communities with low literacy levels or where participants have difficulties in expressing complex ideas (such as changes in environmental conditions). PRAs include construction of charts, maps, or tables where the group agrees on the placement of familiar objects, such as stones or seeds, on a chart to illustrate trends, important events, magnitude, or causal patterns. Timelines, trend analysis, historical transects, seasonal diagrams, and daily activity schedules can be used to assess changes over time or the situation at the baseline reference point (Kumar 2002).

These PRAs have several benefits. Respondents may feel more comfortable expressing themselves in a group with their peers, rather than in a one-on-one interview with an outside researcher. If participants are selected to ensure their representativity, the group consensus can also provide a more cost-effective way to obtain an approximate estimate for the situation of the whole population of interest, rather than having to use a sample survey. Synergistic group interaction also generates new ideas that might not have come up in one-on-one interviews. There are also potential risks: the group may be dominated by a few vocal people, participants may defer to politically powerful, wealthier, or more educated group members, or the group facilitator may inadvertently direct the group toward certain decisions.

Applying Reconstruction Strategies to Fill In Baseline Data for Results-Based M&E

M&E systems often take some time to get established, so there may be a period at the start of the intervention when monitoring data are not being collected. So when setting up the M&E system, a first step should be to check: What key indicators are required for baseline data? Which indicators are available and which are missing? Why are the data missing and how easily can the problems be overcome? Is any important information not being collected during the interim period before the monitoring system becomes fully operational? All of the techniques for reconstructing baseline data can be applied to filling in baseline data gaps.

Results-based M&E systems are usually based on a program theory model that includes how the program is intended to achieve its objectives, implementation and outcome indicators to be measured, key assumptions to be tested, and the time horizon over which different results are to be achieved (Bamberger, Rugh, and Mabry 2006, Chapter 10). Often the program theory model was not defined or fully articulated at the start of the project. In these cases, the evaluator may need to work with the implementing agency and other stakeholders to reconstruct the implicit program theory on which the program is based. Sometimes staff agree on the underlying theory model and a short workshop may be sufficient to put this on paper. However, in other cases, staff may have difficulty articulating the model or may disagree on the purpose of the program, how it will achieve its outcomes, and the critical assumptions on which it is based.[3]

Applying Baseline Reconstruction Strategies for Evaluating Outcomes and Impacts

A wide variety of evaluation designs can estimate project impacts and effects, ranging from strong statistical designs with before-and-after comparisons of project and comparison groups, to statistically weaker quasi-experimental designs that may not include baseline data on the comparison or project groups, to non-experimental designs that do not include a comparison group. Different baseline reconstruction strategies can be applied to different evaluation designs. For weaker quasi-experimental designs and non-experimental designs where no baseline data have been collected for the project and/or the comparison group, all of the baseline reconstruction techniques discussed earlier could be considered. Stronger quasi-experimental and experimental designs all include baseline data for both project and control groups.

However, in most cases only quantitative data are collected (for example, the number of students enrolled in school or patients visiting health centers), and the design would be strengthened by complementing this with qualitative data such as the quality of services, women's participation in household decision making at the time the project began, and how different ethnic groups were received when they visited health clinics.

Quantitative and qualitative evaluations rely on different types of data and data collection procedures. When quantitative researchers collect primary data to reconstruct baselines, they are likely to incorporate recall questions into a structured questionnaire. In contrast, qualitative researchers use a wider range of techniques, including key informants, in-depth individual interviews, focus groups, and PRAs. Both quantitative and qualitative research designs can benefit from incorporating mixed-method approaches to baseline reconstruction so as to combine depth of understanding with generalizability of the findings (Bamberger, Rao, and Woolcock 2010).

Selecting a well-matched baseline comparison group presents special challenges. Participant selection procedures often result in project participants having special attributes that affect, and frequently increase, the probability of successful program outcomes. Often these attributes, termed "unobservables" or "omitted variables," are not included in the baseline surveys. For example, in a microcredit program for women, many of the women who are successful in starting or expanding small businesses might have more control over household decision making than is normally the case in their community, or they may have previous experiences with a small business. These characteristics might affect project outcomes, but this information will usually not be included in the baseline data. The following methods could be used to assess the importance of these omitted variables: key informant interviews (for example, staff of microcredit and other economic development programs), administrative data from the loan programs, focus groups, in-depth interviews with participants and non-participants, and PRAs.

Conclusions

Good quality baseline data that measure the conditions of the target population and the matched comparison group are an essential component of effective monitoring, results-based management, and impact evaluation. Without this reference information, it is very difficult to assess how well a project or program has performed and how effectively it has achieved its objectives or results.

However, many projects and programs fail to collect all of the required baseline data. While some of the reasons for this can be explained by inadequate funding or technical difficulties in collecting the data (particularly for control groups), many of the causes could be at least partially corrected by better management and planning. Many reasons relate to administrative delays in releasing funds, recruiting and training staff, and contracting consultants. While administrative procedures are often difficult to change, ways could probably be found to reduce some of these delays. Other issues concern the relatively low priority that is often given to M&E, particularly when there are so many other urgent priorities during the early stages of a project or program.

Even with the best of intentions, these administrative challenges will never be completely resolved and there will continue to be many situations where the collection of baseline monitoring data is delayed and the commissioning of baseline studies for impact evaluations never takes place. Included in this chapter are a range of strategies, many of them relatively simple and cost-effective, for reconstructing baseline data when necessary. Appropriate tools should be built into results-based M&E and impact evaluation systems as contingency tools for reconstructing important baseline data. While some of the statistical techniques such as propensity score matching have been widely used and their strengths and weaknesses are well understood, others such as recall or the systematic use of key informants have often been used in a somewhat ad hoc manner and more work is required to test, refine, and validate the methods. Finally, many potentially valuable sources of administrative data from the project itself tend to be underutilized and more attention should be given to their development and use.

Notes

1. National surveys that are only repeated every few years can also provide useful baseline data, but it is more difficult to obtain data collected close to the time the project began. The greater the time interval the less reliable the baseline estimates as economic, climatic, and other factors change over time.

2. Other widely-used multi-country surveys include UNICEF's Multiple Indicator Cluster Surveys that now provide 42 indicators of the health and welfare of children and women in more than 100 countries, and the USAID-supported Demographic and Health Surveys that since 1984 have conducted more than 240 surveys providing a broad range of demographic and health data on more than 85 countries.

3. See Bamberger, Rugh, and Mabry (2006, 179–82) for a discussion of the different strategies for reconstructing a program theory model.

Bibliography

Bamberger, M., and A. Kirk. 2009. *Making Smart Policy: Using Impact Evaluation for Policy Making: Case Studies on Evaluations That Influenced Policy.* PREM Thematic Group for Poverty Analysis, Monitoring and Impact Evaluation, Doing Impact Evaluation Series 14, World Bank, Washington, DC.

Bamberger, M., V. Rao, and M. Woolcock. 2010. "Using Mixed Methods in Monitoring and Evaluation: Experiences from International Development." Policy Research Working Paper Series 5245. World Bank, Washington, DC.

Bamberger, M., J. Rugh, and L. Mabry. 2006. *Real World Evaluation: Working under Budget, Time, Data, and Political Constraints.* Thousand Oaks, CA: Sage Publications.

Belli, F., F. Stafford, and D. Alwin. 2009. *Calendar and Time Diary Methods in Life Course Research.* Thousand Oaks, CA: Sage Publications.

Bourguignon, F. 2009. "Toward an Evaluation of Evaluation Methods: A Commentary on the Experimental Approach in the Fields of Employment, Work, and Professional Training." *Journal of Development Effectiveness* 2(3): 310–19.

Deaton, A., and M. Grosh. 2000. "Consumption." In *Designing Household Survey Questionnaires for Developing Countries: Lessons from 15 Years of the Living Standards Measurement Study*, Vol. 3, ed. M. Grosh and P. Glewwe, 91–134. Washington, DC: World Bank.

Gibson, J. 2006. "Statistical Tools and Estimation Methods for Poverty Measures Based on Cross-Sectional Household Surveys." In *Handbook on Poverty Statistics: Concepts, Methods and Policy Use*, 128–205. New York: United Nations.

Krueger, R., and M. Casey. 2000. *Focus Groups: A Practical Guide for Applied Research*, 3rd Edition. Thousand Oaks, CA: Sage Publications.

Kumar, S. 2002. *Methods for Community Participation: A Complete Guide for Practitioners.* Rugby, Warwickshire: Practical Action.

Kusek, J., and R. Rist. 2004. *Ten Steps to a Results-Based Monitoring and Evaluation System.* Washington, DC: World Bank.

Mackay, K. 2007. *How to Build M&E Systems to Support Better Government.* Washington, DC: World Bank.

OED (Operations Evaluation Department). 2005. *Maintaining Momentum to 2015? Impact Evaluation of Interventions to Improve Maternal and Child Health and Nutrition in Bangladesh.* Washington, DC: World Bank.

Patton, M. 2008. *Utilization-Focused Evaluation*, 4th Edition. Thousand Oaks, CA: Sage Publications.

Pradhan, M., and L. Rawlings. 2002. "The Impact and Targeting of Social Infrastructure Investments: Lessons from the Nicaraguan Social Fund." *World Bank Economic Review* 16 (2): 275–95.

Pratt, C., W. McGuigan, and A. Katzeva. 2000. "Measuring Program Outcomes: Using Retrospective Pretest Methodology." *American Journal of Evaluation* 21 (3): 341–49.

Van de Walle, D. 2009. "The Poverty Impact of Rural Roads Projects." *Journal of Development Effectiveness* 1 (1): 15–36.

Vaughan, R., and T. Buss. 1998. *Communicating Social Science Research to Policy-makers.* Thousand Oaks, CA: Sage Publications.

White, H. 2006. "Impact Evaluation: Experience of the Independent Evaluation Group of the World Bank." Independent Evaluation Group, Evaluation Capacity Development Series. World Bank, Washington, DC.

Further Reading

Gorgens, M., and J. Z. Kusek. 2010. *Making Monitoring and Evaluation Systems Work: A Capacity Development Toolkit.* Washington, DC: World Bank.

Khandker, S., G. Koolwal, and H. Samad. 2009. *Handbook on Impact Evaluation: Quantitative Methods and Practices.* Washington, DC: World Bank.

Pretty, J., I. Guijt, J. Thompson, and I. Scoones. 1995. *A Trainer's Guide for Participatory Learning and Action.* London: International Institute for Environment and Development.

Silverman, D. 2004. *Qualitative Research: Theory, Method and Practice,* 2nd Edition. Thousand Oaks, CA: Sage Publications.

Teddlie, C., and A. Tashakkori. 2008. *Foundations of Mixed Methods Research: Integrating Quantitative and Qualitative Approaches in the Social and Behavioral Sciences.* Thousand Oaks, CA: Sage Publications.

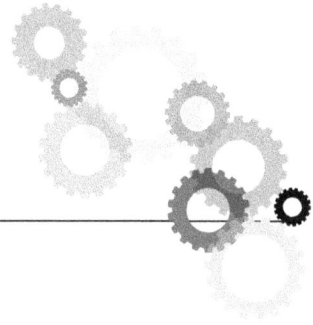

CHAPTER 11

Combining Quantitative and Qualitative Methods for Program Monitoring and Evaluation: Why Are Mixed-Method Designs Best?

Michelle Adato

Over the last decade, development programs in Latin America, Asia, and Africa have increasingly undertaken rigorous impact evaluation. Despite advances, much program monitoring and evaluation (M&E) data have limited utility because of an over-reliance on quantitative methods alone. Survey methods will tell us, for example, the rate of change in attended hospital births, while qualitative methods will explain why some women now go to hospitals to give birth while others will not, despite a program designed to

For their comments, the author thanks Laura Rawlings (Lead Social Protection Specialist, Social Protection Team), and the following members of the Poverty Reduction and Equity Group: Philipp Krause (Consultant), Gladys Lopez-Acevedo (Senior Economist), Keith Mackay (Consultant), and Jaime Saavedra (Director). The views expressed in this chapter are those of the author.

encourage their attendance. Qualitative methods also improve survey design, identify social and institutional impacts that are hard to quantify, and uncover unanticipated processes or outcomes, and trace impact pathways.

Mixed-method approaches are necessary, because whether development programs work as intended depends not only on how efficiently resources and knowledge are transferred, but also on complex economic and social dynamics in households, communities, and institutions. These dynamics cannot be disentangled through surveys alone. When used together, quantitative and qualitative approaches provide more coherent, reliable, and useful conclusions than do each on their own. This chapter provides guidance on how to combine quantitative and qualitative methods for M&E to maximize the ability to assess program performance *and* interpret and act on that information. The chapter includes examples of different mixed-method designs used in Haiti, South Africa, Nicaragua, Turkey, and Zimbabwe.

What Do Mixed-Method Evaluation Designs Offer?

Quantitative methods provide uniform measures of project outputs and impacts, for example the number of farmers trained or vaccines administered, or changes in income, crop yields, school enrollment, or child stunting. Representative sample sizes ensure that findings are generalizable among a wider population. Econometric analysis further enables inferences of causality and relationships between impacts and explanatory variables.

Quantitative methods perform less well in explaining these results, particularly when explanations involve issues that are hard to quantify, but are often fundamental to understanding program results—such as beliefs and perceptions, social relationships, administrative bottlenecks, or institutional dynamics. Qualitative methods better capture these issues because they use more flexible questions, ask for open-ended responses, thoroughly explore the topic, and promote rapport between researchers and research subjects, which results in more candid responses. Observation methods independently confirm or contradict what people say. There is, however, a trade-off between depth and breadth, and smaller sample sizes in qualitative studies mean that findings are rarely statistically representative of a broad population. Quantitative and qualitative evaluation methods compensate for each other's weaknesses, *and each approach provides more value when used in a mixed-method design,* providing information and conclusions that are more coherent, reliable, and useful than those from single-method studies.

BOX 11.1

Examples of Issues Normally Studied Through Quantitative and Qualitative Methods

Quantitative

- Household demographics
- Targeting accuracy
- Participation rates (for example, in training or services)
- Impacts (for example, on production, income, expenditure, employment, education, health, or nutrition)
- Intra-household decision making
- Service quality (for example, waiting times, availability of supplies, accuracy of rations, staff absenteeism)
- Test scores

Qualitative

- Processes in households, communities, and organizations
- Beliefs, norms, values, attitudes, social relationships
- Gender relations and women's status
- Experiences with institutions (for example, government agencies, banks, and hospitals)
- Institutional and political dynamics (for example, interdepartmental cooperation and conflict)
- Service delivery (for example, care practices and attitudes of service providers toward beneficiaries)
- Local satisfaction with program design, targeting, and administration

Some issues tend to be best addressed by either a quantitative or qualitative approach (Box 11.1). Note, however, that categories represent relative strengths for emphasis, but not a dichotomy. Each topic can potentially be addressed in different ways by quantitative and qualitative methods, yielding different types of information. Furthermore, surveys can include questions with open-ended responses, and qualitative data can be quantified.

Most importantly, the approaches work in complementary ways to address a given issue. In the evaluation of the Child Support Grant in South Africa, for example, qualitative methods identified the full range of adolescent high-risk behavior and its economic and social drivers. These were turned into survey questions and responses were carefully tailored to this program context. Furthermore, the focus groups tested a key assumption used to construct the survey's control group, tested respondent stratification and recruitment strategies, and provided data that would later help with interpretation of survey data.

Qualitative methods explain *process*. Quantitative methods can determine, for example, whether dissemination through farmers' organizations

BOX 11.2

Complementarities between Qualitative and Quantitative Methods

Qualitative methods support quantitative survey research through:

- Identifying hypotheses
- Suggesting or confirming the validity of identification strategies, constructs, proxies, assumptions, and instrumental variables
- Identifying and testing topics, questions, response options, and local meanings of language for surveys
- Identifying sampling and measurement error
- Determining the direction of causality
- Identifying unanticipated issues
- Making "unobservables" observable
- Triangulating, confirming, challenging, and explaining survey findings

Quantitative methods support qualitative methods through:

- Identifying topics and questions for investigation
- Identifying a stratification strategy and providing data for drawing a qualitative sample
- Providing background data on households, communities, and institutions
- Comparing profiles of qualitative sample communities or households with broader populations to determine degree of similarity or difference
- Testing the generalizability of qualitative findings
- Triangulating, confirming, and challenging qualitative research findings

leads to increased adoption of an agricultural technology. Qualitative methods will tell us about the social and political relationships that explain why different types of farmers join, and about formal and informal practices—factors necessary for understanding whether such organizations are likely to generate the intended outcomes under different circumstances. Such process issues "can be crucial to *understanding* impact, as opposed to simply *measuring* it" (Rao and Woolcock 2003). The study of process is also an important component of program monitoring. Studying what actually occurs during program implementation can determine whether failure to achieve intended outcomes or impact results from design failure or implementation failure (Bamberger, Rao, and Woolcock 2010).

Quantitative and qualitative methods support each other in a wide variety of ways (Box 11.2). *Triangulation* is a central function of mixed-method M&E designs: comparing quantitative and qualitative datasets to see how each one confirms, challenges, or explains the other. In the evaluation of the conditional cash transfer (CCT) program in Turkey, a survey was used to measure program impacts on attendance rates at school and health check-ups, while the qualitative research collected the full range of economic, political, and socio-cultural explanations for attendance and lack of attendance at both. The survey found, for example, that the CCT program raised secondary school enrollment for girls by 10.7 percent, but enrollment rates were still very low at the secondary level: 38.2 percent for secondary school girls nationally, and lower in some regions. The qualitative study found that socio-cultural beliefs and practices, and especially gender issues, frequently overpowered the financial incentive of the transfer. The issues hindering the success of the CCT program included the belief that women's primary roles are as wives and mothers, the perceived lack of benefits of education, and fear of girls' sexuality and male advances bringing harm to family reputation and honor, exacerbated by inadequate transportation and location of schools that were perceived to put girls at further risk. The findings explained why the CCT was successful in some contexts and not others, and the need for complementary interventions (Adato 2008).

Single-method studies do not have this ability to explain. In the evaluation of a CCT for nutrition in Brazil, the survey found a small *negative* effect of the program on children's weight gain. The evaluators speculated, based on anecdotal information, that mothers might have deliberately kept their children malnourished due to a mistaken belief that they would lose benefits if they gained weight (Morris et al. 2004). Qualitative methods could have been used to test whether this explanation—or a different one—was likely to be correct. In another example, from a study of domestic violence, a survey found a strong correlation between domestic violence and female sterilization. This would have been difficult to explain without qualitative research, which found both that sterilized women tended to be less interested in sex and that husbands became more suspicious of their fidelity due to reduced risk of pregnancy, thereby increasing the risk of violence (Rao and Woolcock 2003). Surveys may be able to further test the generalizability of some of these findings, but qualitative work is necessary to identify these pathways.

Choosing Among Methods

The most common qualitative methods used for M&E are focus groups, participatory appraisal, beneficiary/non-beneficiary interviews, key informant interviews, and observation. These can be used in rapid appraisals, spending a day to several days in a locality or program delivery setting, or as part of extended case studies and ethnographic studies spending several weeks or months in one location. Monitoring systems tend to use these methods through shorter data collection exercises at regular intervals. Which methods are selected depends in part on M&E budgets and time frames, but also on the purpose, stage of M&E at which they are used, and the types of issues to be investigated.

Focus groups and participatory appraisal tend to be best suited for broadly identifying issues and preferences. They are frequently used at early stages of evaluation design to inform the design of surveys, though they can also be used at later stages to provide data on how well a program is functioning and why. A main advantage of focus groups is that a large number of people can be included in the study in a relatively short period of time, maximizing the diversity of experiences and opinions identified while minimizing costs. Another advantage is that a group discussion can stimulate recollection and debate. Participatory appraisal methods, which combine visual exercises with discussions, provide more control and benefits to participants. The main limitations of focus groups are that there is relatively little time to establish rapport and trust, or to investigate issues in depth, and it is difficult to link the information to other datasets. People may also be less willing to discuss sensitive topics in groups (though not always), such as domestic violence or HIV, particularly with respect to their own experience. Finally, minority opinions or those of the less powerful may not be revealed: careful disaggregation of focus groups by categories such as gender, wealth, age, or ethnicity is essential for reducing this risk. Still, these are useful methods for rapid, low-cost identification of issues and for assessing beneficiary or service provider perceptions and experiences.

In-depth interviews and observations can be used at any stage of M&E to identify issues early on and—more frequently—to gather data once a program is under way. These methods allow the fieldworker to pursue a topic until it is well understood. People may be more willing to respond candidly in individual interviews, and observations enable independent confirmation. These data can then be triangulated and analyzed in relation to other individual and contextual data. In evaluation, ethnographic case study methods are sometimes used, where fieldworkers live for a period of time (for example, three to six months) in program communities. These methods permit the most reliable picture of program processes and impacts by providing the time to establish strong rapport and trust with program stakeholders, conduct iterative sets of interviews, and observe household, community, and program interactions and key activities over time. These methods are, however, more time- and resource-intensive compared to focus group methods, and sample sizes are normally smaller.

Key informant interviews are essential for M&E, gathering the knowledge of program officials and staff, service delivery professionals, community leaders, business owners, contractors, and other stakeholders. Key informant interviews provide information and analysis based on day-to-day observations of the program. Another mixed-method approach, particularly valuable for operations or process M&E, are systematic observations of service delivery, combining quantitative instruments to record and rate observed conditions and practices with qualitative interviews and observations.

Key Issues in Mixed-Method Designs

Sequencing of methods. Although sequencing can be done in various ways, a best practice evaluation design might proceed as follows. The evaluation starts with qualitative methods to identify key issues and gather information to inform survey design. This is followed by the baseline survey. The survey data are used to design and select the sample for a new stage of qualitative research and to identify issues for investigation—such as impact findings that need explanation. Following this qualitative study, an evaluation survey mirrors the baseline, but adds new questions identified in the qualitative study. Depending on the length of the program, resources, and needs, additional rounds may follow. For program monitoring, a subset of quantitative indicators and qualitative data can be collected at regular intervals, maintaining common indicators but also adapting indicators based on new findings. Many governments invest substantial resources in monitoring systems that collect large quantities of quantitative data that reflect expected outputs. They typically do not explain the reasons for good or poor performance, which limits the ability to respond. Complementary use of qualitative methods in monitoring systems can help provide these explanations and identify unanticipated issues and outcomes.

Site and household selection. While some qualitative studies involve a convenience sample of locations or households, a more rigorous approach uses survey data to stratify qualitative samples. The qualitative sample would then reflect characteristics of the quantitative sample. Within these stratified categories, households or individuals are often selected *purposively* to ensure inclusion of households across the distribution; if a random sample is used, the sample should be large enough to capture this distribution. In an evaluation of an agro-forestry intervention in Kenya, for example, survey data were used to select a sample of households for qualitative case studies that captured Luo and Luhya ethnic groups; male- and female-headed households; richer and poorer farmers; and agro-forestry early adopters, late adopters, non-adopters, and "dis-adopters" (Place, Adato, and Hebinck 2007). In evaluations of CCT programs in Turkey, Nicaragua, and El Salvador, survey data were used to stratify the qualitative sample between households where children performed well and poorly on the key education and health indicators targeted by the program. In this way, the qualitative research could investigate the conditions and characteristics that explained this different performance, with and without the program (Adato 2008).

Data analysis and integration. Many M&E systems that collect quantitative and qualitative data fail to take advantage of their synergies. For example, data from alternating rounds of surveys and qualitative research are not always used to inform the questions for the alternating next round. Even more common is the failure to triangulate and integrate the findings at the analysis stage—thus losing much of the principle analytic power of mixed-method designs. Under the typical time pressure to complete evaluation or monitoring reports, data are analyzed and reported separately. It is critical that data integration becomes a priority, and that the time and resources needed for data integration at the analysis stage are included in the budget.

What Do We Learn? Findings from Mixed-Method M&E

Examples of mixed-method M&E from three countries are outlined in this section, illustrating the different purposes, designs, and methods discussed above.

Monitoring a food-assisted maternal and child health and nutrition program in Haiti

An operations research approach was used for the M&E system for World Vision's food-assisted maternal and child health and nutrition program in Haiti (Loechl et al. 2005). The objectives were to assess the implementation of service delivery, identify constraints to effective operation, and implement corrective actions. The quantitative method used was structured observations at program delivery points. The qualitative methods were structured and semi-structured interviews with stakeholders and focus group discussions with the program staff. The service delivery points were: rally posts, where targeting, health education and services, and growth monitoring and promotion took place; mothers' clubs, where smaller groups of participants gathered to discuss health and nutrition topics; and food distribution points, where beneficiaries received monthly food rations. Selected findings from the service delivery points include:

Rally posts. These were found to be operating as planned; however, problems identified included crowding, a high participant/staff ratio, long waiting times, bottlenecks at registration, and the lack of supplies and transport for staff. Improvements were needed in the general education sessions and the communication between health staff and caregivers. Measurement errors were also identified in weighing and plotting children's weight on the growth chart; this was a critical area because the growth charts were used for targeting children for recuperative action.

Mothers' clubs. These were found to be highly popular among health staff and beneficiaries. A new behavior change and communication strategy and new materials and techniques were recently developed to improve infant and young child feeding practices. The mixed-method approach enabled an objective assessment of the technical content of the sessions and health staff's facilitation and teaching skills, which were found to have improved. However, ensuring the intended composition of the clubs was identified as an ongoing challenge, and continued supervision and retraining of the staff was recommended.

Food distribution points (FDPs). Observations of the FDPs identified excessive crowding and long waiting times, delays in arrival of the food and staff, and the reasons for these problems: bad road conditions, limited transport facilities, and fuel scarcity. Exit interviews revealed that a large proportion of beneficiaries did not receive the amount of food commodities they were entitled to. The sharing of food commodities among other relatives, neighbors, and others was reported to be widespread. This was determined to be inevitable, and it was recommended that an additional indirect ration be provided to cover this, and that the program should continue to emphasize the use of fortified commodities with micronutrient content targeted to beneficiaries, especially young children.

After implementation of the recommendations, a new round of operations research was conducted to monitor the corrective measures and document improvements in the program.

Evaluation of the conditional cash transfer program in Nicaragua

The evaluation of the CCT in Nicaragua (Adato 2008) involved baseline and follow-up panel surveys with 1,359 households, conducted in 42 administrative units (*comarcas*) with and without the program. Survey data were later used to stratify households by high and low performance in health and education indicators, with a qualitative sample drawn from each category. In total, 120 households were included in the qualitative study in Nicaragua. Fieldworkers lived in the study communities for approximately four months, conducting interviews about program experiences and impacts and people's attitudes and behavior, and observing meal preparation, health and hygiene practices, shopping, beneficiary and community gatherings, health service delivery, health and nutrition education, and other program activities. Some of the benefits of this mixed-methods design are outlined below.

Targeting. The survey found that the program was well targeted, with under-coverage rates of 3 to 10 percent. The qualitative research found, however, that people saw themselves as "all poor" and did not understand why households were selected into or out of the program, resulting in several types of stress and tension in the communities. This led to recommendations to improve program communications and to provide some limited benefits to non-beneficiary households.

Iron supplements. The survey found a large increase in the percentage of children receiving iron supplements: from under 25 percent to nearly 80 percent. However, it found no impact on the high anemia rates in this population. In initial interviews in the qualitative research, mothers said that they gave the supplements to their children. However, over time, the case study methods revealed a different picture: mothers were picking up the supplements but not giving them to their children because of the perception that iron negatively affected children's stomachs and teeth.

"Stuffing" children before weighing. In the first phase of the program, if children twice fell below an established rate of weight gain, benefits could be suspended. Although this policy was dropped, many beneficiaries did not know this. The study found that to avoid losing benefits, some mothers were stuffing their children with food and liquids on the day or days leading up to the weighing. This revealed important information about poorly conceived incentives, as well as the impact of inadequate communications.

Program impacts on gender relations. Concerns have been raised that giving cash transfers to women could cause tensions with their male partners, possibly contributing to domestic violence. The qualitative research was able to explore this delicate topic, but found that men largely supported women receiving the benefit, because they saw the CCT program as for children and believed that women would spend it more wisely. Furthermore, the new resources in households helped to ease tensions. It also found that the program's discourse on women's empowerment and women's receipt of the cash increased their self-confidence and gave them some new autonomy in certain spending decisions.

Evaluation of high yielding maize varieties in Zimbabwe

This evaluation (Bourdillon and others 2007) used data from a panel survey conducted in resettlement areas from 1983 to 1984, 1987, and annually from 1992 to 2000. The surveys contained extensive information on agricultural and non-farm activities, expenditure, assets, and other impacts. Qualitative household case studies, focus groups, and key informant interviews were conducted during a six-month period of fieldwork in 2001. Findings include:

Gender relations and intra-household resource control. Despite a modest reduction in household-level poverty, benefits to men from high yielding varieties (HYVs) of maize undermined women's control of resources. Whereas men operated within the public commercial markets for HYV maize, women preferred the open-pollinated varieties (OPVs), which HYV maize had displaced, because OPV seeds and maize were marketed through informal networks where women operated. Women also did not have access to credit for the commercial fertilizer necessary for HYV maize but not for OPVs. Although money from the sale of HYV maize was called "family money," the qualitative research revealed that "family money" was really the household head's money, kept in his bank account. This family money was often invested in cattle (traditionally male property), and in one case study a woman explained her fear that if her husband died, his relatives would take the cattle away and she would be left with nothing.

The significance of age for extension approaches. The qualitative research revealed generational differences in how farmers value knowledge. Young people trusted the knowledge of the national extension service officers, viewing them as trained and experienced. In contrast, older people trusted their own experiences and demonstration units. Cultural values and beliefs attributed wisdom to age, and older men especially found it hard to admit to limitations in their knowledge, preferring their own practical knowledge to theoretical knowledge.

Culture and magic. In the case study communities, there was widespread belief in the effect of witchcraft on crop performance. People frequently attributed magical powers to those who achieved unusually high yields, and poor yields to theft of crops through witchcraft. In one resettlement area, people would not show interest in the crops of others, because observing how others grew their crops could arouse suspicions of witchcraft. In another area, there was a widespread belief that implements or animals lent to other farmers could be returned bewitched. This had important implications for farmer-to-farmer methods of dissemination and extension, and the expectation that farmers "learn from each other."

Conclusions

Although mixed methods are widely used by governments and international agencies, there are a number of reasons why it is still common to find single-method approaches. The high cost of survey research means that decisions are often made to allocate an entire evaluation budget to a single approach. Second, timelines are often perceived as too tight for iterative rounds of data collection. Third, researchers are usually trained in one approach—quantitative or qualitative—and do not sufficiently understand or appreciate the methods and value of the other. However, research designs can be adapted to fit a given set of conditions, and the benefits are likely to far exceed the costs. Still, it is important to recognize that the open-ended nature of qualitative research methods requires a considerable degree of skill on the part of field researchers to obtain quality data, and that sufficient resources are needed to ensure a strong research design, a sample size large enough to capture heterogeneity, adequate time for fieldwork, and the systematic analysis and integration of data. If both quantitative and qualitative research are undertaken with rigor, then mixed-method M&E will result in a far better understanding of program results than either approach alone. This level of understanding is critical to provide effective feedback that will improve performance and enable programs to meet their goals.

Bibliography

Adato, M. 2008. "Combining Survey and Ethnographic Methods to Improve Evaluation of Conditional Cash Transfer Programs." *International Journal of Multiple Research Approaches* (2): 222–36.

Bamberger, M., V. Rao, and M. Woolcock. 2010. "Using Mixed Methods in Monitoring and Evaluation: Experiences from International Development." Policy Research Working Paper 5245, World Bank, Washington, DC.

Bourdillon, M. F. C., P. Hebinck, and J. Hoddinott, with B. Kinsey, J. Marondo, N. Mudege, and T. Owens. 2007. "Assessing the Impact of High-Yield Varieties of Maize in Resettlement Areas of Zimbabwe." In *Agricultural Research, Livelihoods and Poverty: Studies of Economic and Social Impacts in Six Countries*, ed. M. Adato and R. Meinzen-Dick, chapter 6. Baltimore, MD: Johns Hopkins University Press.

Loechl, C., M. T. Ruel, G. Pelto, and P. Menon. 2005. "The Use of Operations Research as a Tool for Monitoring and Managing Food-Assisted Maternal/ Child Health and Nutrition (MCHN) Programs: An Example from Haiti." FCND Discussion Paper 187, International Food Policy Research Institute, Washington, DC.

Morris, S., P. Olinto, R. Flores, E. Nilson, and A. Figueiró. 2004. "Conditional Cash Transfers Are Associated with a Small Reduction in Weight Gain of Preschool Children in Northeast Brazil." *Journal of Nutrition* 134 (9): 2336–41.

Place, F., M. Adato, and P. Hebinck. 2007. "Understanding Rural Poverty and Investment in Agriculture: An Assessment of Integrated Quantitative and Qualitative Research in Western Kenya." *World Development* 35 (2) 312–25.

Rao, V., and M. Woolcock. 2003. "Integrating Qualitative and Quantitative Approaches in Program Evaluation." In *The Impact of Economic Policies on Poverty and Income Distribution: Evaluation Tools and Techniques,* ed. F. Bourguignon and L. A. Pereira da Silva, 165–90. Washington, DC: World Bank.

Further Reading

Adato, M., R. Meinzen-Dick, P. Hazell, and L. Haddad. 2007. "Studying Poverty Impact Using Livelihoods Analysis and Quantitative Methods: Conceptual Frameworks and Research Methods." In *Agricultural Research, Livelihoods and Poverty: Studies of Economic and Social Impacts in Six Countries,* ed. M. Adato and R. Meinzen-Dick, pp. 20–55. Baltimore, MD: Johns Hopkins University Press.

Kanbur, R., ed. 2003. *Q-Squared: Qualitative and Quantitative Methods of Poverty Appraisal.* New Delhi: Permanent Black.

Maluccio, J., M. Adato, and E. Skoufias. 2010. "Combining Quantitative and Qualitative Research Methods for the Evaluation of Conditional Cash Transfer Programs." In *Conditional Cash Transfers in Latin America,* ed. M. Adato and J. Hoddinott, pp. 26–52. Baltimore, MD: Johns Hopkins University Press.

Plano Clark, V. L., and J. W. Creswell, eds. 2008. *The Mixed-Methods Reader.* Thousand Oaks, CA: Sage Publications.

PART III

M&E Systems in Context

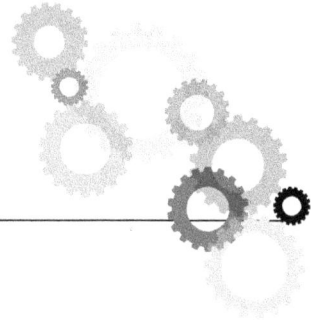

CHAPTER 12

The Mexican Government's M&E System

Gloria M. Rubio

Fifteen years ago, Mexico, like most countries, had conducted a few scattered evaluations, but had not implemented systematic performance measurement. Political changes in the late 1990s generated an increased demand for transparency and accountability. These changes led to new legislation and institutions aimed at strengthening independent government oversight through several channels, including external evaluations, public access to information, and the creation of a supreme audit institution (Figure 12.1). Also in the late 1990s, Mexico implemented Oportunidades,[1] an innovative conditional cash transfer program with a rigorous impact evaluation built into its operational design. The program's evaluation component became a role model within the Mexican public administration.

The development of a monitoring and evaluation (M&E) system in Mexico can be divided into two stages. The first phase, from 2000 to 2006, was characterized by good intentions, but a limited vision on the institutional

The author thanks Amparo Ballivian (Lead Economist, LCSPP), Philipp Krause (Consultant, Poverty Reduction and Equity Unit [PRMPR]), Gladys Lopez-Acevedo (Senior Economist, PRMPR), and Keith Mackay (Consultant, PRMPR) for their comments. The views expressed in this chapter are those of the author.

167

FIGURE 12.1 M&E Legal Framework

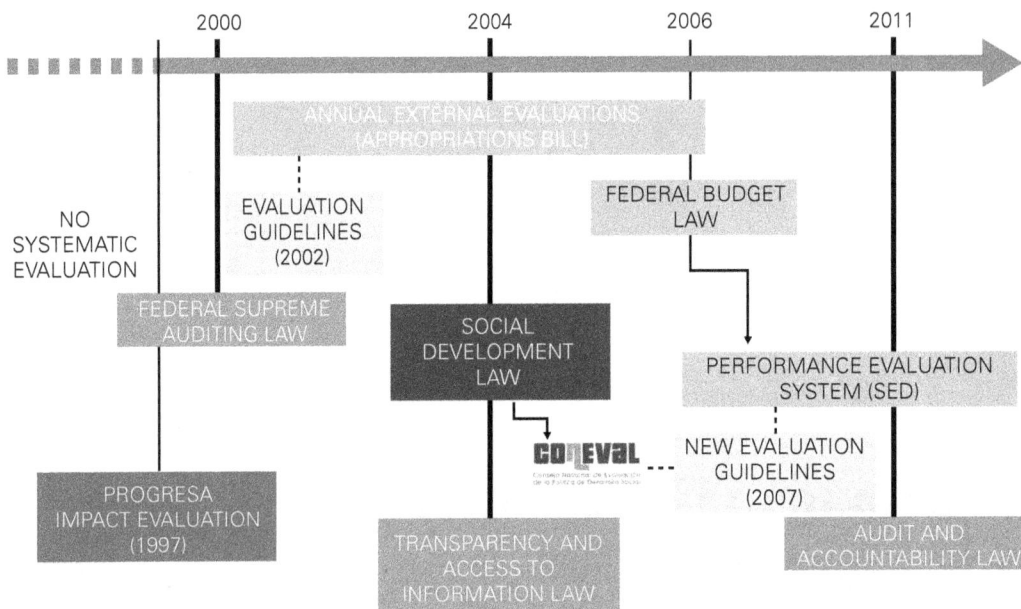

Source: Adapted from Rubio, 2009.

capacity building required for the new evaluation efforts. The budget law compelled federal programs involving subsidies, cash or in-kind transfers, and some infrastructure, health, and education services to carry out annual external evaluations. This requirement provided the necessary push to start systematic evaluation in Mexico. However, it also implied that ministries with incipient experience in this area had to prepare terms of reference, identify institutions capable of conducting evaluations, and supervise their work. At the time, evaluation guidelines did not distinguish between different types of evaluations. Nonetheless, annual external evaluations were expected to address questions ranging from compliance with operation rules, to program impact, to program cost-benefit. This was an overwhelming task given the nascent institutional capacity on both the demand (ministries) and the supply (universities and research institutions) sides.

Despite the overall implementation shortcomings in this period, some ministries made substantial progress in developing sectoral M&E systems. For example, key champions at the Ministry of Social Development (*Secretaría de Desarrollo Social* [SEDESOL]) embraced the M&E agenda. SEDESOL reorganized to create a deputy minister office in charge of planning, analysis, and evaluation, and invested in setting up an adequately staffed and resourced evaluation unit. Following the Oportunidades example and encouraged by the growing evidence-based approach of many professionals in the field, key champions in SEDESOL promoted the use of impact evaluation methodologies in a number of social development programs. They also supported the implementation of various innovations, including the use of logical frameworks and an evaluation feedback mechanism. Furthermore, the key champions participated in pushing legislation institutionalizing evaluation and creating the National Evaluation Council (*Consejo Nacional de Evaluación* [CONEVAL]), an autonomous institution in charge of social program evaluation and poverty measurement.

M&E during the first phase lacked the incentives and institutional arrangements to ensure the use of the findings. More than 500 external evaluations were conducted in this period, but very little of that information was effectively used (Castro et al. 2009). Since the driving force behind M&E was transparency and accountability, there was little attention to the role that evaluation could play in improving government programs. Congress, the Ministry of Finance (*Secretaría de Hacienda y Crédito Público* [SHCP]), and the Ministry of Public Management (*Secretaría de la Función Pública* [SFP]) were the main recipients of the evaluation reports.

The 2006 Federal Budget and Fiscal Responsibility Law established a governmentwide performance evaluation system. This legislation, coupled with a change in administration,[2] provided a new impetus to implement the M&E system. Fiscal concerns increased SHCP interest in promoting public expenditure efficiency and effectiveness. In addition, international experiences from Chile and other Organisation for Economic Co-operation and Development (OECD) countries, along with policy dialogue with multilateral institutions, motivated SHCP to renew efforts to incorporate the performance dimension in the budgeting process.

A key factor leading to the second phase of the M&E system implementation (2007 to present) has been the strategic partnership between SHCP and CONEVAL. The former had the mandate to implement a performance-based budget, but its experience in M&E was limited, while the latter had substantial M&E technical expertise, but no "stick" to ensure that ministries outside the social sector participated in the system. The combination of forces has led to a federal governmentwide M&E system with much better chances of sustained utilization.

In 2007, CONEVAL, SHCP, and SFP jointly issued a revised set of evaluation guidelines that introduced technical criteria for regulating M&E activities and allowed a more selective and strategic approach. Moreover, the guidelines established mechanisms to ensure evaluation quality and utilization, such as standardized terms of reference, uniform procedures to select performance indicators, creation of evaluation counterparts in line ministries, and a systematic feedback mechanism.

Mexico's Performance Evaluation System

M&E in Mexico has gradually evolved into the Performance Evaluation System (*Sistema de Evaluación del Desempeño* [SED]). SED's main purpose is to assess progress in meeting policy and program objectives to inform the performance-based budgeting decision-making process. It also aims at strengthening transparency and accountability. The scope of the system covers federal government spending by executive branch agencies and federally funded programs administered at the local level. This limits the influence of the government performance focus, since the legislature, judiciary, and autonomous agencies, as well as state and municipal-level spending, are not required to participate.[3] SED has three main components: performance indicator monitoring, evaluation, and a feedback mechanism.[4]

Performance indicator monitoring

Performance indicator monitoring has been part of the M&E system since the late 1990s. However, it was initially a challenging exercise. There were multiple overlaps of indicator reporting demands from different actors including SHCP, SFP, and the presidency. The focus of these indicators on outcomes was limited. There was no clear understanding of the difference between process, output, and outcome indicators. Moreover, data quality standards were absent, resulting in different values for the same indicator. Finally, although it had some application for accountability purposes, indicator monitoring was not relevant for decision making.

Since 2007, SED has required programs to identify performance indicators through a logical framework methodology (matrix of indicators for results [MIR]). MIRs are reported regularly through the SED informatics platform. This information is an input for annual performance evaluations. Moreover, a subset of MIR is submitted to Congress as part of the budget request. This subset is reported to Congress quarterly during the fiscal year and included in the federal government final accounts and Government Activities Report.

The logical framework methodology was adopted to provide a unified framework for program planning, monitoring, and evaluation to standardize results measurement. Also, it was expected that the process of building the framework would help improve consistency and quality in program design.

In practice, however, SHCP and line ministry budget officials have struggled to take full advantage of the fairly comprehensive performance measurement provided by the framework, given the need to report quarterly a manageable number of indicators. Thus, programs are often discouraged from registering in SED a broader set of indicators that may take longer—one year or more—to be measured, even if they are necessary to fully account for program outcomes. Another difficulty with SED is setting meaningful targets for indicators resulting from strategic planning exercises. According to the 2008 specific performance evaluation, around 20 percent of indicators achieved levels that were 20 percent higher than the established target value. This raises questions about the merit of the target setting process.

Evaluation

Evaluation has struggled to balance the demand for accountability for all programs and the need to selectively and strategically apply different analytical tools to respond to specific policy questions. After an ambitious start in which evaluations were expected to assess program operation, impact, cost-benefit, and client satisfaction every year, the revised evaluation guidelines introduced an Annual Evaluation Program (*Programa Anual de Evaluación* [PAE]) and a menu of evaluation tools. Each year PAE specifies which evaluation tools will be applied to which programs. Evaluation tools are selected from a comprehensive menu addressing a broad range of policy questions including program design, operation, impact, and overall performance (Box 12.1). The menu of evaluation tools includes various alternatives in terms of purpose, audience, and duration. For example, specific performance evaluations provide rapid feedback for annual program assessment. Impact evaluations require a longer implementation period but respond to more strategic policy questions. The menu also includes the possibility of analyzing strategies, policies, and institutions.

The selection of programs and evaluation tools is made jointly by CONEVAL, SHCP, and SFP by considering programs' relevance, particular policy interest, and previous evaluation results. Ministries can also propose additional evaluations to support policy or management decisions or to get specific program performance information.

Despite the progress made in promoting a more sensible application of evaluation, legislation still requires annual external evaluations of all social programs. This entails a number of challenges: first, development of a low-cost evaluation tool that provides rapid feedback, yet is informative; second, identification of objective and technically sound evaluators to conduct over 100 evaluations every year; third, an organizational structure capable of

BOX 12.1
Menu of Evaluations

Design evaluation is conducted on programs that are in their first year of implementation. The evaluation assesses if a program makes a clear contribution to the solution of a particular policy problem and if the objectives of the program are clearly defined and aligned with the strategic objectives of its ministry. Moreover, it analyzes to what extent there is a sound and evidence-based results chain behind program design. This evaluation only uses secondary information and involves no original data collection. It is mandatory for all new programs and is targeted to inform program managers, budget officials, and other ministry staff. The assessment goal is to identify early on any potential problems or flaws in program design, thereby increasing the effectiveness of interventions. This assessment is also expected to clarify how a new program will add to existing policies, thereby reducing the likelihood of duplication.

Process evaluation appraises the efficiency and efficacy of a program's operational processes and provides feedback for improvement. It allows program managers to identify bottlenecks in the program's service delivery mechanisms and leads to improvements in the program's operation, which then benefit the target population. As such, it should play an important role in providing explanations for low performance. The process evaluation is implemented on a case-by-case basis and is targeted for use by program managers, budget officials, and other ministry staff.

Program consistency and results evaluation is a rapid assessment used to obtain a general and comparative perspective of a program's de-

sign, strategic planning, coverage and targeting mechanisms, operation, beneficiary perception, and results. It is used to highlight specific strengths and weaknesses and to motivate decision makers to consider which of these should be evaluated in a more rigorous way, using the other methods. This type of evaluation only uses secondary information and involves no original data collection. It is targeted at a broad range of users, including program managers, high-level decision makers, and the general public.

Impact evaluation seeks to measure changes in the conditions of well-being of the target population that are attributable to a specific program. This type of evaluation provides the most technically robust evidence about whether a program is working or not. As such, its purpose is to inform high-level officials on whether a program should be continued or not, or if any potential modifications are needed. This kind of evaluation is implemented on a case-by-case basis and is targeted toward more executive levels of government, although it does provide useful information to program managers and all kinds of government officials.

Specific performance evaluation is a rapid assessment of program progress in meeting objectives and annual goals. This type of evaluation analyzes program coverage, MIR monitoring data entered in the SED, as well as progress on implementing previous evaluations' recommendations. It is implemented annually for all federal programs and is mainly for the review of Congress, executive levels of government, budget officials, and the general public.

Source: Updated from Castro et al. (2009).

planning and implementing such a large number of evaluations; and last but not least, a formal process to ensure that evaluation results feed back into policy making.

Feedback mechanism

SED established a feedback mechanism in 2008. Following the completion of annual evaluations, program managers, along with planning, evaluation, and budget units within ministries, are required to prepare an evaluation response document. The document should identify issues for program improvement based on evaluation recommendations and classify them according to the actors involved in their solution (program operation unit, ministry, several ministries, and different government levels) and their relevance in achieving program objectives. In addition, each ministry should develop a two-level (program and institution) implementation plan to deal with evaluation recommendations that can be addressed at the program operation unit and at the ministry level. These plans should outline the improvement actions, the officials responsible for them, and their timeline. They should be published on the ministry's Web site with the evaluation reports.[5]

Undoubtedly, this mechanism has helped evaluations get the attention of program managers as well as other key actors. Moreover, by requiring an institutional plan, it forces ministries to consider sector-wide issues that cannot be addressed at the program level. However, program managers or ministries often commit to addressing the easier-to-solve problems only. They tend to dismiss evaluation findings involving major changes as invalid or unfeasible. Furthermore, although annual performance evaluations should assess the progress in carrying out improvements, this is only a mild incentive to follow up the implementation plan.

Institutional Setup

SED institutional arrangements result from the parallel efforts to promote M&E. In practice, SED is coordinated by SHCP with technical advice from CONEVAL, and some participation by SFP (Figure 12.2).[6] Institution-specific roles and responsibilities have been shaped ad hoc by their broader mandate and technical capacities. Hence, CONEVAL autonomy and academic expertise lend to providing technical leadership in defining the scope, methodologies, and processes of SED evaluation and feedback activities (Box 12.2). Moreover, CONEVAL is responsible for evaluating social sector programs and ensuring that results feed back into policy making. SHCP is in

FIGURE 12.2 SED Institutional Arrangements

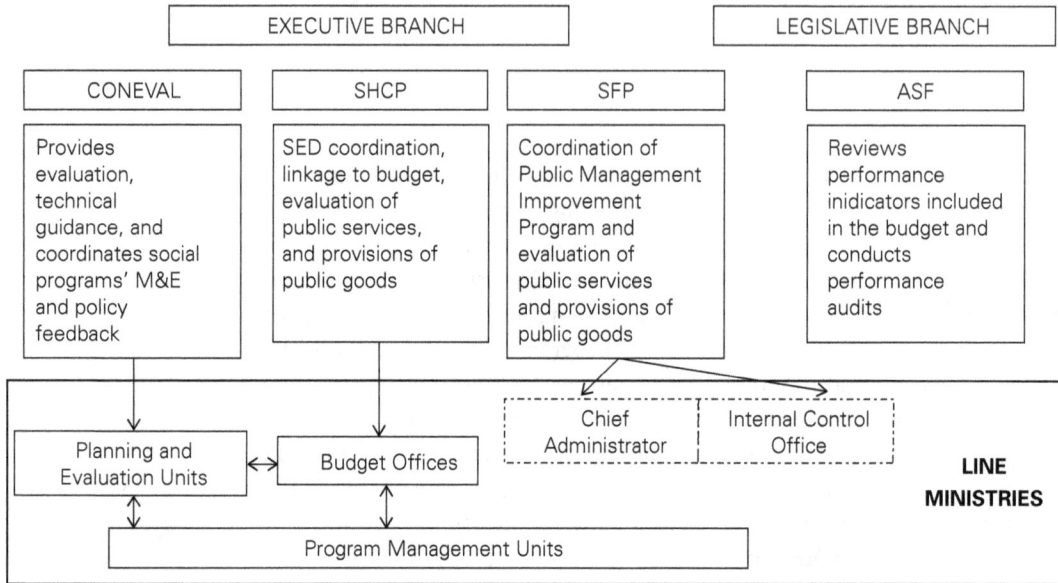

Source: Author's compilation.

charge of the performance-based budgeting initiative. It coordinates performance monitoring activities and, in principle, ensures that this information is used for the budgetary decision-making process. SFP participation is less well-defined: although it has the mandate to coordinate the internal government M&E system, in fact its main focus on oversight has narrowed its perspective on the best way to contribute to SED.[7]

SED institutional arrangements pose some challenges. The fragmented institutional responsibility for different sectors and activities is a potential source of coordination problems (OECD 2009). SHCP's coordinating role is critical in linking M&E with planning and budgeting. However, SFP participation in SED coordination has yet to be thought-out. Moreover, the fact that CONEVAL responsibility is limited to the social sector hinders the even progress of SED implementation across the public administration. Although SED has benefited from CONEVAL's technical guidance, evaluation implementation outside the social sector still lags.

Other key players are the SED counterparts in the line ministries. Traditionally, SHCP's liaison with line ministries is the Budget Office, which is responsible for implementing the performance-based budgeting process. In addition, administrative units in charge of coordinating the contracting, im-

The National Evaluation Council for Social Development Policy—CONEVAL

CONEVAL is the lynchpin of the social sector M&E system in Mexico. CONEVAL coordinates evaluation activities, sets standards and methodologies for the evaluation of social programs, develops evaluation terms of reference, provides technical assistance to ministries and agencies, and undertakes or manages some specific evaluations. It also coordinates with development organizations to plan and undertake evaluation work and to advise national entities and sub-national governments in the implementation of their M&E systems, as well as on how to conduct quality program evaluations.

In addition, CONEVAL prepares and consolidates evaluation reports and disseminates the evaluation findings among Congress, government agencies, and civil society. To accomplish these tasks, CONEVAL has a staff of 73 professionals, including administrative personnel, and for 2011 has an annual budget of about Mex$155 million (US$12.4 million).

One particular feature that deserves attention is the mixed nature of CONEVAL, which is a relatively independent government agency with a unique governance structure. Although it is located within the executive branch and its executive director is appointed by the federal government, leadership of CONEVAL relies on an independent collegiate body made up of six academic advisers chosen from certified academic institutions. They are democratically elected for a period of four years by members of the National Social Development Commission, which includes 32 state government officials responsible for social development, the presidents of the Senate and the House of Representatives Social Development Committees, representatives of the national municipal governments' associations, and the heads of federal government ministries responsible for social development, education, health, agriculture, labor, and environment. The councilors are involved in all of the agency's decisions and the definition and review of evaluation projects. They also provide general guidance on the administrative direction of the institution and play an important role in the methodologies for poverty measurement.

Source: Updated from Castro et al. (2009).

plementation, supervision, and feedback of evaluations within line ministries were introduced in 2007. These units are separate from program operation and their purpose is to ensure that evaluation work within each ministry is conducted independently and with the necessary human and financial resources. Finally, program operating units have the duty of reporting performance information, providing data needed for evaluation, and implementing evaluation recommendations.[8]

SED implementation is complemented by congressional budget oversight through the Federal Supreme Audit (*Auditoría Superior de la Feder-*

ación [ASF]). ASF conducts performance audits to assess program progress in meeting objectives and goals and generate recommendations to improve government results. It also reviews performance indicators included in the budget.

Extent of SED Utilization

SED's implementation progress is to a large extent the result of the combination of the M&E legal framework and the public administration's strong legalistic tradition that provides the incentives to comply with SED requirements. However, sustained SED use depends on shifting to a performance management and evidence-based policy-making culture throughout government. This cultural shift is still in the making, but at least a great deal of attention has been placed on identifying relevant outlets for SED information and formalizing feedback mechanisms. Established procedures feed M&E information back into decision-making processes in four areas. A pending task in SED implementation is to systematically monitor and publish budget and program or policy decisions informed by M&E information.

1. At the program level, the feedback mechanism described earlier provides the connection between evaluation recommendations and program design and operation. At the end of the 2009 evaluation exercise, CONEVAL reported that 78 percent of programs had clearly defined areas for improvement based on evaluation recommendations and a plan to address them. Programs identified on average six subjects for improvement. Most of them are design or operational issues that can be addressed at the program level, and more than half were considered a high priority for achieving program objectives. Upcoming results from the 2010 evaluation should reveal to what extent programs followed the improvement plans.

2. In the budgeting process, the use of evaluation findings is fostered by SHCP through the implementation of performance-based budgeting. With the incumbent administration, the Office of the Presidency has also played a key role in supporting this process by considering performance information when signaling budget priorities and agreeing on total ministry budget ceilings. In preparation for the 2009 budget and building on the logical framework exercise, SHCP analysts discussed with their counterparts in line ministries the progress made in the previous year's performance indicators and proposed indicators and targets for the following year. This information was combined with the ministries' self-assessment

TABLE 12.1 Examples of Use of Evaluation Findings in the 2009 Budget Preparation

Programs	Evaluation findings	2009 Budget
1. Community model for *mestizo* population education	– Need to improve program planning	Programs were merged into a single intervention: Initial and Basic Education for Rural Indigenous Population
2. Community model for indigenous and migrant populations' education	– Duplication of efforts; a single, unified design suggested	
3. Training support	– Limited job skills generation	Program was substituted by a new intervention focused on supporting productivity
4. Efficient use of water and electricity	– Same target population and similar components	Programs were integrated into a new single intervention: Modernization and Technical Improvement of Irrigation Units
5. Hydroagricultural infrastructure use	– Merging would simplify administrative structure and improve monitoring	

Source: Adapted from Castro et al. (2009).

and a traffic light system developed by CONEVAL, using the 2007 Consistency and Results Evaluation, to create a summary picture of the performance of programs and ministries. SHCP top political officials met with the presidency to discuss budget ceilings for each ministry considering fiscal priorities and performance summaries. Anecdotal evidence suggests that a few programs received additional resources for performing well (OECD 2009). In addition, there are some examples of program improvements informed by evaluation findings (Table 12.1).

3. In social policy decision making, CONEVAL presents summary reports of cross-cutting issues revealed by evaluations to the Interministerial and the National Social Development Commissions. These commissions are in charge of coordinating social policy within the federal government and the national level, respectively. For example, some of the 2009 recommendations include implementing at the local level a maintenance scheme of social infrastructure financed by federal programs; simplifying and harmonizing administrative processes across ministries to speed up project approval; and clarifying the role of state and municipal governments in cofinancing and operating federal programs.

4. In congressional budget oversight, ASF revises program performance indicators and issues an official report on their consistency, with binding recommendations for the programs. Unfortunately, the ASF annual report does not summarize the nature of performance audit recommendations or their follow up.

In addition, national media regularly use evaluation and poverty measurement results published by CONEVAL. There are also some examples of civil society organizations beginning to use evaluation findings as a way to exert public influence.

The Sustainability of the M&E System

Efforts to introduce M&E activities have been continuous since the late 1990s. The first attempts to conduct performance M&E started more than a decade ago and continue today. However, the comprehensiveness and suitability as well as the institutional arrangements of the M&E initiatives have varied considerably across the three different administrations governing the country during this period. Although there is still a long way to go in building a successful M&E system, so far the trend has been positive. One explanation for this favorable evolution is the combination of local demand for transparency and accountability and the existing capacity and external technical assistance available from a global trend on performance management.

Nonetheless, the jury is still out on M&E system sustainability, particularly in the case of a change in the governing party. Enabling elements for continuity in building an M&E system include a fairly solid legal framework. Moreover, demand from civil society and Congress for accountability and performance measurement does not seem to be fading away, and the economic and political economy factors that contributed to this demand remain valid and are likely to persist. Furthermore, to the extent that the civil service continues to operate adequately, some public servants who have experienced the change in the way government business is conducted could contribute to sustaining the new evaluation culture. Finally, an encouraging sign is the growing development of M&E initiatives at the state level. A number of states, regardless of their governing party, have created M&E institutions and systems resembling CONEVAL and SED.

A number of risk factors threaten the continuity of the positive trend in building and sustaining the M&E system beyond 2012. First, although some degree of M&E institutionalization has been achieved, progress to date has relied heavily on key champions in the presidency, CONEVAL, line ministries, and SHCP. Many of them are unlikely to remain in office another term. Second, Congress has not fully come to grips with the need of the executive branch to have a strong M&E system that supports its management decisions. Congress tends to favor the view of M&E as an accountability tool that should be in the hands of control and oversight entities such as ASF or SFP.

This is a potential threat to SED credibility and its institutional setup. Finally, it is inevitable that new administrations will want to make their mark in policy making. In some cases, changes may be merely cosmetic or even improve the system. However, there are also examples from members of the Organisation for Economic Co-operation and Development (OECD) of well-functioning M&E activities or systems that have suffered changes compromising effectiveness when a new administration takes over. Hence, the challenge will be to adapt the system to the new administration's vision while retaining the soundness of the critical elements.

Lessons Learned and Challenges Ahead

SED is the result of a confluence of several factors over time that have led to a federal M&E system. Political economy changes since the late 1990s have increased the local demand for accountability and transparency, thus producing a legal framework promoting M&E. During the early stages, the political and technical leadership of key champions helped pilot M&E activities and created crucial institutions such as CONEVAL. Sectoral experience served as an example to design and implement a national M&E system to support a renewed performance-based budgeting initiative. Performance-based budgeting was motivated by fiscal concerns and OECD country experiences. Here again, key champions in SHCP, the presidency, and CONEVAL promoted the application of sound M&E tools and the use of results in budget and policy decisions.

Policy dialogue and external technical assistance from different institutions, including the Economic Commission for Latin America (ECLAC), the Inter-American Development Bank (IDB), the OECD, and the World Bank, have played a key role in strengthening institutional M&E capacity. In particular, external support has been critical in generating momentum for reforms, ensuring continuous training, learning from other country experiences, and getting access to top-notch technical advice. For example, the World Bank supported SEDESOL through an Institutional Development Fund grant to design and implement a sectoral results-based M&E system. ECLAC technical assistance helped introduce the use of the logical framework methodology, first in the ministry and then across government as part of SED. SHCP benefited from technical assistance and a grant from IDB.

Mexico's well-trained public service has facilitated SED implementation. In addition, sustained capacity building through constant training has helped overcome limited experience with some M&E methodologies. Continuous training also contributed to maintaining institutional capacity despite staff turnover during the change in administration. The introduction of the logical framework has been accompanied by widespread instruction of government officials and evaluators. There is also regular training and guidance for line ministry counterparts to implement SED activities, particularly performance indicator monitoring and annual performance evaluations.

Despite its progress, the M&E system in Mexico faces a number of challenges. First and foremost is sustaining use of the M&E system in budget decisions and policy making. The incentives to move toward evidence-based policy making and performance budgeting are weak or vulnerable to the leadership of key actors. Higher utilization depends on the full engagement of four players: Congress, SHCP officials, line ministries, and civil society. As OECD (2009) pointed out, the role of Congress in using performance information is yet to be fully realized. Congress's role is critical in holding government agencies accountable for their performance and ensuring the use of M&E information to inform budget decisions and policy making. M&E information should be seen as a means for improving public policy effectiveness and government performance rather than as an instrument for controlling the executive.

Budget officials in SHCP and line ministries are critical players for using M&E in performance budgeting. Hence, it is necessary to change their mindset from detailed line item costing and regulation compliance to policy effectiveness and government performance. Their recruitment and training should emphasize more policy and analytical skills, including evaluation. Internal discussions as well as external negotiations with line ministries and Congress will benefit from an enhanced policy and performance focus.

Internal use of performance information is heterogeneous across ministries, as is their institutional capacity to implement evaluations. Social ministries tend to be at the forefront, in part due to CONEVAL guidance, while the rest lag behind. It is important to level the capacity across ministries and provide incentives for performance management at the program level, for example, through benchmarking and showcasing good practices. Executive training for top and middle-level management, particularly program managers, should include performance management principles and practice.

Finally, it is necessary to generate broader demand for the use of performance information outside the government. The media, academia, and civil society organizations can use publicly available M&E information to hold Congress accountable for its decisions, as well as government officials for their performance. The media are already regular users of evaluations, but they need to focus more on discussing policy issues rather than attacking the government. Academia and civil society organizations could strengthen their role in monitoring SED implementation, as well as the use of performance information by Congress and the government.

A second challenge of M&E system implementation is the fragmented institutional arrangements and ad hoc coordination mechanisms. The strategic alliance between SHCP and CONEVAL is highly beneficial for the system, but it is vulnerable to changes in leadership and does not take full advantage of each institution's potential. SED coordination should remain in SHCP, but CONEVAL's voice and vote in SED design and implementation should be institutionalized. Ideally, CONEVAL's mandate should be expanded to all sectors, making the necessary adjustments to its organizational structure. However, Congress has rejected this proposal in the past. SFP's role in SED should be reexamined to profit from its comparative advantage and avoid unnecessarily cumbersome arrangements. Care should be taken not to replicate the pitfalls of institutional arrangements at the central level among planning, budgeting, and evaluation units within the line ministries.

Last but not least is the challenge of producing quality performance information. Specifically, a long-term effort involving other partners such as the National Statistics Institute (*Instituto Nacional de Estadística y Geografía*) is required to improve weak ministerial administrative records and data management systems. Moreover, it is important to take advantage of national surveys, particularly for higher outcome monitoring. Finally, given Mexico's M&E system's strong reliance on contracting out external evaluations, it is necessary to build capacity and expand the evaluators' market to ensure the objectivity and soundness of performance analysis.

Notes

1. PROGRESA (Education, Health, and Nutrition Program) was launched in 1997 and it was renamed Oportunidades in 2001.
2. A new administration from the same ruling party came into office at the end of 2006.
3. A constitutional reform in 2008 led the way to introducing evaluation at the state and municipal level, so the process of building sub-national M&E systems is just starting.
4. SED comprises M&E and a Medium-Term Program (*Programa de Mediano Plazo* [PMP]) to increase public spending efficiency and reduce administrative costs, which has not been fully implemented yet. This chapter focuses only on M&E.
5. Since 2004, ministries are required to publish all external evaluations on their Web sites.

6. Although it is not formally a part of SED, the National Institute for Women (INMUJERES) participates in some M&E activities, such as revising the gender focus of the MIR.

7. SFP is supposed to spearhead the Program for Improving Public Management (PMG), in which one of the inputs is recommendations from evaluations. However, this initiative has not gotten off the ground.

8. According to PMG plans, the chief administrator is the SFP liaison within line ministries in charge of coordinating PMG activities with the collaboration of the Internal Control Office.

Bibliography

Castro, Manuel F., Gladys Lopez-Acevedo, Gita Beker Busjeet, and Ximena Fernandez Ordonez. 2009. "Mexico's M&E System: Scaling Up from the Sectoral to the National Level." Evaluation Capacity Development Working Paper Series 20, Independent Evaluation Group, World Bank, Washington, DC.

Consejo Nacional de Evaluación de la Política de Desarrollo Social. 2007. "Normatividad para la Evaluación de los Programas Federales." Gobierno Federal, Mexico City.

———. 2010. *Informe de Seguimiento a los Aspectos Susceptibles de Mejora de Programas Federales 2009*. Proceso de Evaluación Externa 2009 del Gobierno Federal, Mexico City.

OECD (Organisation for Economic Co-operation and Development). 2009. "OECD Review of Budgeting in Mexico." *OECD Journal on Budgeting* 2009: Supplement 1.

Rubio, Gloria M. 2009. "Integrating Impact Evaluation into Decision Making: The Mexico Experience." Presentation at the Regional Impact Evaluation Workshop, Beijing, China, July 20–24. Available at: http://siteresources.worldbank.org/ INTISPMA/Resources/383704-1184250322738/ 3986044-1250881992889/ Mexico_Experience(Rubio)_EN.pdf.

SHCP (Secretaría de Hacienda y Crédito Público). 2008a. "Sistema de Evaluación del Desempeño." Gobierno Federal, Mexico City.

———. 2008b. "Acuerdopor el que se establecen las disposiciones generales del Sistema de Evaluación del Desempeño." Diario Oficial de la Federación, Marzo 31. Mexico City.

Web Sites

CONEVAL: http://www.coneval.gob.mx/

Sistema de Evaluación del Desempeño, SHCP: http://www.apartados.hacienda.gob. mx/sed/

Programa de Mejora de la Gestión, SFP: http://www.funcionpublica.gob.mx/index. php/ programas/pmg

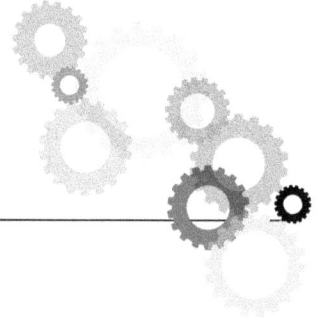

CHAPTER 13

Chile's M&E System

Mauricio I. Dussauge Laguna

The Chilean Management Control and Evaluation System (*Sistema de Evaluación y Control de Gestión*) is internationally regarded as an example of how monitoring and evaluation (M&E) can be successfully put into practice. Chilean M&E tools are the product of both cross-national lesson-drawing, and national policy learning experiences. The main M&E tools are centrally coordinated by the Ministry of Finance's Budget Office (*Dirección de Presupuestos*—DIPRES) and promote the use of M&E information in government decision-making processes, particularly those related to the budget.

Elements of the Chilean M&E system are discussed very favorably in other chapters of this volume. Authors particularly underline the technical quality of the instruments and tools used in Chile. This overall very positive depiction is not contradicted by the fact that in Chile as everywhere else, there are also shortcomings in practice, and that the system as such is embedded in a particular political and institutional context. The experience

The author would like to thank Fernando Rojas (former Lead Public Sector Specialist, Public Sector, Latin America and the Caribbean), the following members of the Poverty Reduction and Equity Unit: Philipp Krause (Consultant), Gladys Lopez-Acevedo (Senior Economist), Keith Mackay (Consultant), Jaime Saavedra (Director), and Álvaro Ramírez Alujas (Associate Researcher, Instituto Universitario de Investigación Ortega y Gasset) for their comments. The views expressed in this chapter are those of the author.

described below does not necessarily offer a "model" that can, or should, be easily transferred to other countries with different institutional contexts. However, the Chilean experience summarized here, covering the period of 1994–2010, provides interesting examples and highly relevant lessons about the benefits and limitations of M&E design and implementation.

The Development of Chile's M&E System

Chile's M&E system originates in a series of reform efforts that go back to the 1990s. During the presidencies of Patricio Alwyn (1990–94) and particularly Eduardo Frei (1994–2000), an administrative modernization agenda gained currency among political and technocratic elites. While democratization advanced in the political realm, the new governing coalition faced a number of administrative and managerial challenges for which the Chilean bureaucracy was ill-prepared, such as how to ensure policy coordination within the central government, how to assess the performance of public programs and the effectiveness of government policies, and how to better monitor the use of public resources.

In response to these challenges, during the 1990s a set of reform initiatives were implemented, including the "first generation" of some of the tools that would later become the M&E system that was put in place during 2000–10. For example, the first round of performance indicators sponsored by DIPRES was implemented in 1994, and the first program evaluations and a preliminary version of the General Management Reports were both developed in 1997. A first round of Programs for Management Improvement took place in 1998.

These and other efforts triggered a process of trial and error within the central government. In fact, some of these initiatives were voluntary and deemed to be part of a long-term process of M&E capacity building (Marcel 2006). Public officials thus received training in M&E tool design and implementation, and actively participated in target-setting and evaluation exercises. Although neither the quality of performance indicators nor the reliability of the information produced were ideal (Arenas and Berner 2010), the experience and institutional learning process that accompanied these years were definitely helpful assets when the M&E system was introduced in 2000.

Whereas the development of these M&E tools originated in Chile's own political transition to democracy, inspiration and some of the initial "technical" ideas came partly from abroad (Marcel 2006; Armijo 2003). Chilean policy makers studied "best practices" through documentation and interviews with government officials in Australia, the United Kingdom, and New Zealand, among other countries. Then a series of seminars took place in Santiago in the mid-1990s, in which administrative modernization strategies and M&E practices from these and other countries were discussed by national and international experts. Additional information was gathered via the study of public management reforms, communications with World Bank experts, and the participation of DIPRES officials at the Organisation for Economic Co-Operation and Development (OECD) senior budget officials meetings. In the end, Chilean officials did not "copy" any particular foreign model. However, these cross-national policy learning activities were essential to inform them about methodologies and tools used by other countries, which could be eventually adapted to fit the Chilean administrative environment.

The Chilean M&E System

An M&E system was formally introduced in 2000, centrally coordinated by the Ministry of Finance's DIPRES. Since the 1990s, DIPRES played a key sponsorship/management role in developing and implementing M&E tools. The Chilean M&E system eventually comprised eight tools (Guzmán 2005, 2010; Arenas and Berner 2010), which are listed in Table 13.1 and briefly described below.

Monitoring tools

Strategic definitions were introduced in 2000 to provide information about each organization's mission, strategic objectives and products (public goods and services provided), and its clients, users and/or beneficiaries. Every year

TABLE 13.1 Chile's M&E Tools

Monitoring tools	
Strategic definitions	2000
Performance indicators	1994; redesigned in 2000
Comprehensive management reports	1997; redesigned in 2000
Programs for management improvement	1998; redesigned in 2000
Evaluation tools	
Government program evaluations	1997; redesigned in 2000
Impact evaluations	2001
Comprehensive spending evaluations	2002
Evaluations of new programs	2009

Source: Author, based on Arenas and Berner (2010).

public institutions are asked to prepare their strategic definitions on the basis of information provided during the previous year. They also take into account the government's priorities set by the Ministry of the Presidency (MINSEGPRES) as well as the budgetary priorities defined by DIPRES in the Budget Law submitted to Congress.

Strategic definitions go hand in hand with *performance indicators,* which are quantitative measurements supposed to reflect targets/results to be achieved annually by each institution in the provision of public services and goods. Institutions prepare their performance indicators on the basis of those submitted in previous years, in order to facilitate comparisons across time and thus provide information about institutional performance. Indicators are designed by each institution, but according to formats and internationally accepted quality criteria set out by DIPRES. Indicators can be process-oriented, product-oriented, or results-oriented, and are required to measure effectiveness, efficiency, economy, or quality of service factors. Institutions are required to notify DIPRES about the means used to verify the validity of information used. Performance indicators are then included in the Budget Law proposal submitted to Congress.

Comprehensive management reports are a third monitoring tool used by the Chilean government. While they have existed since the mid-1990s, the ones introduced in 2000 seek to incorporate broader institutional information, such as organizational structure, strategic definitions, human resources management, financial management, the description and justification of target achievement, and links between this information and the budgetary resources used. Comprehensive management reports are prepared by each institution following formats and criteria set by DIPRES, and are sent yearly to Congress. According to DIPRES, they are also used to comply with the 2003 State Financial Administration Law, which requires that central government organizations provide information about their institutional performance.

Programs for management improvement (PMIs) are designed around five management areas established by DIPRES: human resources, user service quality, planning and control, financial administration, and gender focus. Ministries/agencies that have completed these areas advance to a further stage which includes ISO-9000 certification. Specific indicators and targets are agreed upon between DIPRES and each institution, so that the latter improve their managerial capacity and organizational performance. Progress assessment is carried out by an "experts network" and overseen by the Tri-Ministerial Committee comprised of DIPRES, the Ministry of Interior, and MINSEGPRES. PMI annual results are tied to salary increases, and are also taken into account when agency funding levels are discussed during budget formulation (Guzmán 2005; Zaltsman 2009).

FIGURE 13.1 **Chile's Monitoring Tools and Actors Involved**

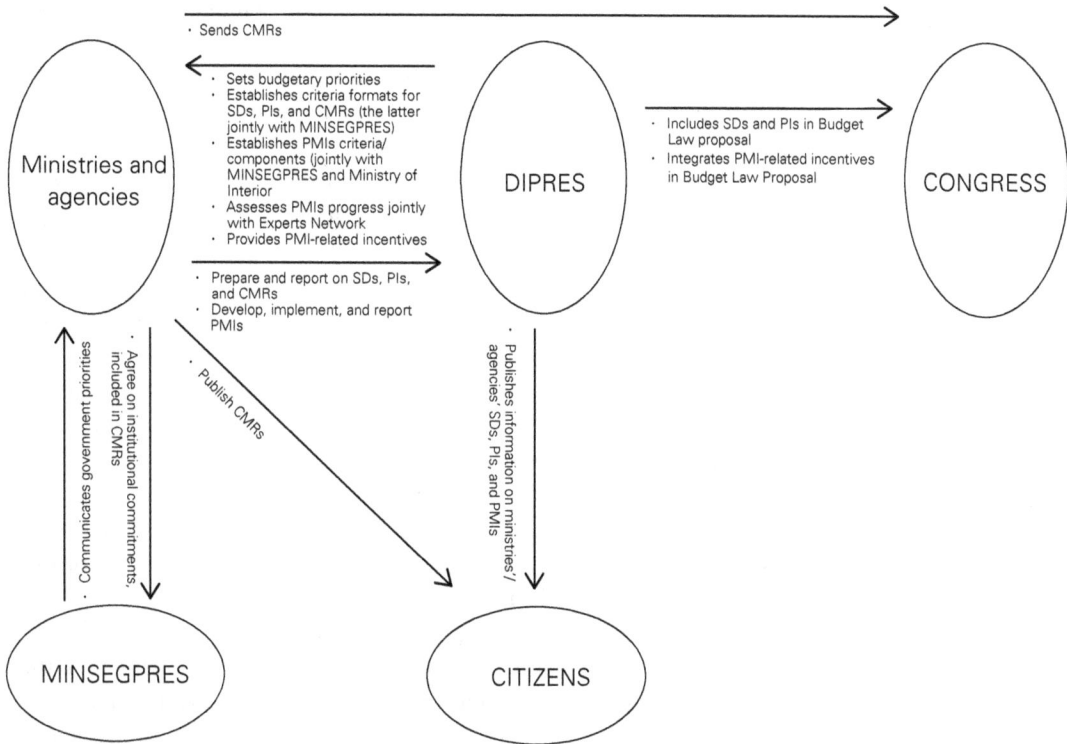

Source: Author.
Notes: SDs = Strategic Definitions; PIs = Performance Indicators; CMRs = Comprehensive Management Reports; PMIs = Programs for Management Improvement.

Figure 13.1 summarizes the relationships among different actors in managing and implementing monitoring tools in the Chilean system during 2000–10.

Evaluation tools

The Chilean M&E system for 2000–10 has also used four evaluation tools. These are coordinated by DIPRES on the basis of priorities set out by the Interministerial Committee for Evaluation, which is integrated by DIPRES, MINSEGPRES, and the Ministry of Planning and Co-operation (MIDEPLAN). A key defining feature of all evaluations conducted in the Chilean government has been the central role assigned to external experts (consultants and academics), who are selected through public tendering procedures managed and paid by DIPRES. Furthermore, all evaluation practices are meant to follow principles, such as independence, transparency, reliability, and timeliness of the findings, as well as cost-effectiveness (Arenas and Berner 2010).

Government program evaluations—introduced in 1997—are conducted by panels of three external experts, including one expert in evaluation practices, one in the policy field/sector under analysis, and one in program/public management (Guzmán 2010). On the basis of "logical frameworks," which map out the foundations of each program, these experts assess the soundness of the program's design, objectives, internal organization and management, and results. Evaluations usually begin in January of each year and last for about six months, so that DIPRES can use evaluation findings for budget proposal formulation.

Impact evaluations started in 2001 as a means to know how public programs ultimately affect their beneficiaries. Impact evaluations usually take about 18 months to implement, are based on a combination of qualitative and quantitative information, and use a completely different methodological approach. Instead of logical frameworks, they are based on quasi-experimental methods, in which evaluators compare two groups or "populations": one integrated by beneficiaries of the program, and another integrated by people who did not receive the goods/services provided. Evaluators also measure the variables under study before and after the program has been implemented, thus seeking to eliminate potential measurement biases due to external factors.

Comprehensive spending evaluations were introduced in 2001 in response to a congressional petition. Instead of evaluating a program or agency, comprehensive spending evaluations try to evaluate the whole set of institutions that integrate a given policy sector. As the name implies, these evaluations assume a more comprehensive perspective, and thus usually take a year or so to evaluate a varied number of factors, including the links between institutional and sector objectives, management processes, organizational structures and functions, and services/products provided.

Evaluations of new programs were introduced in 2009. It seeks to provide relevant baselines to more effectively evaluate future performance of new programs. These evaluations include the selection of a control group from the beginning, and are planned to cover an evaluation period of between two and three years in total. This type of evaluation is supposed to receive technical support from an international advisory panel and the University of Chile's Economy Department (Arenas and Berner 2010).

The findings and recommendations obtained through the various evaluation tools are sent to Congress and are made publicly available through DIPRES's Web site. Within the central government, evaluation results are discussed between the ministry or agency involved and DIPRES to deter-

FIGURE 13.2 Chile's Evaluation Tools and Actors Involved

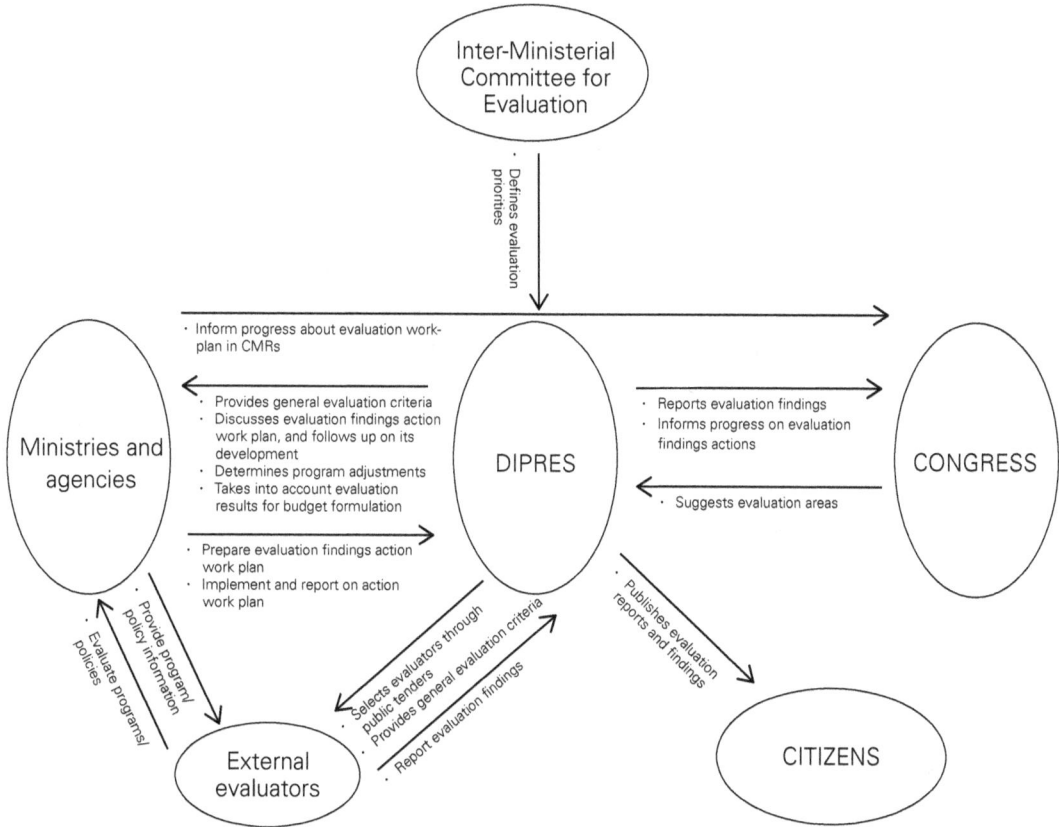

Source: Author.
Note: CMRs = Comprehensive Management Reports.

mine whether the program requires minor adjustments, modifications in its design or in some of its management systems, a substantial redesign, an institutional relocation, or termination. Evaluated institutions and DIPRES then elaborate work plans, which establish a set of commitments to be implemented during the following two or three years. Institutions report progress in their comprehensive management reports and to DIPRES, which then includes relevant information in the Budget Law proposal submitted to Congress. Figure 13.2 broadly synthesizes the different activities performed by the actors involved in evaluation activities until 2010.

As the previous description shows, the Chilean M&E system for the period 2000–10 contained a number of different tools designed to serve a variety of information demands, as well as a number of actors and institutions taking part in the design and implementation of the tools. Ministries and agencies have been, of course, the main producers of relevant information. Similarly, they have been responsible for adjusting their institution's management, organization, and policy in response to their performance reported in indicators and PMIs and evaluation findings and recommendations. Some particular ministries, such as MINSEGPRES, the Ministry of Interior, or MIDEPLAN, have played important albeit limited roles at certain points or with regard to specific M&E tools. Congress has received all relevant information through comprehensive management reports or as part of the Budget Law proposal prepared by DIPRES. While Congress has had some influence in determining areas for evaluation, it has remained a rather passive consumer of M&E information.

At the other extreme, DIPRES has played the crucial role in every phase of the system. DIPRES has overseen the production of targets and performance indicators, had the final word regarding which evaluations should be conducted, set the general criteria and procedures to select evaluators, coordinated information gathering, followed up on institutional improvements, and has been in charge of linking monitoring data and evaluation findings with budget preparation and proposals.

Achievements of the Chilean M&E System 2000–10

What were the main achievements of the Chilean experience during the period of 2000–10? First, the Chilean M&E reforms have contributed to developing a "measurement"-orientated culture across central government ministries and agencies. This is recognized by current and former DIPRES officials, public servants in other ministries, and various academic and international assessments. Nowadays, central government officials seem to understand the relevance of measuring outputs, setting targets, assessing programs, and evaluating policy impacts. Furthermore, they apparently see these as regular activities that are both an essential component of Chile's management and control system and of contemporary public management practices.

Second, data produced by the various M&E tools has been used for making budgetary policy decisions (Arenas and Berner 2010; Rojas et al. 2005; Zaltsman 2009). As mentioned above, high levels of PMI achievement are linked to salary increases, which in turn have impacted budget levels for incumbent agencies. Similarly, evaluation results have sometimes affected agency appropriations, as evaluation recommendations require increased resources for implementation. DIPRES has also been more open to increase budget appropriations proposals for high performing agencies. By the same token, poor performing agencies (those with low results in their PMIs or with poor evaluation results) have been occasionally "punished" by DIPRES, either in terms of budget reductions or by rejecting budget increase requests (Zaltsman 2009). This link between M&E tools and budgetary policy making acquires particular relevance when one takes into account the following data for the period 1997–2004 (Rojas et al. 2005): about 64 percent of Chile's budget had been subject to various kinds of evaluations even then. Between 2000 and 2008, 393 evaluations were carried out. Sixty-four percent of these recommended major adjustments or substantial redesign of the evaluated program, a further 23 percent recommended minor adjustment. Eighty-two percent of these recommendations were subsequently implemented fully, and a further 11 percent implemented partially (see also the discussion in Chapter 3, Figure 3.1).

Third, the Chilean government has made a significant effort to use evaluation results for making policy and management decisions (Guzmán 2005, 2010; Rojas et al. 2005). Information produced by impact evaluations, for example, has been employed to refocus links between policies and beneficiaries. Government program evaluation results have been used by agencies to improve internal management processes as well as for redesigning logical frameworks or performance indicators. Evaluation results have also informed decisions about institutional relocation of programs or, in some cases, have even led to policy termination. All of this has been possible because of DIPRES's forceful role in agreeing to program changes with ministries/agencies, monitoring the extent of implementation, and enforcing compliance through its high level of power and influence. This has been possible, in turn, because of Chile's institutional setting (constitution and budget legal framework), which provide DIPRES with a leverage potential that is not that common in other OECD countries.

Fourth, Chile's M&E system has introduced mechanisms for promoting the objectivity, impartiality, and reliability of evaluation procedures and findings. As described above, external experts (consultants and academics) have been involved in the design and implementation of evaluations. This has served to increase the expertise with which evaluations are carried out, as well as their validity and reliability.

Lastly, the Chilean M&E system of 2000–10 has acquired a high level of institutionalization within the central government administration. Based on a continuous work that spans more than a decade, evaluation units have been created in almost every government ministry and agency. Many public servants have been (and continue to be) involved in M&E and broader administrative modernization activities. M&E activities have been coordinated by DIPRES's Management Control Division, which was created explicitly for that purpose in 2000. Implementation of most M&E instruments has taken place on a regular basis during the past decade, with formats and methodologies that are by now well known by ministries and agencies.

Limitations of the Chilean M&E System 2000–10

Despite the achievements described above, various analysts, users, and managers have also pointed out important limitations in the design and management of the Chilean M&E system as it has worked during 2000–10. First of all, DIPRES's crucial role in promoting and ensuring the use of the M&E system has brought with it some significant issues. For instance, M&E information has in the end been mainly used by DIPRES, but less so by other bureaucratic actors, Congress, or the Chilean society (Rojas et al. 2005). Similarly, DIPRES's control over the design and management of the M&E tools has introduced a strong budgetary-centered perspective, which has left aside alternative values (planning, participation) that are present in other international experiences. These might need to be addressed in the future if the M&E system seeks to contribute to public results and democratic accountability considerations, and not only to budgetary policy making and internal bureaucratic control.

A second limitation, closely related to the previous one, has been the downside of the high level of centralization achieved by DIPRES (May et al. 2006; Rojas et al. 2005). Relationships between DIPRES and the other participating agencies have been rather asymmetrical, with the latter having limited influence on defining performance indicators and evaluation criteria. This has significantly affected the degree of ownership from senior civil servants in agencies and ministries regarding evaluation results and recommendations. Moreover, according to a recent study by Zaltsman (2009, 455), "certain aspects of Chile's budgetary process limit the benefits that can be gained from use of performance information. One of them is the relatively little room for maneuvering that agency officials have to decide on allocation of their appropriated resources without DIPRES approval." These features have limited the system's legitimacy among central government institutions, as well as its potential transferability to other nations.

A third set of limitations are in the technical dimension of the Chilean M&E system. A World Bank study of Chile's evaluation tools carried out in 2005, for example, pointed out that the quality of some early evaluation reports has not always been in line with international standards (Rojas et al.

2005). Another World Bank study (2008) also pointed out that the PMI might be too complex to manage and verify, as well as too homogenous for the heterogeneous conditions of the Chilean public administration. A recent document by DIPRES similarly states that the quality and relevance of the performance indicators and targets used in the budget preparation process require further refinement, and that the various monitoring and evaluation tools have yet to achieve better integration (Arenas and Berner 2010). Furthermore, broader "inter-sectoral" indicators and evaluation frameworks are missing for situations where multiple institutions share both tasks and responsibility over a given policy/program (May et al. 2006, 17). Lastly, some observers have suggested that the Chilean government should actually dedicate more resources to evaluations, and even spend a higher amount of public resources in individual evaluations of programs that might be particularly relevant because of their social impact (May et al. 2006; Guzmán 2010).

Finally, two central limitations of the sometimes called "Chilean model" relate to the nature of the system as it has evolved during 2000–2010. The World Bank study stated that Chile's evaluation program "has not showed yet the specific way or degree in which it contributes to increasing the effectiveness and efficiency of public expenditure" (Rojas et al. 2005, 16). Furthermore, the M&E system may not have become systematically linked to other monitoring frameworks developed within the Chilean government during the same period. In particular, this has been the case with regard to MINSEGPRES's scheme for monitoring ministerial goals and indicators, which has been in place since the early 1990s. While these are issues that affect other countries as well, they will certainly remain central challenges for the Chilean government in the near future. These limitations do not necessarily undermine the high technical quality achieved by most of the elements that comprise the M&E system. They show, however, that when M&E is implemented in a particular context, there are always tradeoffs between competing priorities and constraints to overcome.

Concluding Remarks

This chapter has offered a brief introduction to Chile's M&E system, from its origins in the mid-1990s to the way it functioned during the period 2000–10. The experience of the Chilean system provides useful information about the way M&E works in practice, the benefits M&E can have for decision-making processes, policy implementation, and program evaluation, and the potential limitations that governments elsewhere might face when developing M&E tools.

The case of Chile offers a set of interesting lessons about the "nuts and bolts" of M&E systems, including both its advantages and potential limitations. For example, Chile's various M&E tools have been designed to solve specific government needs, and not because of external international pressures or fashions. Performance indicators were implemented when measurements of agency performance across time were deemed to be necessary, and impact evaluations were introduced when it was considered that government program evaluations were not providing enough information about policy effectiveness. Similarly, the Chilean experience exemplifies how timely and relevant M&E information can enrich decisions about budgetary policy making, as well as about program management or policy refinement/termination.

The case of Chile suggests how a strong institutional leadership (in this case that of DIPRES) might be key for ensuring a system's institutionalization and continued relevance, but might also "bias" the purpose of the system and the way information is eventually used/owned. In the end, the Chilean experience exemplifies how M&E capacity building is a long-term process, in which methodologies need to be adjusted, practical shortcomings have to be periodically addressed, and the design and use of M&E tools require continuous adaptation.

Bibliography

Arenas de Mesa, Alberto, and Heidi Berner. 2010. "Presupuesto por Resultados y la Consolidación del Sistema de Evaluación y Control de Gestión del Gobierno Central." DIPRES.

Armijo, Marianela. 2003. "La evaluación de la gestión pública en Chile." In Nuria Cunill and Sonia Ospina, eds., *Evaluación de Resultados para una Gestión Pública Moderna y Democrática: Experiencias Latinoamericanas*. Caracas: CLAD-AECI/MAP/FIIAPP, 43–142.

Guzmán, Marcela. 2010. "Challenges for Evidence-Based Decision Making: The Experience of Chile and Features of Its Design, Implementation, and Use of Information." In Gladys Lopez-Acevedo, Katia Rivera, Lycia Lima, and Helena Hwang, eds., *Challenges in Monitoring and Evaluation: An Opportunity to Institutionalize M&E Systems*, 13–22. Washington, DC: World Bank and Inter-American Development Bank.

———. 2005. "Sistema de Control de Gestión y Presupuesto por Resultados: La Experiencia Chilena." DIPRES.

Marcel, Mario. 2006. "Reflexiones acerda del proceso de modernización del Estado en Chile y desafios futures." *Reforma y Democracia* 34.

May, Ernesto, David Shand, Keith Mackay, Fernando Rojas, and Jaime Saavedra, eds. 2006. *Towards the Institutionalization of Monitoring and Evaluation Systems in*

Latin America and the Caribbean: Proceedings of a World Bank/Inter-American Development Bank Conference. Washington, DC: World Bank-IDB.

Rojas, Fernando, Keith Mackay, Matsuda Yasuhiko, Geoffrey Shepherd, Azul Del Villar, Ariel Zaltsman, and Philipp Krause. 2005. *Chile: Análisis del Programa de Evaluación del Gasto Público.* Washington, DC: World Bank.

World Bank. 2008. *Chile: Estudio de Evaluación en Profundidad del Programa de Mejoramiento de la Gestión (PMG).* Washington, DC: World Bank.

Zaltsman, Ariel. 2009. "The Effects of Performance Information on Public Resource Allocations: A Study of Chile's Performance Based Budgeting System." *International Public Management Journal* 12: 450–83.

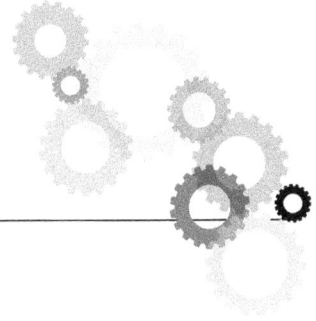

CHAPTER 14

The Australian Government's M&E System

Keith Mackay

Countries from all over the world have shown an interest in Australia's experience in creating a monitoring and evaluation (M&E) system that supports evidence-based decision making and performance-based budgeting. The Australian M&E system, in existence from 1987 to 1997, was generally considered to be one of the most successful in the world and was driven by the federal Department of Finance (DoF). This chapter discusses the genesis, characteristics, and success of this particular system and briefly considers the Australian government's approach to M&E after the system was abolished. The contrast between these two periods provides many valuable insights into success factors and challenges facing M&E systems, and into implementing evidence-based decision making more broadly.

By the early 1980s, Australia was facing a very difficult economic situation—not unlike the current difficulties faced by many developed and developing countries. A reformist Labor government was elected in 1983, and it

For their comments, the author thanks Jim Brumby (Sector Manager, Public Sector Governance), Philipp Krause (Consultant, Poverty Reduction and Equity Unit [PRMPR]), as well as Gladys Lopez-Acevedo (Senior Economist, PRMPR), and Jaime Saavedra (Director, PRMPR). The views expressed in this chapter are those of the author.

was committed to a substantial reorientation of public spending toward the poor, while also significantly reducing budget spending. By 1989–90, the Labor government had reduced the budget share of gross domestic product (GDP) from 30 to 23 percent—a major reduction by international standards. The fiscal pain of budgetary cuts was shared by the federal, state, and territorial governments. The federal government collects the bulk of taxes in Australia, and it provides considerable funding to other levels of government. Most public services are the responsibility of the states and territories.

The federal government wanted not simply to reduce spending, but also to significantly improve its efficiency and effectiveness and thereby receive greater value for its money from government expenditures. A number of public sector reforms were implemented to encourage this new approach, including a substantial devolution of powers and responsibilities to government departments known as "letting the managers manage." The reforms also included a series of changes to streamline the budget system and enable the budget process to focus on "big picture" policy issues rather than on smaller details. Thus, Australia led the world in introducing a medium-term expenditure framework, a system of budget forward estimates, and consolidated running costs.

DoF was a major driver of these public sector reforms and had the active support of other central departments and a number of reform-oriented government ministers. The senior leadership of DoF wanted to shift the departmental focus from relatively minor spending issues to higher-level policy issues, as spelled out in its policy analysis and briefings prepared for the annual budget process.

While DoF leadership had hoped that sector departments and agencies would conduct M&E to help them manage their own performance, it was evident that they were not prepared to do so. DoF therefore asked the Cabinet to agree to a formal evaluation strategy to force departments (and agencies) to plan and conduct evaluations on a systematic basis (Box 14.1). Cabinet agreement was formalized in a cabinet decision. In Westminster systems of government, such decisions virtually have the force of law, and few public servants would dare to defy them. An advantage of such decisions is that they can be taken quickly; a disadvantage is that the lack of a legislative basis means they can easily be reversed when there is a change in government.[1]

Main Characteristics of the M&E System

Evaluation was the most important component of the M&E system. Evaluation was stressed because it was considered to be much more valuable than

BOX 14.1

The Australian Government's Evaluation Strategy

There were four formal requirements:

- That every program be evaluated every 3–5 years

- That each portfolio (that is, comprising a line department plus outrider agencies) prepare an annual portfolio evaluation plan, with a 3-year forward coverage, and submit it to DoF—these plans were to comprise major program evaluations with substantial resource or policy implications

- That ministers' new policy proposals include a statement of proposed arrangements for future evaluation

- That completed evaluation reports should normally be published, unless there exist important policy sensitivity, national security, or commercial-in-confidence considerations, and that the budget documentation that departments table in parliament each year should also report major evaluation findings.

performance information due to the detailed insights it could provide into issues of causality. Some effort was paid to the collection and publication of monitoring information, but mainly from 1995 onward.

The evaluation strategy had three main objectives. The first, and arguably the most important, objective was to provide fundamental information about program performance to aid Cabinet decision making and prioritization, particularly in the annual budget process when a large number of competing proposals are advocated by individual ministers. The second objective was to encourage program managers within departments to use evaluations to improve their programs' performance. Lastly, the strategy aimed to strengthen accountability in a devolved environment by providing formal evidence of program managers' oversight and management of program resources. The strategy thus had the important element of letting the managers manage.

It was the responsibility of individual departments to conduct their own evaluations: they decided which programs to evaluate, the focus of each evaluation, and the evaluation techniques that would be used. Many different types of evaluations were conducted, including rapid evaluations, which can take at least three to four months to complete; rigorous impact evaluations taking 12–18 months; and cost-benefit analyses, which were conducted mostly for infrastructure investments. A sample of these evaluations showed that their cost ranged from about $56,000 to $560,000 (in 1993 prices); their average cost was about 1 percent of the annual cost of the program being evaluated. Departments could decide not to evaluate a program if it had recently been subject to a performance audit by the national audit office, since these audits were also regarded as a form of evaluation.

Although features of the evaluation strategy were devolved, key aspects were centralized. The strategy itself was designed and managed by the DoF. By overseeing the strategy, DoF played a strong quality assurance role, and it could amend the strategy when it deemed an element to be ineffective. DoF also used its significant power and influence as the central budget agency (and as the overseer of departments' financial estimates) to promote the benefits of evaluations, and to point out to departments if they were not investing sufficient effort into evaluation. The DoF desk officers (and also the desk officers of the Treasury and the Department of the Prime Minister and Cabinet) who "shadowed" each line department and agency would frequently attempt to influence the evaluation plans of the line departments. The key aspects of evaluation plans were the decisions about which programs would be evaluated, when, and which particular issues would be addressed in each evaluation. DoF involvement was intended to ensure that evaluations addressed the difficult issues of program performance (rather than bland, uncontroversial issues) in an honest and objective manner. Major disagreements concerning evaluation planning priorities would often be escalated to the ministerial level. DoF desk officers would also seek to become involved in major evaluations, usually through participation in evaluation steering committees and by commenting on draft evaluation reports. Figure 14.1 represents the evaluation planning and reporting relationships among the key stakeholders inside and outside government.

The evaluation strategy lasted from 1987 to 1997, and continued to evolve over this entire period. It required effort to create the M&E system, and it was also found to be important to monitor the M&E system itself, so that DoF and other stakeholders could understand what was working well and what was not, and identify areas for improvement. A lot of trial and error was needed to progressively refine the M&E system.

By the mid-1990s, about 160 major evaluations were under way at any point in time. Evaluations were defined as "major" if they related to programs that involved large expenditures or were of major policy significance. This level of evaluation activity involved considerable effort on the part of DoF, as well as on the part of departments and agencies.

While Australia's overall M&E system stressed evaluation, it became clearer in the 1990s that insufficient attention had been paid to the regular collection, reporting, and use of performance information. DoF had hoped

FIGURE 14.1 Evaluation Planning and Reporting Flows

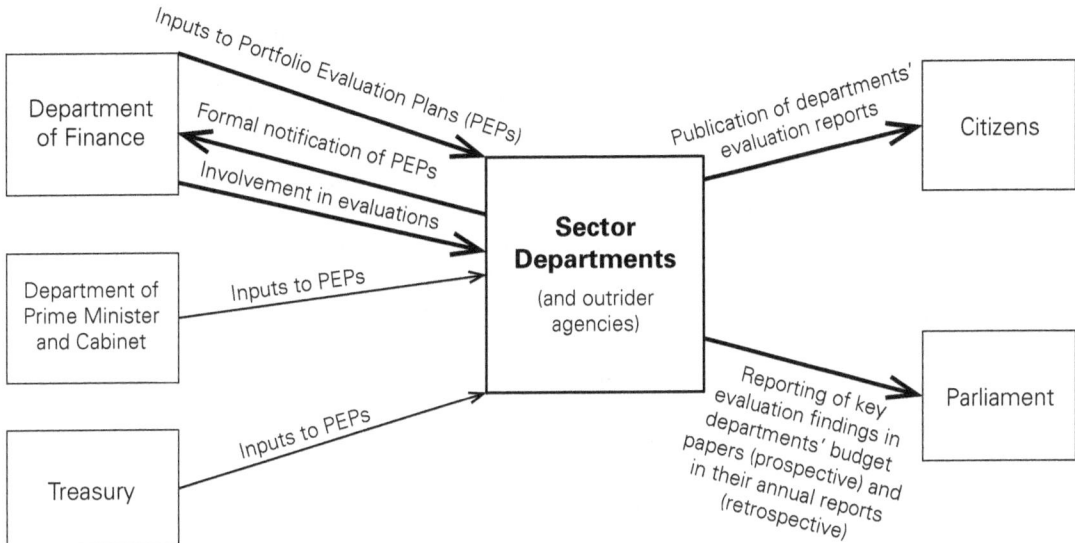

Source: Author.

that by stressing the planning and conduct of evaluations, which can be technically difficult, departments would be induced to improve their collection of performance information. However, DoF reviews found evidence that program performance was not being well measured nor reported using performance information. Thus in 1995, DoF secured the Cabinet's agreement to a rolling series of in-depth reviews of the objectives and key performance information for every government program. These reviews were conducted jointly by DoF and each line department. They provided the new government elected in 1996 some of the groundwork for shifting the emphasis to performance information.

Another initiative related to performance information was the publication, from 1995 onward, of annual reports on service delivery by the federal, state, and territorial governments.[2] These reports included public hospitals, schools and vocational training, public housing, police, court administration, and prisons. Initially these reports covered $38 billion in annual expenditures, or about 9 percent of GDP, and their coverage has since expanded.[3] The purpose of these reports was to provide greater transparency and accountability for government programs. In addition, it was hoped that the reports would both support and spur improved performance by enabling comparison across different jurisdictions—described as "yardstick competition"—and thus help to identify best practice.

Success Factors and Obstacles

The fact that M&E information—especially evaluation findings—was frequently used was due to a number of factors. The strong support of reform champions at the most senior levels of DoF, and of reformist ministers in the government, was particularly important. DoF was highly active in managing the M&E system and in both coercing and supporting departments to undertake M&E. DoF's incentives included carrots, sticks, and sermons. The carrots included the evaluation advisory support provided by DoF, such as evaluation handbooks, introductory M&E training, and identification of good practice departmental M&E arrangements, as well as access to resource agreements to help line departments improve management of their underperforming programs. The sticks included DoF's ability to influence line departments' budget allocations and to escalate department disputes to the ministerial level. DoF also had the option of embarrassing departments by releasing the comparative rankings it prepared concerning departments' approaches to the planning and conduct of evaluations. The sermons included persistent advocacy by the secretary and senior executives of DoF, as well as explicit evaluation support from some powerful ministers.

Another success factor was cultural change within DoF. Its budget analysts were capable, tough-minded, and very conservative. Thus it was a challenge to change their mindset from focusing on detailed line item costs to focusing on high-level policy concerned with the performance of government programs. This required strong leadership and advocacy by successive DoF secretaries. Staff turnover was also required, with more emphasis on research and policy skills and less emphasis on accounting skills. Evaluation experience became one of the selection criteria in the annual recruitment rounds for section heads in DoF.

The availability of evaluation findings helped DoF and line departments improve the quality of their policy advice to ministers: advice became more evidence-based. It became understood that the budget process was a "marketplace of ideas," where evaluation findings could provide a competitive advantage. As the government's chief microeconomic adviser recently stated:

> Policy decisions will typically be influenced by much more than objective evidence, or rational analysis. Values, interests, personalities—in short, democracy—determine what actually happens. But evidence and analysis can nevertheless play a useful, even decisive, role in informing policy makers' judgments. Importantly, they can also condition the political environment in which those judgments need to be made. Without evidence, policy makers must fall back on intuition, ideology, or conventional wisdom—or, at best, theory alone. (Banks 2009, 3)

Of course, having plentiful M&E information and having good quality policy advice are not sufficient. If governments are not influenced by this information and advice, then there might be little point in creating an M&E system. But a powerful success factor in Australia was having reformist ministers who were not only receptive to M&E information, but who actively demanded it—as seen in a number of Cabinet policy and budget debates where evaluation findings were explicitly discussed by ministers.

The M&E system was not perfect, and it ran into several obstacles. One obstacle was the lack of available training in advanced evaluation techniques, as well as a shortage of trained evaluators in departments and agencies. These entities often responded to formal evaluation requirements by relying on their operational program managers and their staff to be responsible for conducting the evaluations. However, the staff usually possessed few evaluation skills and also lacked experience in outsourcing evaluations. On the other hand, this devolutionary approach helped ensure that the evaluations drew on the staff program expertise and that there was a high level of ownership of the evaluation findings—both of these may be difficult to achieve with externally conducted evaluations.

Some departments successfully addressed the need for more advanced skills and experience by setting up a central evaluation unit to provide advice on methodology and training in research and evaluation and participate in evaluation steering committees. Although the national audit office and DoF both advocated such central units as examples of good practice, most line departments chose not to follow this approach. Therefore the lack of evaluation skills resulted in a reduction in the quality of some evaluations—the national audit office found that over one-third of a sample of evaluation reports suffered from methodological weaknesses of one kind or another. Of course, if line departments relied on poor quality evaluations in the new policy proposals that their ministers sent to the Cabinet, DoF would certainly advise the Cabinet that the evaluation was unreliable.

Extent of Utilization of the M&E System

Clear evidence indicates that evaluations were used intensively in the budget process during the 1987–96 period. DoF conducted several surveys on the extent to which evaluation findings influenced budget proposals prepared by line department officials for submission to the Cabinet. The survey participants were DoF officers, who carefully analyzed all new policy proposals and who typically attended all Cabinet meetings concerned with budget issues. Because of their involvement, these DoF officers had first-hand knowledge of the influence of evaluation findings on the budget proposals of line ministers and on the meetings of Cabinet ministers who made the final decisions on budget allocations. The close familiarity of DoF officers with these proposals and with any evaluations or reviews on which they were drawn, and also their participation in Cabinet budget meetings, gave them an insider's perspective on the influence of evaluation findings.

In the 1990–91 budget, some US$230 million of new policy proposals submitted by line ministers were judged to have been directly or indirectly influenced by the findings of an evaluation. By 1994–95, the last year for which estimates were available, this had risen to US$2.3 billion. Measured in dollar terms, the proportion of new policy proposals influenced by evaluation findings rose from 23 to 77 percent over that period; and for most of these, the influence of evaluation was judged by DoF officers to be both direct and major. These results indicate that line department staff and ministers felt that it was important to use evaluation findings to strengthen their new policy proposals. Ministers often expressed that it was valuable to them to have evaluation findings available for their Cabinet debates. Overall, it was very helpful to have had the active support of key Cabinet ministers to encourage portfolios to plan and conduct high-quality evaluations. This support was also reflected by the many Cabinet decisions that called for evaluations of specific programs or issues.

Evaluations can have a significant influence on the "savings options"[4] put forward by DoF or by portfolios for Cabinet consideration in the budget process. In 1994–95, about US$500 million of savings options—or 65 percent of the total—were influenced by evaluation findings, and this influence was usually judged to be major. This emphasis on evaluation findings was encouraged by the nature of the budgetary system in the Australian government. Australia had a well-functioning policy decision-making mechanism that made the costs of competing policies transparent and encouraged debate and consultation among stakeholders within government.

DoF officers were also surveyed for their opinions on the extent to which evaluation findings had influenced the Cabinet's final decisions—separate from the influence of evaluation on the proposals drafted by officials and submitted by sector ministers to the Cabinet—in the 1993–94 and 1994–95 budgets. While the evidence is mixed, it indicates that evaluation findings played a substantive role. In 1994–95, evaluation findings were assessed to have influenced the Cabinet's decision in 68 percent of the US$3.74 billion of proposals considered (new policy proposals plus savings options). The corresponding proportion for the 1993–94 budget, however, was only 19 percent of proposals. One important reason for this difference was the substantial revision of labor market, industry, regional, and aboriginal policies in the

1994–95 budget—the major policy review on which these decisions were based had been heavily influenced by a number of evaluations commissioned specifically to help guide the policy review.

The observation of the Auditor-General is worth noting:

> In my view, the success of evaluation at the federal level of government . . . was largely due to its full integration into the budget processes. Where there was a resource commitment, some form of evaluation was necessary to provide justification for virtually all budget bids. (Barrett 2001, 13)

It is interesting to speculate on whether the returns to M&E declined over the decade in which the evaluation strategy was in existence. When the evaluation strategy was created in 1987, there would have been a number of underperforming programs, and subsequent evaluations could be expected to have revealed their poor efficiency, effectiveness, or appropriateness. This would usually have led to the programs being improved (especially if they were an important government priority) or else cut or even abolished. But by the time the strategy was abolished in 1997, most programs would have been evaluated more than once, and it might be expected that the marginal returns to M&E would have declined. However, the heavy reliance on M&E information in the 1994–95 budget does not lend support to this possibility. Because there is no information on the changing returns to M&E over time, this issue cannot be investigated further.

A survey conducted in 1997 by the national audit office found that evaluation findings were highly utilized by line departments for ongoing operations and internal management. The survey also found that the impact or use of evaluation findings by line departments was most significant for improvements in operational efficiency and, to a lesser extent, for resource allocation decisions and the design of service quality improvements to benefit clients. This high level of utilization was a strength of the Australian evaluation system: evaluation was essentially a collaborative effort involving DoF, other central departments, and line departments. Although responsibility for evaluation was largely devolved to line departments, the involvement of the central departments in the planning and oversight of major evaluations helped achieve broad ownership of the evaluations themselves and of their findings.

The Sustainability of the M&E System

While the future sustainability of any existing M&E system can be difficult to predict, that question has been answered for the M&E system created in Australia in 1987: it was abolished in 1997 following the change in government in 1996. By far the most significant component of the M&E system was evaluation, and the evaluation strategy that DoF had centrally managed was abolished. There had been considerable opposition on the part of line department secretaries to the creation of the evaluation strategy in 1987, mainly on the grounds that it was an intrusion into their areas of responsibility. However, once the strategy was established, there was little opposition during the following decade. This changed with the change in government in 1996. The new conservative government distrusted the public service, which it downsized by 20 percent over three years, and it also wanted to significantly simplify public administration. Line departments took this opportunity to highlight the burden of planning and conducting evaluations. These arguments immediately found a receptive audience with the new government, which had decided to devolve many central functions to line departments and agencies, thus freeing them from most central controls and requirements. Evaluation was only one of many central requirements that were abolished or significantly weakened; while evaluation was officially encouraged, the decision to conduct evaluations was essentially left to line department secretaries. The government placed much more emphasis on the collection and reporting of performance information, mainly for accountability purposes. However, there was little central oversight of this information by DoF, and no real attempt at quality control, with the result that the published performance information was severely criticized by a number of parliamentary committees, the national audit office, senior officials, academics, and others.

Other devolved functions included the setting of pay and conditions for public servants (individual employment contracts were also introduced) and responsibility for financial estimates. DoF was downsized considerably, most of its policy analysis areas were abolished, and its responsibility for maintaining and overseeing the financial estimates of line entities—a traditional core function of any central budget agency—was removed. At the same time, the new government decided to rely heavily on sources outside the civil service for advice on policy issues, such as business consulting firms in the private sector.

Instead of the evaluation strategy, the new government created a new Outcomes and Outputs Framework that required all departments and ministers to specify the government outcomes (that is, objectives) toward which they were working, and also to specify the departmental outputs, such as service delivery for specific target groups, that would be produced to help achieve these outcomes. By 2004, departments and agencies collectively had 199 outcomes and usually between one and 10 outputs each. These outcomes and outputs (including their quantity, quality, and costs) were required to be reported to the Parliament in each department's annual report and in their budget documentation. However, this framework suffered from a number of fundamental conceptual and implementation difficulties (discussed by Mackay 2011a, b), including:

- Poor specification of outcomes, using only broad, aspirational terms.
- Poor logical links between many outputs and outcomes.
- Lack of reporting on unmet targets, or on areas where performance was poor.
- Different specifications of outputs and outcomes by different departments, making it very difficult to make comparisons.
- Continuing changes in definitions over time, making it very difficult to conduct time series comparisons.

This performance framework is widely judged to have been a failure, and it was abolished by a later government in 2009.

Although the M&E system was abolished in 1997, it had been hoped that an evaluation culture would take hold within the departments and agencies, and that these entities would have been more than willing to continue to conduct evaluations for their own purposes—to aid their own policy development, prioritization of activities, ongoing program management, and for accountability purposes. By 2003, six years after the deregulation of evaluation, some departments still devoted considerable priority to evaluation, and some could be considered good practice in a number of respects, including the departments of family and community services, employment, and health.[5] However, even these departments tended to conduct evaluation less frequently, to address only particular issues on a selective basis. It is not clear whether any departments continued to conduct evaluations as regularly or as systematically as they did under the previous evaluation strategy. There has been no analysis of the reasons why these islands of good practice evaluation persisted after the ending of the government's evaluation strategy. However, one likely reason includes the personal commitment of some key individuals in these departments—that is, champions of M&E. Another reason could be the corporate culture and mindset of professional staff in the areas of health and education, whose professional training emphasized the value of research, evaluation, monitoring, and statistics. The reality that most departments and agencies appear to engage in little evaluation activity would suggest that a wholly devolutionary approach to evaluation is insufficient—both for purposes of internal management and to support evidence-based decision making.

It is important to speculate on possible reasons why a broader evaluation culture did not persist. One reason may be that many departmental secretaries and their ministers are naturally disinclined to conduct evaluations. While positive evaluation findings are always welcome, adverse findings can pose significant political and reputational risks. Another important risk factor was the departure of key reform champions—not just reformist ministers, but also the leading champions of M&E in the central departments, who were either advised to retire or were moved to less influential positions. It is well known from other countries that the existence of such champions is a key factor for the creation and sustainability of a successful M&E system.

The main factor that led to the dismantling of the M&E system was the change in government in 1996. The new government believed the civil service to be caught up in red tape and inherently less efficient than the private sector. The new government also changed the entire policy process by: relying less on the civil service and much more on non-government sources of advice; substantially weakening the role of DoF, which had been the main guardian of fiscal rectitude; concentrating policy and budget decision making in the Prime Minister's Office; making many expenditure decisions after the end of the formal budget process; and basing many government decisions on ideological considerations, with relatively little attention to hard evidence such as M&E information. This approach can perhaps be regarded as the antithesis of evidence-based decision making. It was considerably facilitated by the economic good fortune that Australia enjoyed as a result of booming exports (largely due to a very strong resource sector), and especially by the continuing high levels of budget surplus. Thus, just as difficult macroeconomic circumstances can provide a powerful motivator for public sector reform and for greater effort to be devoted to getting the most value from government spending, abundant prosperity can have the opposite effect by undermining these reforms.

The Australian M&E system endured for a decade, and it achieved a considerable level of utilization during this period. However, based on the definition of a "successful" M&E system presented in Chapters 1 and 2—which includes the concept of sustainability—its eventual abolition means that it cannot be regarded as having been wholly successful. The demise of the system was not due to a careful consideration of its benefits and costs—most objective observers would judge the system to have a high benefit/cost ratio. Rather, the system was abolished for what were essentially ideological reasons, and government decision making came to rely much less on hard evidence about value for money from government spending.

A new government elected in 2007 has taken a number of initiatives that collectively are likely to increase the supply of and demand for monitoring information and evaluation findings. The initiatives include a fresh approach to monitoring that replaces the Outcomes and Outputs Framework and reintroduces program budgeting. There is also a renewed focus on evaluation and review, with substantive interest from DoF in creating a whole-of-government system that avoids the weaknesses of the earlier evaluation system. More emphasis is also being placed on developing the policy skills of the civil service in the context of government decision-making processes, which will provide greater scope for policy advice. Only time will tell if the current efforts to reinvigorate monitoring and evaluation in the Australian government are successful.

Notes

1. Note that this evaluation strategy related to the federal government's own spending, not to the services provided by lower levels of government.
2. See www.pc.gov.au/gsp.
3. Coverage currently relates to US$136 billion in annual expenditures, or 13 percent of GDP.
4. Savings options are areas of government expenditures that could be reduced or abolished entirely.
5. It is interesting to note that these were the same departments that had created specialist evaluation units during the period of the formal evaluation strategy.

Bibliography

Banks, Gary. 2009. *Challenges of Evidence-Based Policy-Making*. Canberra: Productivity Commission and Australian Public Service Commission.

Barrett, Pat. 2001. "Evaluation and Performance Auditing: Sharing the Common Ground: A Review of Developments." Address to the Australasian Evaluation Society, Canberra, October 10.

Mackay, Keith. 2007. *How to Build M&E Systems to Support Better Government*. Independent Evaluation Group. Washington, DC: World Bank.

———. 2011a. "The Australian Government's Performance Framework." World Bank ECD Working Paper 25. World Bank, Washington, DC.

———. 2011b. "The Performance Framework of the Australian Government, 1987 to 2011." *OECD Journal on Budgeting* 11, no. 3: 75–122.

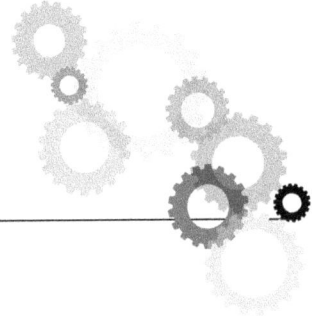

CHAPTER 15

The Canadian M&E System

Robert Lahey

Performance measurement, monitoring, and evaluation have long been a part of the infrastructure within the federal government in Canada. With over 30 years of formalized evaluation experience in most large federal departments and agencies, many "lessons" can be gained from this experience, not the least of which is the recognition that the monitoring and evaluation (M&E) system itself is not static. The Canadian government has a formalized evaluation policy, standards, and guidelines and these have been modified on three occasions over the past three decades. Changes have usually come about due to a public sector reform initiative, such as the introduction of a results orientation to government management, a political issue that may have generated a demand for greater accountability and transparency in government, or a change in emphasis on where and how M&E information should be used in government. This chapter provides an overview of the Canadian M&E model, examining its defining elements and identifying key lessons learned.

For their comments, the author thanks Richard Allen (Consultant, Public Sector Governance), Philipp Krause (Consultant, Poverty Reduction and Equity Unit [PRMPR]), Keith Mackay (Consultant, PRMPR), as well as Gladys Lopez-Acevedo (Senior Economist, PRMPR), and Jaime Saavedra (Director, PRMPR). The views expressed in this chapter are those of the author.

Evaluation in public sector management in Canada dates back to 1969, with the initiation of formalized and centralized evaluation practices. The centrally-led approach was replaced in 1977 with the first government-wide Evaluation Policy that established the model upon which the practice of evaluation still functions in the government. The introduction of evaluation was inspired by the notion of "letting the managers manage"; that is, allowing deputy ministers[1] of federal government departments to assume greater responsibility but also be accountable for the performance of their programs and the prudent use of public funds. The model is based on a strong central management board that oversees and holds deputies accountable. One of the mechanisms to do this is performance evaluation.

Main Characteristics of the Canadian M&E System

The structure of the Canadian M&E system is characterized by three defining elements:

1. Internal evaluation units in most federal departments, with central leadership

The Canadian M&E system distinguishes itself from many other countries by its "departmental delivery–central leadership" structure, where rule-setting is done by the central agency, the Treasury Board Secretariat (TBS), and evaluations are conducted by internal evaluation units established in each federal department.

To assist in rule-setting, capacity building, and oversight of the system, a Centre of Excellence for Evaluation (CEE) was established within TBS. As results-based monitoring and reporting became increasingly popular starting in the 1990s, relevant policy areas were established in TBS to provide guidance to departmental managers and oversight in these areas. This central leadership structure guides departments and agencies with performance measurement and reporting aspects of results-based management and, system-wide, the results orientation of government.

2. An emphasis on both monitoring and evaluation as tools of "performance measurement"

The Canadian M&E system relies on *both* ongoing performance monitoring *and* the conduct of planned evaluations as tools to measure program and policy performance. Both are recognized as key tools to support good governance, accountability, and results-based management.

Within individual government departments and agencies, the deputy head has some flexibility in resourcing these tools to be appropriate to the size and needs of their organization. The expectation is that both tools are used in managing a department and helping a deputy achieve the organizational goals for which they are being held accountable. It falls upon individual program managers to put in place the necessary results-based monitoring systems and upon the internal evaluation unit to plan for and carry out evaluations that generally provide deeper understanding of program performance. Considerable time and effort has been expended by the central agency to provide appropriate guidance to both technical experts and program mangers across government.

3. **A well-defined foundation setting the rules and expectations for performance measurement and evaluation—policy, standards, and guidelines**

The requirements and standards of practice for both monitoring and evaluation have been built into administrative policies of government, developed by the central agency, and rolled out for all government departments and agencies to adhere to. The formalized policies and guidelines help clarify the government's expectations and the roles and responsibilities of all key players in the M&E system. It also reinforces the use of oversight mechanisms to monitor the health and use of M&E across government. Embedded as they are in administrative policies, these policies and guidelines have been adjusted and improved as more experience has been gained with the M&E system.

Roles and Responsibilities of the Key Players

The Canadian M&E system has two key focal points for the delivery and use of M&E information: the TBS that sets the rules and individual government departments that measure the performance of their programs and policies.

Centre of Excellence for Evaluation—the government's evaluation policy center

While the TBS plays a strong role in both the practice of evaluation as well as performance monitoring within departments, the CEE within TBS acts as the government's evaluation policy center. This unit, which currently employs 14 staff, plays a variety of roles in support of the evaluation function across the system:

- Community development to assist in capacity building, including: development of competency profiles for evaluators, a community development strategy, an internship program, and evaluation tools.
- Leadership and "champion" for evaluation by establishing evaluation networks and providing guidance related to M&E practices, including maintaining an up-to-date Web site.
- Operational oversight and quality control via monitoring standards and quality of evaluation practices in individual departments and system-wide.
- Facilitating the use of evaluation results by linking departmental evaluations with TBS program analysts to help ensure that results information is used in program funding decisions and the broader Expenditure Management System.
- Government-wide evaluation, which is a feature of the new 2009 evaluation policy.

TBS policy centers for performance monitoring and reporting

TBS provides formal guidance and support to departments in developing department and program-level performance measurement frameworks and ongoing performance monitoring systems. Additionally, TBS oversees annual performance reporting, including reviewing every departmental performance report required by all federal departments and agencies before sending it to Parliament.

Another important player in the M&E system is the Office of the Auditor General (OAG), which periodically monitors and reports to Parliament on the functioning of various aspects of the M&E system.

Organization of M&E in a government department

All major government departments and agencies are required to dedicate resources for evaluation, at a capacity appropriate to the size and needs of the organization. In addition, each department must put in place a senior-level evaluation committee chaired by the deputy minister, annual and multi-year planning for evaluation, a departmental evaluation policy reflective of the government's policy, and the mechanisms needed for delivering credible evaluation products. TBS/CEE monitors departments on all of these aspects, including the quality and use of evaluation, and reflects this in an annual assessment of each deputy minister.

A critical part of the evaluation infrastructure in a department is the internal evaluation unit, led by the "head of evaluation." This position plays a pivotal role in ensuring that the government's policy requirements as well as the priorities of the deputy minister are reflected in departmental evaluation work. To help ensure independence, the position generally reports to the deputy minister or at least has unencumbered access to the most senior official in the department.

Deputy ministers are also required by TBS policy to develop a corporate performance framework (the so-called Management Resources and Results Structure—MRRS) that links all departmental programs to expected outcomes. This articulation of program architecture serves as the basis for performance monitoring and reporting, and its development is watched closely by TBS to ensure adherence to the MRRS policy. Performance monitoring is an ongoing responsibility of individual program managers, though evaluation specialists often support the development of monitoring systems. In theory, ongoing performance monitoring provides much of the data needed for program evaluation; in practice, however, this does not always happen.

Scale and cost of Canada's M&E system

Virtually all large departments and agencies (37) have a stand-alone evaluation unit, as do most mid-size agencies, resulting in some 550 evaluation professionals currently working in the Canadian federal public service.

Given the flexibility allowed by the government's policy, departmental evaluation units range in size from one individual up to 60 evaluators, with contract budgets for hiring external consultants ranging anywhere from zero to over $8 million. The average size is now in the order of 12 professionals. The salary for internal evaluators has historically represented some 25 percent of all funds spent on evaluation in a department, though this number is likely rising as a result of the 2009 evaluation policy.

Spending on evaluation government-wide has risen substantially over the 2000s. It was $32 million in 2005–06 (still below the estimated resource need of $55 million), but it has continued to rise sharply, most recently in response to the greater demands put on departments by the 2009 evaluation policy.

How Is the M&E System Used?

Many uses and users for M&E information

M&E is not viewed as an end in itself. The intent of M&E in the Canadian system is to provide results information that will serve a variety of needs and users at different levels throughout the system—at an operational or program level, at an individual department, at a government-wide level, and in a legislative context. In broad terms, much of this need has been driven by various public sector reforms and, most recently, the government's management agenda, Results for Canadians, as well as its efforts around renewal of the Expenditure Management System. As such, M&E is seen and used as both a management/learning vehicle as well as a means to support accountability in the design and delivery of government policies, programs, services, and the use of public funds.

Informing decision making with M&E information

In the mid-2000s, the CEE reported that some 230 evaluations were being completed a year. Historically, the prime focus for a large proportion of these evaluations was for internal management purposes, largely program improvement, and to support performance accountability to external audiences such as Parliament, parliamentary committees, or TBS. Increasingly over the past decade, however, a government-imposed requirement to evaluate all "grant and contribution" programs prior to their funding renewal has resulted in more evaluations being used to assess program effectiveness, with the information being used by TBS analysts and Treasury Board ministers in decisions around future program funding. The formal requirement to table an effectiveness evaluation at the time of discussions around funding renewal has helped institutionalize the use of evaluation information in program funding decision making. Currently, federal departments and agencies are on track to evaluate all grant and contribution programs over a five-year cycle, representing coverage of some $43.8 billion, or 40 percent of all government direct program spending. In all cases, the M&E information gets used by the TBS program analyst as part of the decision making on future funding and program renewal.

The 2009 evaluation policy is bringing M&E closer to funding decisions on *all* direct government program spending (some $112.3 billion in 2010–11). This is happening as part of a broader government-wide expenditure management requirement faced by all deputy heads to carry out a strategic expenditure review every four years to ensure value for money, effectiveness, efficiency, and alignment with government roles and priorities of all programs. Deputy heads are using M&E information drawn from formalized evaluations and other sources to make these determinations. Faced with frozen budgets across government, the M&E information is becoming even more important as an input to budget planning and decision making regarding the need to change, improve, or replace programs.

Reporting and accountability to Parliament

On a corporate level, M&E information is a required input to a number of important documents that regularly inform ministers or Parliament on government and program performance: submissions to Treasury Board ministers, memoranda to Cabinet, departmental performance reports tabled in Parliament each year, and reports to parliamentary committees. Since the OAG's mandate does not include assessing effectiveness of government programs (OAG audits focus on issues of efficiency and economy), departmental evaluations and results reporting in the above documents represent an important use of M&E information in general and evaluation in particular in keeping elected officials abreast of government performance and how well programs are meeting their objectives.

Incentives to Help Promote and Drive the Use of the M&E System

Formal requirements for using M&E information in government

A number of centrally-driven administrative policies introduced over the 1990s and 2000s have served as key "drivers" for M&E. Some have had a direct impact on building M&E capacity in departments, including the evaluation policy (most recently renewed in 2009), Management Resources and Results Structure Policy (2005), the Federal Accountability Act (2005), and the Policy on Transfer Payments (updated in 2008). Others serve broader needs but have also generated demand for systematic and credible performance information. These include the government's management agenda Results for Canadians (2000), government requirements for departments to annually report to Parliament via the report on plans and priorities and the departmental performance reports, the Results-based Management and Accountability Frameworks Policy (2000), the Management Accountability

Framework annual assessment of departmental performance (2003), and the strategic expenditure reviews (2007) and Expenditure Management System (2007).

While these have all served to drive the development of M&E in Canada in one way or another over the last fifteen years, they do *not* represent a master plan for M&E. Rather, they reflect the government's long-term commitment to build a results orientation into public sector management and a recognition that performance M&E are critical tools to make this happen.

Checks and balances to support the independence and neutrality of the evaluator

An internal evaluation function could potentially be criticized for not having the necessary independence to "speak truth to power." To deal with this challenge, the Canadian model has put in place infrastructure and oversight mechanisms aimed at ensuring that internal evaluations of departmental programs or policies are credible and objective. Some of these elements are at the level of the individual department while others are enforced centrally. All are intended to reinforce the independence and neutrality of the evaluation process and the reporting on the findings, conclusions, and recommendations of the evaluation study. A listing of some of the main checks and balances is provided in Box 15.1.

The 2009 revision to the evaluation policy dropped the word "independence," replacing it with "neutral," defined as "an attribute required of the evaluation function and evaluators that is characterized by impartiality in behavior and process." The rationale for this change was in part to ensure that evaluators would not operate at arm's length from key stakeholders (as an internal auditor might, to maintain independence). It formally recognized that stakeholders, including managers whose programs are being evaluated, need to be involved in the conduct of the evaluation, during both design and implementation.

A strong set of oversight mechanisms to reinforce credibility and quality control

Oversight mechanisms in the system serve as a "challenge" function and, in the process, provide quality control and help reinforce the credibility of the system. Oversight in the Canadian model is implemented at three levels: (i) an individual evaluation study; (ii) at an organizational level; and, (iii) at a whole-of-government level.

BOX 15.1

Checks and Balances to Support the Independence and Neutrality of Internal Evaluation

- Deputy head of a government department is required by the government's evaluation policy to establish an internal evaluation function that is both "robust" and "neutral."

- The policy requires that the head of evaluation has "direct and unencumbered access" to the deputy head of the individual department or agency, to help ensure independence/neutrality/impartiality in the conduct and use of evaluation results.

- The government's Directive on the Evaluation Function outlines the principle that "heads of evaluation, as primary departmental experts in evaluation, have final decision-making authority on technical issues, subject to the decision-making authority of deputy heads."

- Each department has a senior-level departmental evaluation committee in place that plays a variety of roles regarding evaluation planning, conduct, and follow-up, including assessing the performance of internal evaluation.

- The head of evaluation is encouraged by the government's policy to make use of advisory committees, peer review or, as appropriate, external review panels (independent experts, for example) for the planning and conduct of individual evaluation studies.

- The government's evaluation policy stresses the "neutrality" of both the evaluation function and the evaluator ("impartiality in behavior and process"). This is specifically defined in the policy document.

- Standards for evaluation identify four broad requirements intended to ensure that evaluations produce results that are credible, neutral, timely, and produced in a professional and ethical manner.

- Operational oversight is provided through ongoing monitoring by the TBS/CEE.

- The performance of each department and deputy head is formally assessed each year by TBS through the Management Accountability Framework process, which includes assessing M&E in the department.

- The OAG carries out an oversight role through periodic audits of the implementation of the government's evaluation policy and the quality of performance reporting. As an independent body reporting directly to Parliament, OAG reports represent a public disclosure of information that reinforces both independence and transparency.

The oversight role is carried out by both the OAG and the TBS/CEE. This oversight role provides an additional incentive to help drive a well-performing M&E system in departments and across the system.

At an operational level, TBS monitors departmental M&E initiatives at various points—planning, implementation, and reporting phases. The CEE for example, monitors evaluation planning and conduct in all departments, including coverage and quality of individual studies. Performance measurement and monitoring in general is monitored by the TBS, both at the time of the development and approval of a department's MRRS, the basis for its corporate performance reporting, and annually during the review of departmental performance reports, submitted to TBS by each department prior to their tabling in Parliament.

Additionally, since 2003, TBS assesses each department/deputy head annually against a number of criteria (including the use of results and performance information). This is the annual Management Accountability Framework process that is linked to compensation received by deputy heads. This formalized framework is an important way to provide a vehicle for a dialogue between the central agency and senior departmental officials that could point to areas where improvements may be needed.

At a whole-of-government level, the OAG conducts periodic performance audits that monitor the effectiveness of M&E implementation across the full system. This could include a system-wide audit of the implementation of the government's evaluation policy or the quality of results measurement and reporting. Results of these audits are reported directly to Parliament and generally receive high media exposure, particularly if the findings point to issues with the effectiveness of government policies and/or need for change. Such audits highlight the importance and role of M&E in public sector management and catch the attention of legislators, both at the time of reporting and in follow-up discussions that may take place in the Public Accounts Committee. The independence of the OAG and the transparency of its public reporting to Parliament are key elements for the external auditor.

The Sustainability of the M&E System

One of the defining characteristics of a successful M&E system is its sustainability. The longevity of the Canadian model, with over 30 years embedded in the federal public sector, has likely been influenced by four factors discussed below.

Flexibility and willingness to learn and adjust

Flexibility and avoiding a "one size fits all" approach has been a hallmark of the M&E model in Canada. Along with this flexibility has been recognition of the need to learn and adjust as required and a willingness to pilot new requirements and adjust as needed before the cross-government roll-out. This approach was used to introduce the concept of corporate performance reports, with several adjustments to the guidelines and directives introduced through the late 1990s and early 2000s.

The fact that the government has had four versions of its evaluation policy over the past 34 years is a testament to a willingness to move from the status quo. This has been made easier by the fact that the government-wide requirements for evaluation are largely based on administrative policies rather than embedded in legislation.

Transparency as an underlying value of the M&E system

To be effective, there needs to be an enabling environment for M&E, both in organizations and across the whole system. This rests in part on a willingness to carry out performance M&E of government programs in full public view.

In Canada, transparency is a critical dimension underlying the government's M&E system. The 2009 evaluation policy makes officials accountable for "ensuring that complete, approved evaluation reports along with management responses and action plans are made easily available to Canadians in a timely manner." Public disclosure laws have played an important role in increasing accessibility of M&E studies to the general public, including the media. Additionally, OAG reports have increased public focus on performance and results of government programs. Added to this is the increasing access to and use of departmental and central agency Web sites where M&E information is made accessible to the general public.

An ongoing commitment to capacity building

An adequate supply of trained human resources (HR) with the needed skill sets is critical for sustainability of an M&E system. HR capacity development is an ongoing issue for the Canadian system, given the large number of professional evaluators working in government (currently over 550).

Several sources have traditionally been relied on for HR training and development, including community development initiatives led by the CEE as well as workshops, seminars, and professional development and networking opportunities generated by professional associations and the private sector. Recently, a network of universities across Canada started offering evaluation certificate programs, providing more in-depth training needed to work as an evaluation practitioner.

Substantial efforts have been made over the last three years to establish a recognized set of competencies for evaluators, and with this, an accreditation program. The Canadian Evaluation Society recently introduced the "Credentialed Evaluator" designation, as a means to define, recognize, and promote the practice of ethical, high quality, and competent evaluation. The CEE is also working to address the issue of further professionalizing evaluation.

A central commitment to accountability and good management practices

The origins for the Canadian M&E system were linked to a desire to strengthen good governance and accountability. The broad set of government initiatives put in place is a testament to this central commitment that has been sustained through various changes of government over the past 30 years. This strong support for M&E can be summed up in the words of the Auditor General recently speaking before the Public Accounts Committee: "The evaluation of effectiveness is absolutely critical to making good decisions about program spending so that we can know whether programs are actually getting the results that were intended . . . this is even more critical in the current economic times we are going through, because government does have to make difficult choices, and it should be making those decisions based on good information."

Lessons Learned from 30 Years of M&E Development in Canada

1. Lesson Learned: Drivers for M&E

M&E should not be considered as an end in itself. Potentially, there are many "drivers" for M&E that may be political, operational, be associated with a major reform agenda, and/or brought on by fiscal measures. Whatever the case, it is important to understand who the key audiences are for M&E information, what their needs are, and what questions need to be answered. Some lessons relating to the drivers for M&E from the Canadian experience are provided in Box 15.2.

2. Lessons Learned: Implementing the M&E system

Implementation of M&E is long-term and iterative—and not costless. As such, senior level commitment and "champions" at both senior and operational levels are important elements to ensure sustainability through the long period of development and implementation. Eventually, the goal is to move M&E beyond the point of being a "special project" to a point where it

BOX 15.2

Some Lessons Concerning Drivers for M&E

1.1 Building and using M&E capacity requires more than resources and technical skills—it requires a political will and sustained commitment. Central leadership and a plan are very important.

1.2 M&E information is not an end in itself—it needs to be linked to particular management and decision-making needs, particularly in the context of public sector reforms or government agendas.

1.3 To be effective, it is important to build both a capacity to do evaluation and gather performance information, plus a capacity to use M&E information within organizations and across the system. A supply of good evaluations is not enough—a reasonable demand for evaluation is key.

1.4 The capacity to use M&E information relies on the incentives in the system for managers to demand such information and actually use it as part of their normal operations. This could take the forms of sanctions for not complying, or rewards for meeting requirements.

1.5 Internal infrastructure on its own is likely insufficient to sustain an M&E system. A number of formal requirements associated with its use, at both a departmental and central level, and in the context of both management and accountability, will force program and senior managers to take the time and effort to invest in M&E development.

1.6 Managing the expectations about the role of evaluation is important in avoiding unrealistic expectations. Evaluation can and should inform decision making, but it is generally only one of many sources of information. Questions about the performance of government programs generally do not have simple yes/no answers.

is a normal part of doing business and the management practices of the organization. Box 15.3 offers some lessons on "implementing the M&E system" from the Canadian experience.

3. Lesson Learned: Building M&E capacity

In considering training needs, it is important to consider not simply technical training but also M&E training and orientation for non-technical officials (that is, the *users* of M&E information). Additionally, building capacity needs to address an oft-ignored area—data development and establishing credible databases. The national statistics office (in Canada, Statistics Canada) should play a central role in data development, data warehousing, oversight, and quality control associated with data capture and public surveying. Key lessons regarding M&E capacity building are outlined in Box 15.4.

BOX 15.3

Some Lessons Concerning Implementing an M&E System

2.1 There needs to be sufficient communication and for information-sharing across organizations about the role of M&E and how it can help management so as to link the demand for and supply of M&E information; that is, to ensure that what gets produced is what is needed, and delivered in a timely way.

2.2 A formal policy document is a useful basis for clarifying roles, responsibilities, and accountabilities of key players—deputy heads, evaluation specialists, program managers, and central agency officials.

2.3 The distinction between the "M" and the "E" need to be clarified, including what each contributes to results-based management and what each requires re capacity building.

2.4 A central agency champion for evaluation in government can play a key role in the M&E system. In Canada, the CEE serves as the policy center for evaluation, provides guidance, leads and promotes capacity development, and provides oversight to help ensure quality control.

2.5 In developing the M&E system in Canada, a number of requirements have been phased in by the central agency, under the general philosophy of "try, adapt, learn, and adjust." This allows for a period of learning and an ease of adjustment if needed, and recognizes that building an M&E system is long-term and iterative.

2.6 In establishing internal evaluation units in departments and agencies, some flexibility is important to take account of the unique circumstances associated with each organization. Recognizing that one size does not fit all, deputy heads in Canada are given some flexibility in implementing the government's evaluation policy, though all are equally accountable for the performance of their individual organization.

2.7 Oversight by the national audit office is important in giving broad and public exposure of how well the M&E system is being implemented and whether adjustments are needed.

2.8 It is important from the outset to think in terms of years, not months, to getting to a mature M&E system.

Note

1. In the Canadian system, the deputy minister of a government department (or deputy head of an agency) is the most senior non-elected official in charge of and accountable for the department and its programs. They report to a minister, an elected politician.

Bibliography

Canadian Evaluation Society Professional Designations Program: http://www.evaluationcanada.ca/ site.cgi?s=5&ss=6&_lang=EN)

Centre of Excellence for Evaluation: http://www.tbs-sct.gc.ca/cee/index-eng.asp

Treasury Board of Canada Secretariat: www.tbs-sct.gc.ca/tbs-sct/index-eng.asp

BOX 15.4
Some Lessons Concerning Building M&E Capacity

3.1 Building an adequate supply of human resource capacity is critical for the sustainability of the M&E system. Additionally, "growing" evaluators requires far more technically-oriented M&E training and development than can usually be obtained via one or two workshops.

3.2 Both formal training and on-the-job experience are important in developing evaluators. Two key competencies for evaluators have been determined to be: cognitive capacity and communication skills.

3.3 Developing communication skills for evaluators is important to help ensure that the message of evaluation resonates with stakeholders. "Speaking truth to power" and knowing how to navigate the political landscape are both critical.

3.4 Building a results culture within organizations requires program and senior managers to have enough understanding that they trust and will use M&E information. This likely requires a less technical form of training/orientation on M&E and results-based management.

3.5 There are no quick fixes in building an M&E system—investment in training and systems development is long-term. A mix of both formal training (given by the public sector, private sector, universities, and/or professional associa-

tions) and job assignment and mentoring programs is likely needed as a cost-effective approach.

3.6 In introducing an M&E system, champions and advocates are important to help sustain commitment over the long term. Identifying good practices and learning from others can help avoid fatigue of the change process.

3.7 Evaluation professionals have the technical skills to advise and guide program managers on the development of appropriate results-based performance monitoring systems, starting with the performance measurement framework and identification of relevant indicators and measurement strategies.

3.8 Ongoing performance monitoring (the "M") and the conduct of periodic evaluation studies (the "E") should be complementary functions that together form the basis for an appropriate and cost-effective performance measurement strategy.

3.9 Data quality is critical for the credibility of an M&E system and likely requires implementation of a long-term strategy to develop sufficient data to populate results indicators. Key support can come from the national statistics office and officials responsible for IM/IT.

Further Reading

A more detailed description and discussion of the Canadian M&E system can be found in Robert Lahey, "The Canadian M&E System: Lessons Learned from 30 Years of Development," ECD Working Paper Series 23, Independent Evaluation Group, World Bank: November 2010. In particular, details can be obtained on the following:

- The key policies and procedures supporting the M&E system in Canada.
- The roles and responsibilities of key players within the M&E system
- Performance of the Canadian M&E system and assessments by the OAG.

ECO-AUDIT
Environmental Benefits Statement

The World Bank is committed to preserving endangered forests and natural resources. The Office of the Publisher has chosen to print *Building Better Policies* on recycled paper with 50 percent postconsumer fiber in accordance with the recommended standards for paper usage set by the Green Press Initiative, a nonprofit program supporting publishers in using fiber that is not sourced from endangered forests. For more information, visit www.greenpressinitiative.org.

Saved:
• 11 trees
• 1 million Btu of total energy
• 1,052 lb. of net greenhouse gases
• 4,744 gal. of waste water
• 300 lb. of solid waste

green press
INITIATIVE

www.ingramcontent.com/pod-product-compliance
Lightning Source LLC
Chambersburg PA
CBHW080327270326
41927CB00014B/3130